D0537060

ART CENTER COLLEGE OF DESIGN
3 3220 00029 4210

FARE THEE WELL

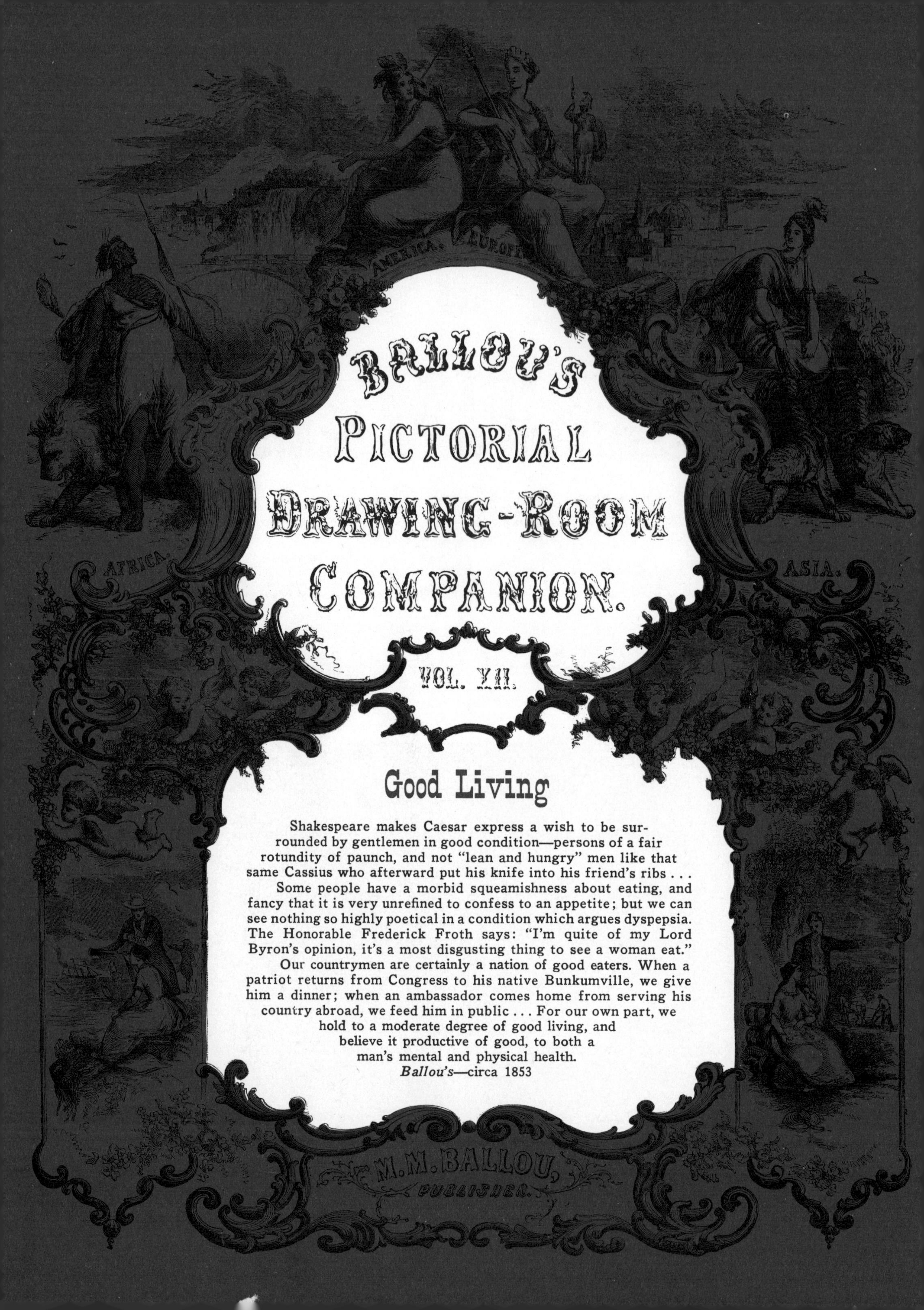

Good Living

Shakespeare makes Caesar express a wish to be surrounded by gentlemen in good condition—persons of a fair rotundity of paunch, and not "lean and hungry" men like that same Cassius who afterward put his knife into his friend's ribs . . .

Some people have a morbid squeamishness about eating, and fancy that it is very unrefined to confess to an appetite; but we can see nothing so highly poetical in a condition which argues dyspepsia. The Honorable Frederick Froth says: "I'm quite of my Lord Byron's opinion, it's a most disgusting thing to see a woman eat."

Our countrymen are certainly a nation of good eaters. When a patriot returns from Congress to his native Bunkumville, we give him a dinner; when an ambassador comes home from serving his country abroad, we feed him in public . . . For our own part, we hold to a moderate degree of good living, and believe it productive of good, to both a man's mental and physical health.

Ballou's—circa 1853

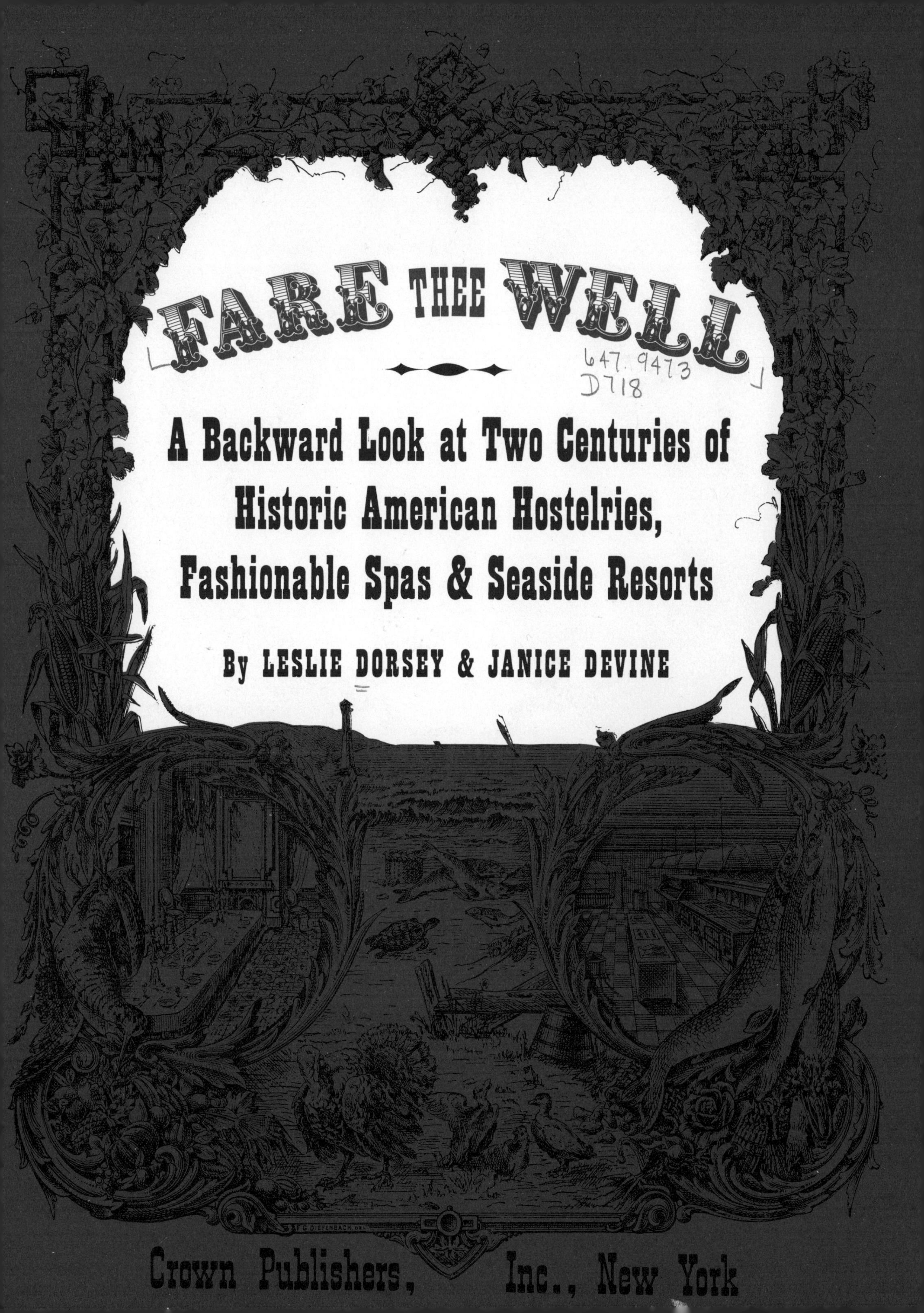
FARE THEE WELL
A Backward Look at Two Centuries of
Historic American Hostelries,
Fashionable Spas & Seaside Resorts
By LESLIE DORSEY & JANICE DEVINE
F.G. DIEFENBACH DEL.
Crown Publishers, Inc., New York

Library of Congress Catalog Card Number: 64-21911

Printed in the United States of America

Designed by Leslie Dorsey

FARE THEE WELL
is dedicated to a bygone time—to the follies thereof as much as to the virtues.

And, in honor, to my mother,
Lillian Maud Dorsey
L. D.

FIRST OF ALL

A Calendar of Hotel Innovations

Just as the Tremont House in Boston was the first real hotel in America, so it was the pace-setter for many new-fangled accessories and conveniences. Among its interesting "firsts" are:

1829—First bellboys (the Tremont called them Rotunda Men).

1829—First inside water closets (Tremont) signalling disappearance of the old outhouses.

1829—Debut of the now ubiquitous hotel clerk, complete with company smile (Tremont).

1829—A matter of some dispute is the appearance of French cuisine on Yankee menus, but most historians give the nod to the Tremont.

1829—No argument here; the Tremont had the first menu cards.

1829—Annunciators placed in Tremont rooms.

1829—Room keys to give Tremont guests a degree of privacy.

1829—Start of permanent residency in hotels—Tremont again showed the way.

1829—Mostly for the ladies, the Tremont set aside a quiet Reading Room.

1817—A disputatious date. Nobody quite agrees about the first hotel to have gaslight, but since Baltimore, Maryland, had the first public gas works in the country, Barnum's City Hotel in that city, lays claim to a gaslight first.

1836—New York's City Hotel was the first to offer clubs a regular meeting place.

1836—House rules first defined by the Astor House and posted in guest's rooms.

1840—Washington Hall in New York first instituted the European Plan.

1846—Eastern Exchange Hotel, Boston, had first central heating system.

1848—The New England Hotel, Boston, offered first safe deposit boxes for the protection of cash brought in by the merchants who were staying there.

1875—Floor clerks installed by the Palace Hotel, San Francisco.

1882—Electric lights first dazzled guests in New York's Hotel Everett.

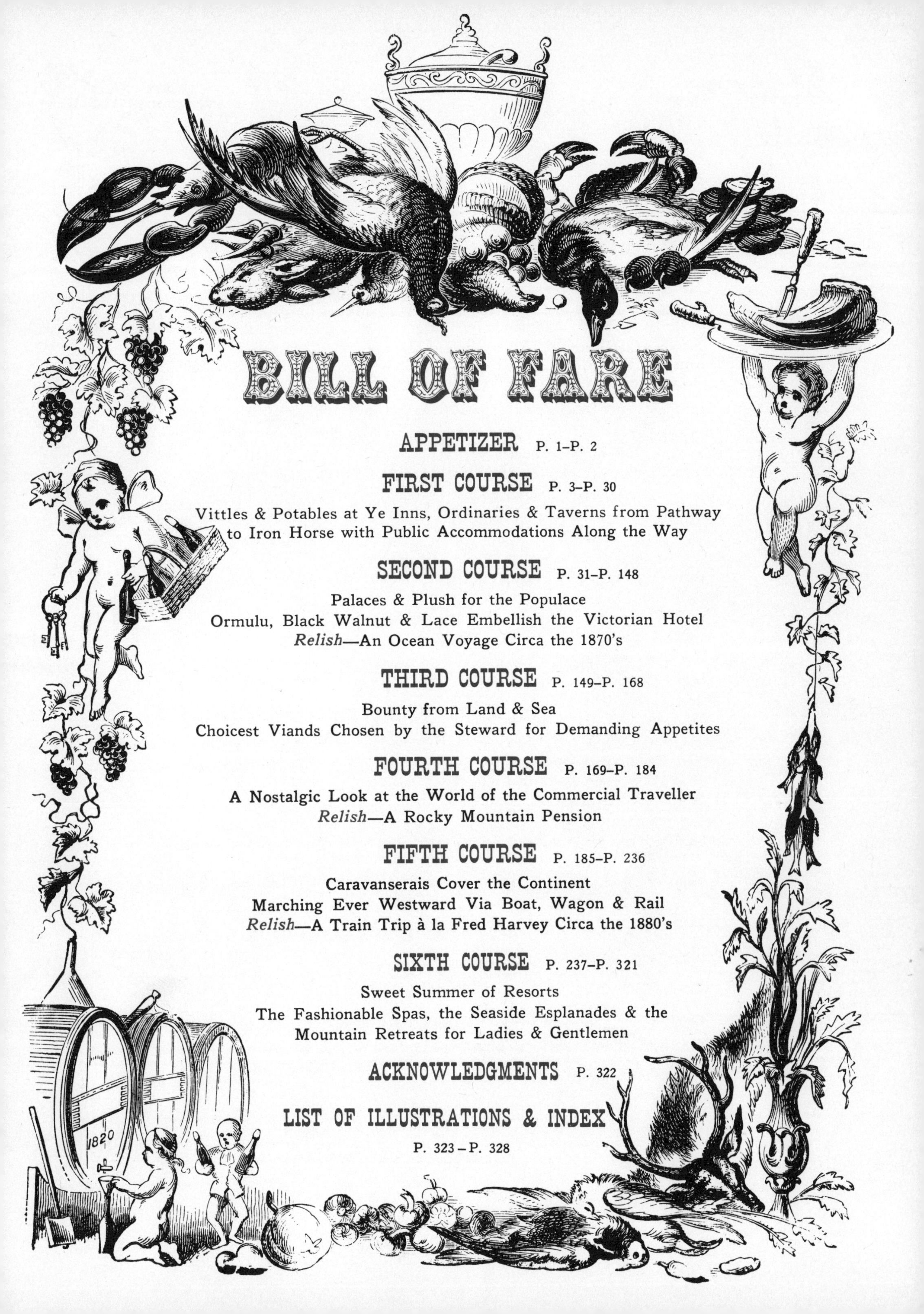

BILL OF FARE

APPETIZER P. 1–P. 2

FIRST COURSE P. 3–P. 30

Vittles & Potables at Ye Inns, Ordinaries & Taverns from Pathway to Iron Horse with Public Accommodations Along the Way

SECOND COURSE P. 31–P. 148

Palaces & Plush for the Populace
Ormulu, Black Walnut & Lace Embellish the Victorian Hotel
Relish—An Ocean Voyage Circa the 1870's

THIRD COURSE P. 149–P. 168

Bounty from Land & Sea
Choicest Viands Chosen by the Steward for Demanding Appetites

FOURTH COURSE P. 169–P. 184

A Nostalgic Look at the World of the Commercial Traveller
Relish—A Rocky Mountain Pension

FIFTH COURSE P. 185–P. 236

Caravanserais Cover the Continent
Marching Ever Westward Via Boat, Wagon & Rail
Relish—A Train Trip à la Fred Harvey Circa the 1880's

SIXTH COURSE P. 237–P. 321

Sweet Summer of Resorts
The Fashionable Spas, the Seaside Esplanades & the Mountain Retreats for Ladies & Gentlemen

ACKNOWLEDGMENTS P. 322

LIST OF ILLUSTRATIONS & INDEX

P. 323 – P. 328

WADE DEL

APPETIZER

The United States is the most traveling nation on earth. We are a restless people—we have been ever since those first fearless families set forth in toy-size ships for an unknown New World.

This book is a chronicle of traveling Americans . . . how they ate, drank, and slept while on their way from Here to There.

The journey we have planned for you in pictures and words spans some three centuries, from the candlelit ordinary of Colonial days to the plush palace-hotels of our twentieth-century big cities. The journey ends on the eve of World War I . . . the end of an era, the end of a way of life.

The American hotel, at its best and at its worst, has had to be a composite of its own time and place. Wars were plotted there, political stratagems contrived, fortunes made and lost. Hotel chefs changed the eating habits of the entire country as they launched Waldorf salads, Crab Newburg, Saratoga chips, and tongue-tangling French dishes. High fashion went on parade in lobbies and ballrooms, love affairs flourished or died as hopeful mamas put their eligible offspring on display. In short, the American hotel has always represented American life in microcosm.

We hope that you will have as much fun and excitement as we have had, taking a backstage look at the precarious business of providing bed and board for some twelve generations of Americans on the move. Around the old menus and pictured dining rooms is the aura of America's sheer joy of eating, which has occupied armies of men and women, from pastry cooks and salad chefs to the makers of fine damask and glass and china. Painters, gas fitters, carpenters, engineers . . . how much our national economy owes to the keepers of taverns and hotels!

And how much we, the authors, owe to the keepers of books and archives! We say thank you to them all at the end of this book.

Now, on to the First Course.

Washington Hotel.

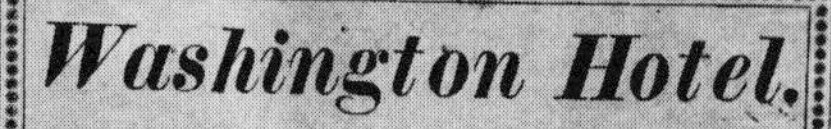

TIMOTHY BOSTON,

HAS the pleasure to inform his friends and the public generally, that he has recently enlarged his establishment in the *Brick Building* near the Hay Scales, where he can for the future, accommodate Gentlemen and Ladies with private apartments, such as will render their tarry with him pleasant and agreeable.

Delegates to the Convention, and all others, will find every convenience and accommodation they can possibly wish or expect.

He also has a very large and commodious Stable, constantly provided with the best of Hay, and Provender, and good Ostlers.

Portland, Sept. 28, 1819.

BOSTON, Decr 3d 1803

SIR,

THE MASSACHUSETTS CHARITABLE SOCIETY, whereof you are a Member, is to meet on Monday next, the 5th of December at Six o'Clock, at the Green Dragon at which Time and Place you are desired to give punctual Attendance.

Nathl Noyes Sec'y.

To Mr. George Homer

SIGN OF THE

INDIAN QUEEN.

THE Subscriber takes this method to inform his Friends and the Public in general, that he has opened A HOUSE of PUBLIC ENTERTAINMENT, at the Sign of the INDIAN QUEEN, No. 37, Marlborough Street, formerly occupied by Mrs. WHITE, where every attention will be paid to give satisfaction to his Customers—and the smallest Favor most gratefully acknowledged, by the Public's

Humble Servant,

ZADOCK POMROY.

Boston, June, 1779.

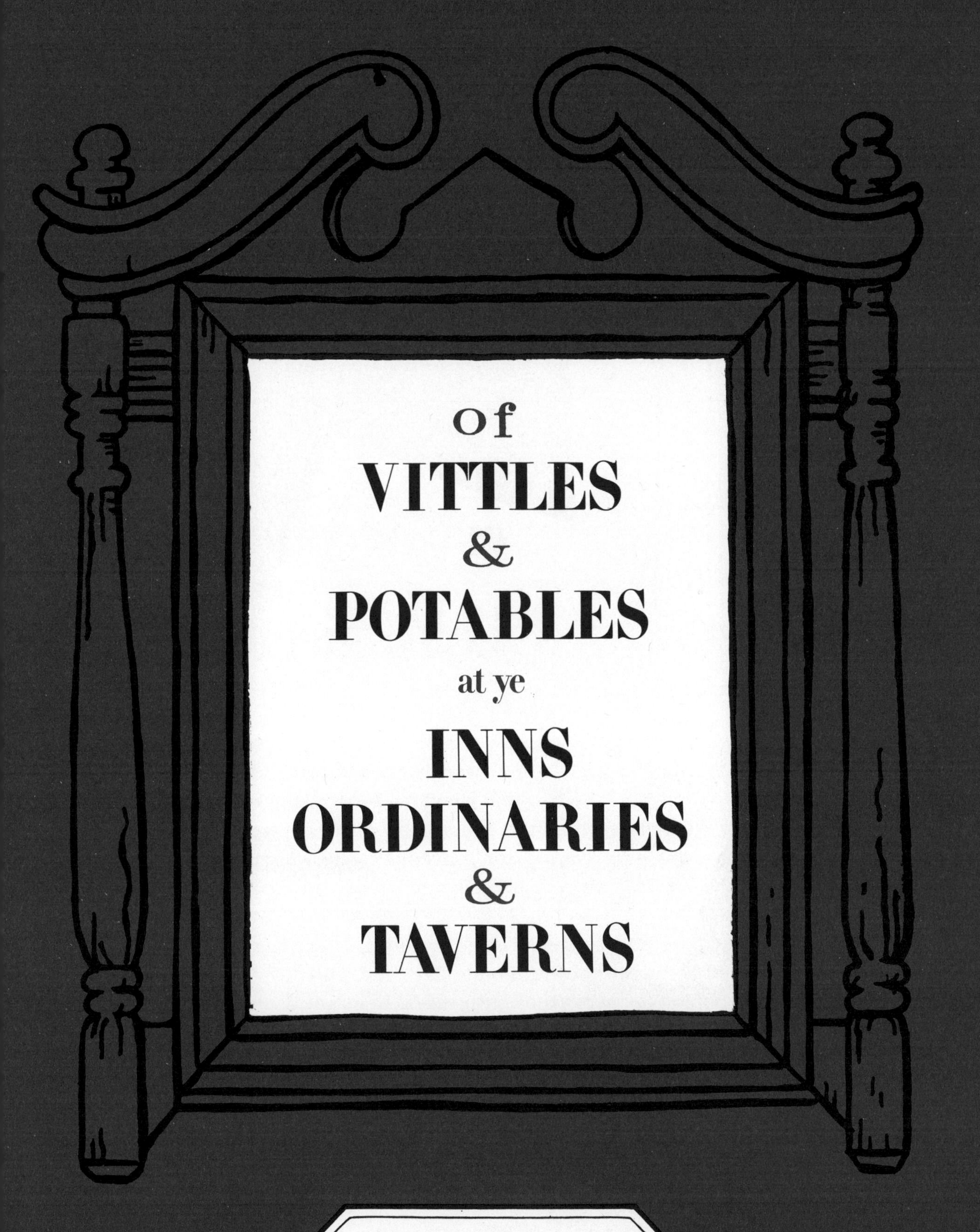

FIRST COURSE

Every Accommodation & Convenience

Close by the lovely white church spires of early New England stood the town ordinaries. They were so important to our fledgling social life that the Massachusetts General Court passed a law penalizing any town that failed to provide this convenience. The historic town of Concord paid its fine accordingly, then hastily persuaded one of its citizens to hang out his sign and serve vittles and potables.

"Every accommodation and convenience" often meant sleeping on the floor of the "long room," with one's feet turned toward the fireplace and one's head on a rolled-up coat, alongside a dozen or more other persons of both sexes. It meant a quick cold-water wash in an outdoor basin and gingerly use of a communal towel. A warning blast on the landlord's cow-horn meant all hands to table, ready to tackle breakfast with fingers and knives—forks were a curiosity and a luxury. Governor Winthrop is said to have brought the first fork to America in 1633, and he carried it about in its own velvet-lined leather case.

Most ordinaries had a few precious pewter mugs, but the breakfast beer or cider was more likely to arrive in a tankard of wood or leather. There would be a steaming bowl of suppawn (cornmeal and milk boiled in molasses) or perhaps of samp, (pounded corn and butter with milk poured over).

Breakfast coffee, now the morning eye opener for millions of Americans, was virtually unknown in the 1600's. Even as late as 1713 a guest at Phillips' Ordinary in Virginia warned that "coffee cannot be prepared without some training and people who are not accustomed to elegant living had better leave it alone."

Johnnycake was a seventeenth-century stand-by in Colonial America. For such an unpretentious concoction . . . cornmeal flour and water baked on a shingle in the fireplace . . . Johnnycake received an inordinate amount of publicity.

Connecticut was labeled the "land of Johnnycake and wooden nutmegs." Rhode Island claimed it as well, and Thomas Robinson Hazard of that state wrote the famous "Jonny-cake Papers," in which he insisted that the genuine article must be made with white, water-ground cornmeal from the eastern coast of Rhode Island and be mixed on a wooden tray, then baked on a red oak Johnnycake board and balanced before an open fire on a heart-shaped flatiron. All else was counterfeit.

Other authorities claimed that the proper name was "Journey-cake" since it was baked hard enough for travelers to carry.

At any rate, it was served by practically all the inns and ordinaries in the Colonies and a favorite way to eat it was by dunking it in cider.

Inns and ordinaries were as important to their own communities as they were to travelers, since they provided shelter, refreshment, and relaxation for churchgoers who came many miles to attend the marathon sermons and half-day services of those times. Between morning and afternoon sessions, the men flocked to the local ordinary, to warm their toes by the fire in winter, to cool off in summer from the sun-baked meetinghouse. They drank beer, ale, and cider, and often something stronger.

Almost everyone drank in those days, but in Puritan New England it was a circumscribed drinking. A man who was clocked at more than half an hour at his beer tankard during a weekday was guilty of "idleness" and could be fined. Drinking was all right with the Puritan fathers, but drunkenness was not, as witness Robert Coles of Boston, who, on September 3rd, 1633, was "fyned ten shillings and enjoyned to stand with a white sheet of paper on his back, whereupon DRUNKARD shall be written in large letters, and to stand therewith as long as the Court find fit, for abusing himself shamefully with drinke."

REGULATIONS
OF THE
HOUSE.

Family worship to be attended in the gentlemen's parlor at 9½ o'clock in the evening and half an hour before breakfast in the morning; the time to be announced by the ringing of the bell.

No intoxicating liquor to be sold or used in the house. Smoking of cigars not allowed on any part of the premises. The food used on the Sabbath, will be prepared, as far as possible, the evening previous, that all the members of the family may have an opportunity of attending public worship.

No money to be received at the office on the Sabbath; nor will any company be received on that day, except in cases of necessity.

Persons going away in the evening, are requested to settle their bills in the morning; and those intending to leave in the morning, to settle the evening previous.

"Kings Arms" inns and taverns sprouted all over the Colonies in the eighteenth century . . . and after 1776 faded faster than you could say "Declaration of Independence."

Since a great many people could not read, inn signs tended to be pictorial. There were "Red Lions," "Golden Bulls," "White" and "Black Horses," and, soon after the Revolution, a rash of "George Washingtons," some hastily painted over the face of a British monarch. Some were excellent art. There is a persistent legend that the distinguished artist Gilbert Stuart painted at least one inn sign . . . that of the King of Prussia Inn in Pennsylvania.

The years following the Revolution found post roads threading their way from the major ports, and as roads went so went the inns and taverns. But it was still a long, arduous trip from Boston to New York in the 1790's when an English clothier, Henry Wamsey, set down his impressions of Captain Flagg's Inn at Weston, Connecticut, where he had "veal cutlets, beef-steaks, coffee, bacon and eggs with toast and butter" on a hot August morning, and "the very sight of these things took away my appetite."

Molasses, which John Adams called "an essential ingredient in American independence," was also an ingredient important to inns and taverns. Aside from the end product, rum, molasses enhanced cakes, cookies, even stews of venison that had been "y-mynced," hacked, diced, or "skerned."

New York in 1676 (it was still the New Netherland settlement) had six wine and four beer taverns. One, a low stone building near the present Pearl Street and Coenties Slip, was built in 1642 and was probably the town's first tavern, paid for by the West India Company which paid the tab for visitors to this port. Lodging rates were regulated in the late seventeenth century: three and four pence a night, with meals at eight pence and a shilling, brandy six pence a gill, French wines fifteen pence a quart, four pence for a quart of cider, three for beer.

A typical tavern of the early 1800's, according to a journal titled *Reminiscences of a Hotel Man,* averaged about twenty-five rooms, was painted white with green blinds and trim, and inside had a "public parlor, dining room and bar-room" with a fireplace big enough to burn a cord of wood. On the other side of this barroom "stood a long, broad box serving as a seat by day and a bed for the hostler by night, its interior containing all the essentials of a bed, screening the same from the common gaze by day."

"The gastronomical critic," adds the Hotel Man in his reminiscences, "would shudder to see a slice of ham lifted to its doom on a sausage knife . . . The fundamental idea of the diner is to convey the food from the table to his teeth . . . the precise method of conveyance being a matter of subsidiary concern."

During stagecoach days, inns and taverns served as post offices and news and gossip headquarters. Tales emanating from them are legion and many no doubt apocryphal. George Washington and Abraham Lincoln are heroes of at least a pair of these yarns.

The one about Washington is set in a New England inn where the General arrived on horseback at a late hour for supper. He found every place at the table full. Pausing, he asked whether the innkeeper had any oysters for his horse. The diners looked up. Hadn't any of these people ever seen a horse eating oysters, he inquired? Apparently not. The anxious innkeeper whisked outdoors with a plate of oysters, followed by the curious patrons. Mr. Washington sat down and ate a quiet supper while the others crowded around the bewildered horse trying to stuff oysters down its throat.

As for Mr. Lincoln, the tale about him concerns an inn in the Middle West. He had scarcely begun his breakfast when the departure of his stage was announced. Mr. Lincoln went on eating. Suddenly he called out to the landlord that a number of silver knives and spoons were missing from the table. The landlord, assuming that the silver was aboard the stage, rushed a boy off to catch it and demand its return. The stage came back, Mr. Lincoln smilingly produced the missing silverware, and then boarded the coach, well fed and content.

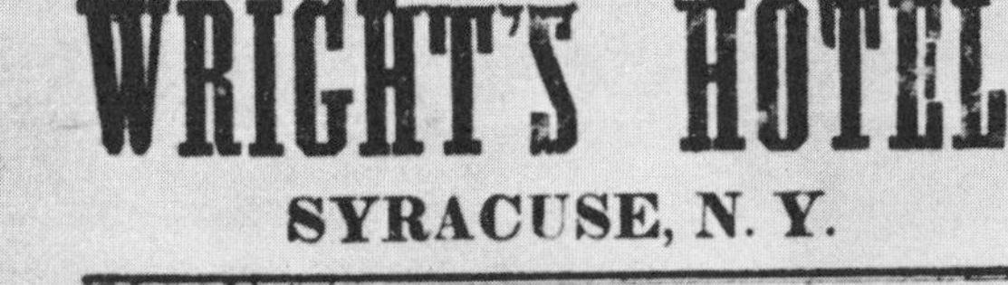
WRIGHT'S HOTEL,

SYRACUSE, N. Y.

East End of Rail Road Depot.

On right hand, as you enter the Depot, going West. On left hand, as you leave the Depot going East, only 10 feet from Depot.

Passengers dining in Syracuse will find this the most convenient house, it being the nearest. Express trains remain in the place thirty minutes.

Meals, 25 Cts. Each,

And satisfaction given or no charges. Ample notice will be given in the dining room on the departure of each train, so there will be no danger of being left.

This House has been newly built and furnished within the past year. The rooms are large and airy. We are confident that we can please all who may favor us with a call.

Board One Dollar per Day.

N. B.—We pay our Porters good wages and allow no dunning for portage money. If they ask it of our guests we should like to be informed of the fact.

☞ Stages leave this House morning and afternoon for Homer, Cortland, Phœnix, Marcellus, Brewerton, Central Square, Pulaski, Bridgeport, Fayetteville, Manlius, Cazenovia, De Ruyter, Fabius, Pompey, &c.

Yours with respect,

Syracuse 1852 CHASE & FRISBIE

Various Old Rum Bottles

Wondrous Flips, Slings & Bounces

Tavern bars carried no such polychrome varieties of liquor as arrived on the scene during the great hotel era. Rather, their heavy glass decanters offered gin, brandy, Medford rum, port wine, and other "remedies." Whiskey, rye, and bourbon were virtually unknown. The bar always had a bottle of Stoughton Bitters, a bowl of cut loaf sugar, a toddy stick . . . and a dice box to determine who paid for the drinks.

Edward Field, in *The Colonial Tavern,* reports that beer was the most common drink of all and that, in general, people "drank water only from necessity."

In the earliest Colonial days, New England ordinaries and taverns were spied on by that happily vanished official, the Tithing Man, who smugly turned in the names of those he decided were "idlers" or "gamers." One John Josselyn, visiting from England, complained bitterly about these officials who thrust themselves into the company, uninvited, and often decided what each man's drink capacity was and then ordered the landlord not to serve him one drink beyond that capacity.

Flip Glasses, Logger Head & Toddy Stick

Flip Glasses & Nutmeg Holders

Sweet wines went by the name of "sack" in the early days, and a "rule" for making Sack Posset appeared in the *New York Gazette* of February 13, 1744:

"A Receipt for All Young Ladies That Are Going to be Married to Make a Sack Posset"

From famed Barbadoes on the Western main
Fetch sugar, half a pound; fetch sack from Spain
A pint; and from the Eastern Indian Coast
Nutmeg, the glory of our Northern toast.
O'er flaming coals together let them heat
Till the all-conquering sack dissolves the sweet.
O'er such another fire, set eggs, twice ten,
Newborn from the crowing cock and clucking hen;
Stir them with a steady hand and conscience pricking
To see the untimely end of twenty chicken.
From shining shelf take down your brazen skillet.
A quart of milk from gentle cow will fill it
When boiled and cooked, put milk and sack to egg,
Unite them firmly like the triple league,
Then covered close, together let them dwell
Till Miss Twice sings; you must not kiss and tell.
Each lad and lass snatch up their murdering spoon
And fall on fiercely like a starved dragoon.

Nutmeg was the favorite flavoring for the flips, slings, and bounces that gladdened Colonial hearts. A nutmeg tied with ribbon was a treasured gift, and many people carried their own pocket-size nutmeg boxes, complete with miniature grater. Thus "the exquisite traveler could always be sure of a dainty, flavored wine." Elegant nutmeg boxes came in Battersea enamel, with graters of silver.

The best-kept secret in drinking history is probably the makings of Philadelphia's Fish House Punch, first concocted in 1732 at what was then called "The Castle of the State in Schuylkill on the Delaware." There have been only 400-odd members in all the years of the club's existence, but thousands of guests have sampled the famous punch made in a nine-gallon bowl brought from England 150 years ago on a clipper ship.

1733

—And hardly a soul was then alive who dreamed that in slightly less than half a century, in this small Wright Tavern in Concord, Massachusetts, one Major Pitcairn, about to command British troops in the Battle of Concord, would prick his finger and stir the blood into his brandy, predicting that the blood of "those rebels" would be flowing by nightfall.

Pumpkins, Parsnips & Walnut Tree Chips

They were all used for "liquor to sweeten our lips," according to an old jingle. Taverns such as Wright's (above) were taking on the grace of paneled walls and polished wood as the eighteenth century found Americans traveling tirelessly and drinking lustily. Here are some of the beverages they favored.

They Flipped

SCOTCHEM

Applejack and boiling water made this a simple but rather challenging drink.

CHERRY BOUNCE

New rum, five gallons of it, and the same of new cherries, sealed in a keg for one year. Guaranteed to bounce.

They Sipped

CIDER-ROYAL

A concentrate and most authoritative, it was made by reducing four barrels of cider in the boiling to one barrel.

EBULUM

The boiled, sweetened juice of elderberry and juniper berries was a favorite with the young.

They Flipped

FLIP

Was often made of strong beer and rum and was sweetened, sometimes with dried pumpkin.

RUM FUSTIAN

Made of beer, sherry, gin, egg yolks, sugar, nutmeg, with a red-hot loggerhead. Called Fustian, no doubt, because there was no rum in it.

They Sipped

BEVERIDGE

An innocent refresher of vinegar mixed with water, "useful after a hot journey."

NIBBEL & SIPS

A lumb of sugar in a saucer was as harmless as Nibbel & Sips sounds, for it was simply intended to be "nibbeled" with a cup of tea.

Major Pitcairn sipping his blood & brandy at Wright Tavern, Concord, Massachusetts

BLACK STRAP

Rum and molasses stirred up with various "simples." Of it John Adams said, "Of all the detestable drinks on which our inventive genius has exercised itself, this Black Strap is truly the most dangerous."

METHEGLIN

"For those who wanted to be loose-bodied," Metheglin had honey as its base with water, spices, pepper, and mead added. Mead and Metheglin were ancient Druid drinks. True Metheglin was said to be only an infusion of herbs mixed with fermented honey and water.

TEA

In Salem, Massachusetts, housewives were not exactly *au courant* with the classic brewed tea the English prize today. In fact, some New England housewives used to serve the tea leaves with butter and salt, while in Dutch New Amsterdam the tea leaves were often served with sugar while the infusion was poured away.

NATIVE TEAS

With nothing else at hand to concoct a warm beverage, seventeenth-century Americans frequently used dried goldenrod, sage, and blackberry leaves to make a breakfast potable.

They Flipped

ARRACK PUNCH

Its secrets were as carefully guarded and its formula as disputatious as Mint Julep is today. Thomas Jefferson's father on a bet won forty acres of land at the price of "the Raleigh Tavern's biggest bowl of Arrack Punch." The Raleigh Tavern, in Williamsburg, Virginia, served this punch with Tipsy Cake, a confection whose various layers were sprinkled with sherry, spread with strawberry jam, almonds, and apricot jam, and topped with whipped cream.

They Sipped

COFFEE

The first coffee arriving in America apparently presented a problem, as no one knew exactly how it was to be used. Often the whole beans were cooked and served in a bowl, with the liquid in a cup to be drunk separately.

A GRATEFUL SUMMER DRINK

Sweet cider diluted with water and flavored with nutmeg and sugar was described as "a grateful summer drink."

A TAVERN-BILL,

Rated at the GENERAL QUARTER-SESSIONS held at ~~Salem~~ Bridgetown for the County of ~~Salem~~ Cumberland the twenty fifth Day of February Anno Domini 1790 — January 1791

Item	Measure	Price	Amended
THE best Dinner or Supper, with a Pint of good Beer or Cyder,		0..1..6	1/10½
Second best or Family ditto, with ditto,		1..2	1/3
Best Breakfast of Tea, Coffee or Chocolate, with Loaf Sugar,		1..0	1/3
Ditto of cold Meat, with a Pint of good Beer or Cyder,		..10	—
Good Madeira Wine,	per Pint,	3..6	3/9
Other good Foreign ditto,	per ditto,	1..6	2/
Fruit Punch of good Spirits and Loaf Sugar,	per Quart Bowl,	1..6	1/10½
Mim of good Rum and Loaf Sugar,	per Quart,	1..0	1/3
Mull'd Cyder,	per ditto,	9	/10d
Egg or other Sling, with a Gill of West-India Rum in it and Loaf Sugar,		9	/11d
West-India Rum,	per Half Pint,	10	1/
Ditto,	per Gill,	5	/6d
Cherry ditto,	per ditto,	5	/6d
Gin or Brandy,	per ditto,	6	/8d
Cyder-Royal,	per Pint,	6	/8d
Metheglin,	per ditto,	9	/11d
Good double Beer,	per Quart,	6	/9d
Good Cyder,	per ditto,	6	/6d
A good clean Bed, with clean Sheets, for a single Person,	per Night,	6	/6d
Ditto with two Persons in a Bed, each Person,	per ditto,	4	/4d
Oats ~~or Corn,~~ Corn	per Quart,	2 / 3	[illegible]
Good Pasture for a single Horse, per Night, or 24 Hours,		8	[illegible]
Good Stabling for ditto, Clover or Timothy Hay, per ditto,		1..6	[illegible]
~~Baiting with Clover Hay for an Hour, before Oats or Corn,~~		/6d	
~~Ditto in good Pasture, in the like case,~~			

By order of Court.

Giles, Clk.

The above is a price-setting "tavern-bill rated at General Court sessions held at Bridgetown [now Bridgeton] in the County of Cumberland [New Jersey] on the 25th day of February anno domini 1790." The last column on the right shows prices amended in January of the following year. The pens used were quill, the blotting paper sand, the currency anything from shillings and pence to Spanish doubloons.

MIMBO

A simple and rather awesome drink, Mimbo was simply straight rum diluted with loaf sugar.

COMFORT TEA

Also called Lady Tea, this was fancied by abstemious ladies who made it from hot water, a dash of milk, and a little sugar.

They Flipped

WHISTLE-BELLY VENGEANCE

Distinctly unappetizing in name, Whistle-Belly Vengeance was apparently just as bad as it sounded, for it was made of sour beer, molasses, Injun-bread simmered, then drunk piping hot.

HAILSTONE

An inn in Lexington, Kentucky, made a variation of the Mint Julep by topping it with a generous dash of brandy and dubbing it a Hailstone.

SNOWSTORM

The same Lexington inn served the same julep with the same brandy, except that, when it was a Snowstorm, it was considerably weaker than its Hailstone counterpart.

They Sipped

SASSAFRAS TEA

Brewed from the dried bark of sassafras and steeped like regular tea. Highly recommended to "thin the blood" as springtime approached.

RUM SWITCHEL

Needless to say, the innocent Switchel carried to working men in the field was not quite the same as their cider and water with a large measure of rum added. (Perhaps it should be in the "Flipped" instead of the "Sipped" column!)

PROHIBITION

Was rearing its ugly head as early as 1774 when a book by one Anthony Benezet was published in Philadelphia, with the awesome title: *The Mighty Destroyer Displayed, In Some Account of the Dreadful Havock Made by the Mistaken Use as Well as the Abuse of Distilled Spiritous Liquors.*

"ONE GROAT, SIR"!

That's what a barmaid of Colonial New England might have charged for a sack posset, made of sack (a heavy white sherry), ale, eggs, and cream seasoned with nutmeg and simmered two hours. A groat was an obsolete English coin worth four cents which frequently turned up in the Colonies. It was a barmaid in the auspicious year of 1776 who is credited by some historians as the inventor of the American cocktail. Her name was Betsy Flanagan, the inn Halls Corners at Elmsford, New York. Her bar was decorated with the brightly colored tail feathers of cocks and Betsy had the fanciful notion of adding to each drink, as a sort of stirrer, a "cock tail" feather.

September Sixteen 1797 The following persons were recommend to the Governor as fit persons to keep Publick Houses of Entertainment within the County of Dauphin for the ensuing year —

Andrew Kapp Shaeffers Town
Nicholas Ott Harrisburgh
Peter Fanstler Londonderry
4 Michael Stroch Bethel Township
5 Joseph Snyder Middletown
6 Samuel Franklin M. Paxton
7 Jacob Noss Coxestown
8 Michael Kemperly Middletown
9 John Eraugh Hallifax
10 John Norton Harrisburgh
11 Jacob Forney Do
12 Jacob Henning Do
13 Valentine Sprengler Coxestown
14 George Zigler Harrisburg
15 John Gilchrist Do
16 Samuel Weir Do
17 Jacob Greer Do
18 Tobias Seybolth Do
19 Andrew Berryhill Paxton
20 Hugh Montgomery Harrisburgh
21 Samuel Elder Do
22 William Dougherty Do
23 George Deffelbaugh Coxestown
24 Frederick Youse Harrisburgh
25 John Kapp Do
26 Joseph Green M. Paxton
27 Daniel Sweigart Harrisburgh
28 Christian Coppel Lebanon
29 Martin Tridley Hummelstown
30 William Crabb Middletown
31 Michael Moyer W. Hanover
32 John Leitzler Harrisburgh
33 Jacob Geigar Lebanon Township
34 John Tinny W. Hanover
35 Joseph Dearmond London Derry
36 John Lytle M. Paxton
37 Andrew Lee Harrisburgh
38 Matthias Flam M. Paxton
39 George Shaver U. Paxton
40 James Ainsworth W. Hanover
41 John Hoover Paxton
42 Archibald McAlister Paxton

...to harbour riotous Company

was to lose the coveted license. From earliest Puritan settlement, police and town officials had the right to pass on "fit persons" who were deemed capable of running decent inns and taverns. Innkeepers had to put up a bond of fifty pounds and were forbidden to allow cock fighting, dice, gaming, or shuffle-board on the premises. During the Revolution, tavern licenses in New York were limited to two hundred to keep within bounds the "daily evils" of too much drinking.

September, 1797:—"The following persons are recommended to the Governor as fit persons to keep publick houses of entertainment within the County of Dauphin (Pennsylvania) for the ensuing year."

...and a tab of ten Shillings

was the credit limit imposed by law on tavern proprietors of the 1770's. Philadelphia ordinaries, as early as 1683, had a fixed price of six pence for what William Penn described as "a good warm meal." Tavern keepers had to fill out forms like this one every time new price levels were approved. A standard price at wayside inns of the time was three shillings a day, for lodging, meals, "a fire if needed," and beer "as required."

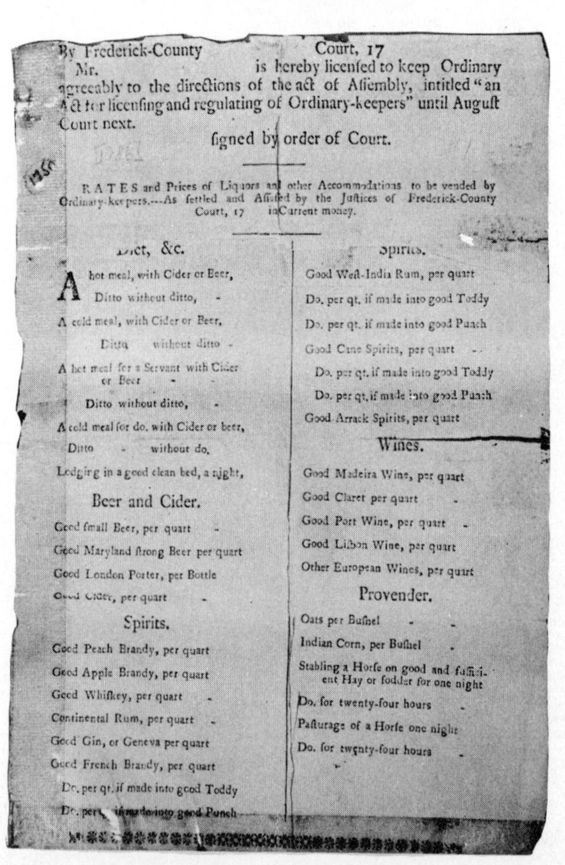

By Frederick-County Court, 17
Mr. is hereby licenfed to keep Ordinary agreeably to the directions of the act of Affembly, intitled "an Act for licenfing and regulating of Ordinary-keepers" until Auguft Court next.

figned by order of Court.

RATES and Prices of Liquors and other Accommodations to be vended by Ordinary-keepers.---As fettled and Affeffed by the Juftices of Frederick-County Court, 17 in Current money.

Diet, &c.

A hot meal, with Cider or Beer,
Ditto without ditto, -
A cold meal, with Cider or Beer,
Ditto without ditto -
A hot meal for a Servant with Cider or Beer - -
Ditto without ditto, -
A cold meal for do. with Cider or beer,
Ditto - without do.
Lodging in a good clean bed, a night,

Beer and Cider.

Good fmall Beer, per quart -
Good Maryland ftrong Beer per quart
Good London Porter, per Bottle
Good Cider, per quart -

Spirits.

Good Peach Brandy, per quart
Good Apple Brandy, per quart
Good Whifkey, per quart -
Continental Rum, per quart -
Good Gin, or Geneva per quart
Good French Brandy, per quart
Do. per qt. if made into good Toddy
Do. per [illegible] made into good Punch

Spirits.

Good Weft-India Rum, per quart
Do. per qt. if made into good Toddy
Do. per qt. if made into good Punch
Good Cane Spirits, per quart -
Do. per qt. if made into good Toddy
Do. per qt. if made into good Punch
Good Arrack Spirits, per quart

Wines.

Good Madeira Wine, per quart
Good Claret per quart -
Good Port Wine, per quart -
Good Lifbon Wine, per quart
Other European Wines, per quart

Provender.

Oats per Bufhel - -
Indian Corn, per Bufhel -
Stabling a Horfe on good and fufficient Hay or fodder for one night
Do. for twenty-four hours -
Pafturage of a Horfe one night
Do. for twenty-four hours -

A Price-Fixing Form of 1786

HOW THEY LOOKED...

OUTSIDE...

Historic Monroe Tavern in Lexington, Massachusetts, was typical of the stout four-square New England inns of the eighteenth century. Its chimneys indicated ample fireplaces needed for cooking as well as for the unequal battle against bitter winter nights. Here, on April 18, 1775, lay the uneasy head of Lord Perry, who knew that in nearby Buckman Tavern a rally of minutemen had been held the previous day and that trouble was pending. The 19th saw the Battle of Lexington—eight minutemen killed, six wounded—the war was on!

...& INN

In the fireplace, according to poet James Russell Lowell, "there dozed a fire of beech logs," and the host behind his polished cage of a bar dispensed good cheer. Taverns as commodious as the Monroe usually had parlors where ladies could repair and where an English bowl of punch was passed discreetly. Even the parsons occasionally imbibed. At the ordination of one minister in the 1780's, persons assembled in his honor at the local tavern consumed thirty bowls of punch before Meeting time . . . forty-four bowls after, plus rum, brandy, and wine.

Sangree drams & hay...

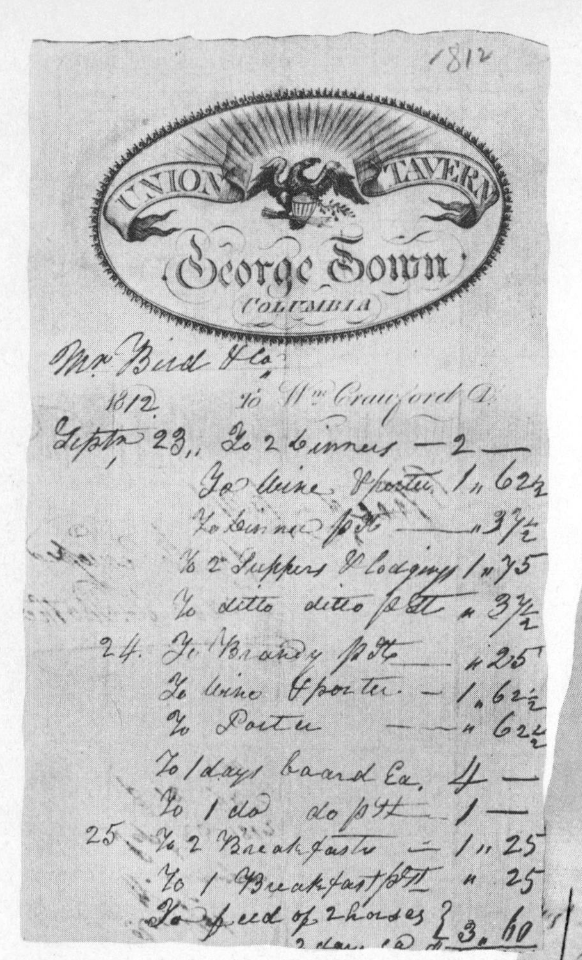

1812

UNION TAVERN
George Town
COLUMBIA

Mr Bird & Co.
1812 To Wm Crawford Dr

Septr 23	To 2 Dinners	2 —
	To Wine & Porter	1 „ 62½
	To Dinner pd	„ 37½
	To 2 Suppers & Lodging	1 „ 75
	To ditto ditto pd	„ 37½
24.	To Brandy pd	„ 25
	To Wine & Porter	1 „ 62½
	To Porter	„ 62½
	To 1 days board Ea.	4 —
	To 1 do do pd	1 —
25	To 2 Breakfasts	1 „ 25
	To 1 Breakfast pd	„ 25
	To feed of 2 horses	3 „ 60

T. S. Manning, Printer.

No. 11 South Sixth Street.

HEISKELL's HOTEL,
Sign of the Indian Queen,
No. 15 South Fourth Street, Philadelphia.

Mr. Jones Dr.

To Supper & Lodging		
Breakfast		42
Dinner		75
	2	25

Recd Payment

...and mind your P's & Q's

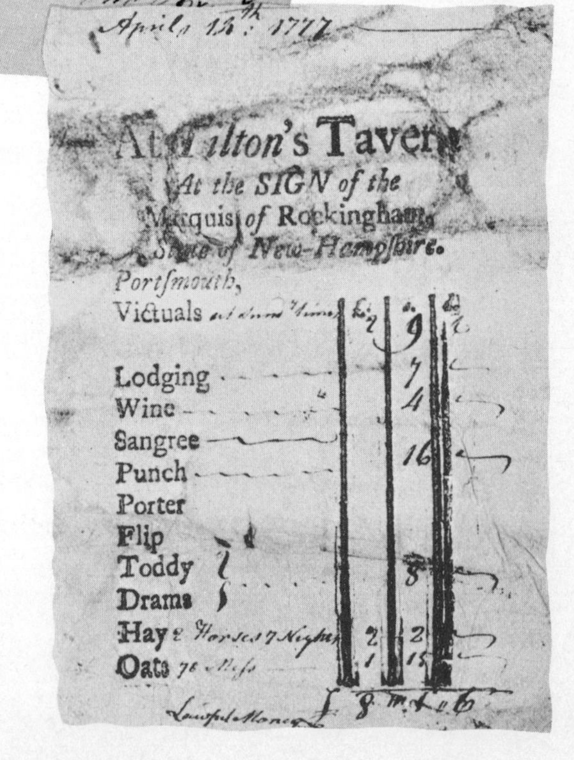

April 15th: 1777

At Tilton's Tavern
At the SIGN of the
Marquis of Rockingham,
State of New-Hampshire.
Portsmouth,

	£	s	d
Victuals	2	9	
Lodging		7	
Wine		4	
Sangree		16	
Punch			
Porter			
Flip			
Toddy		8	
Drams			
Hay & Horses 7 Nights	2	2	
Oats	1	15	

Lawful Money £ 8 ..

The first Indian Queen at 15 South Fourth Street in Philadelphia cherished a legend that Thomas Jefferson wrote a part of the Constitution there. Actually, Jefferson stayed at an excellent boardinghouse next door, run by a Frenchman, John Francis, and his wife. They also had as a guest John Adams, who went from there to be inaugurated the second President of the United States. By the 1820's, Thomas Heiskell owned the house which boasted an Indian Queen signboard painted by John A. Woodside, famous for his fire engine decorations and tavern signs. Heiskell's bills always carried the Indian Queen engraving and a common item listed on them was "Hay & Horses." Bills of that era sometimes listed a lump price for "victuals," sometimes itemized such engaging dishes as ladyfinger potatoes, pigeon pie, and pickled oranges. Puddings were served in "twiffles," milk came to table in a ewer, sugar was often brought in a container called a "sneak pot."

The Buckhorn Tavern, 22nd Street & Broadway, New York City, 1812.

...the Bouwerie Boys...

had already made the street infamous by 1868 when saloons like this one combined drinking with a game of billiards or bowling, and dished up indifferent food for indifferent diners. The Bouwerie, of course, was named in its tree-shaded years of seventeenth-century peace and quiet, "Bouwerie" being Dutch for "street of trees."

...the wits of the day...

assembled at the Old Shakespeare Tavern on the southwest corner of Fulton and Nassau Streets. There De Witt Clinton, later Governor of New York, talked over grandiose plans for the Erie Canal. Fitz-Greene Halleck came there, as did James Fenimore Cooper, and a sprinkling of poets known variously as "queer" or "mad" read their latest brain children. The National Guard was organized at the Old Shakespeare in 1824.

Curb Service

For man and beast . . . man to call out his order for ale, beer, porter, or whatever, while beasts under saddle or harness had a self-service water supply at hand. Halfway House, seen here in 1862, was way uptown in what is now New York's traffic merry-go-round, Columbus Circle. Coaching parties found it a pleasant stopover on a day's outing.

Fraunces Tavern

"a dull & dirty little town"

So a visitor described New York City in 1789 when Fraunces Tavern was in its glory. Built in 1719 by Colonel Van Cortlandt, the mansion remained a private residence until about 1757 when the occupants, as New Yorkers have been doing ever since, moved "uptown." The sturdy old brick building became an inn in 1782, when "Black Sam" Fraunces came from the West Indies to supervise its operation. The proud hostelry at the corner of Pearl and Broad Streets was the scene of exciting happenings during the Revolution and the early years of the new nation. A group of businessmen met there on April 8, 1768, to organize the first Chamber of Commerce.

By the 1880's it had fallen into a dowdy old age and looked like the sorry stepchild shown here.

"off with her head"!

And so literally, the restoration workmen did "guillotine" the ugly top story added in the 1800's. Now Fraunces Tavern looks as it does opposite, standing serene in the jet-propelled twentieth century, with dormered roof and pillared entrance, with fourteen fireplaces and a "most excellent kitchen."

THE NEW YORK TEA PARTY

The long room of Fraunces Tavern was the scene of New York's own Tea Party in 1774, when the Sons of Liberty and the Vigilance Committee met there to plan a protest against taxation without representation. They marched from the tavern to the waterfront, boarded the ship *London,* and dumped the contents of her tea chests into New York Harbor.

The Fraunces was chosen by George Washington for his Farewell Dinner to his officers on December 4, 1783.

Washington's bill, rendered him by the tavern for November 26-December 4, 1783, was for 95 pounds, 15 shillings and six pence.

By 1893, the long room was as down-at-the-heel as the exterior. Early eighteenth-century drawings such as the one above helped the researchers and architects to restore the room to its wood-paneled simplicity. It is authentic, now, with historic portraits and museum-piece furnishings. Its luncheon menu follows the Colonial tradition, the most popular items being Red Snapper Turtle Soup and Turtle Steak.

Pleasantly Located

FOR THE TRAVELER

AMERICAN HOTEL,

NEAR THE

Eastern & Western Railroad Depot.

BY F. McCARTHY,

Successor to J. C. Wells,

STATE STREET, ROCHESTER, N. YORK.

MEALS, 25 CENTS.

The American Hotel is pleasantly located, being near the centre of the City. Gentlemanly and obliging Porters will be at all the conveyances, to take charge of Baggage for Guests of the House.

Persons wishing to take the Steamers for Canada, Cobourg and Toronto, or Oswego, Kingston, Montreal and Lewiston, will find an OMNIBUS running from this House to the Steamboats, Packets and Cars

Stages leave this House for Avon, Geneseo, Mt. Morris, Angelica, Dansville and Lima.

"An obliging host, beautiful scenery and pleasant summer retreats" were the beguilements offered by J. M. Dunlap at his Hurlgate Ferry House in the early 1800's. Located at the end of what is now 86th Street in New York City, the Ferry House overlooked the East River and could be reached "by Murphy's Stages from City Hall, Pell Street and the Bowery." These stages ran every twenty-five minutes and carried passengers at a fare of six cents each. Excursionists loved to make summertime trips aboard side-wheelers such as the *Knickerbocker,* glimpsed in the view of the inn above. The Ferry House offered "refreshments of the first quality" and boats to hire for fishing parties.

As steamboats began to push up the rivers and across the lakes, and as railroad tracks forged a shiny new trail westward, so did inns and taverns spring up along the way. This sign for the American Hotel at Rochester, New York, situated conveniently near the Eastern and Western Railroad Depot, promised that "gentlemanly and Obliging Porters" would be waiting at all the conveyances to take charge of baggage for guests of the house. Omnibus service was provided, too, for persons wishing to take steamers to Toronto or other points.

COFFEE HOUSES

A Sharp Deal & Strong Brew

The concept of today's giant New York Stock Exchange grew from this eighteenth-century Coffee House Slip (above), where Colonial traders and merchants adopted the English habit of transacting business over coffee. The first establishment here is believed to have been opened in Boston in 1670, when a "dame" was given permission to serve coffee and chocolate. In the same year, a Widow Roberts announced a coffee house "for the entertainment of gentlemen," offering as well "the constant attention of hostesses." Even the Indians took to coffee—and a "Coffee Cooler" was the nickname given to an Indian who would sign practically any treaty or agreement in return for a cup of coffee. New York's famous Merchant's Coffee House set a new pattern in 1784 by inaugurating a Directory "to prevent the many disappointments that daily happen to returned citizens, or others, enquiring for their friends, connections or others that they may have business with." The Directory or Register was kept at the back of the Coffee House and in it, alphabetically, a gentleman could insert his name and place of residence. Boston's Exchange Coffee House, opened in 1804, was seven stories tall—a sort of Colonial skyscraper—and in it President James Monroe maintained a suite where he entertained the political and military "Who's Who" of his day at elaborate dinners.

Navigation was a timely subject in 1786 when Mr. Colles invited a group of gentlemen to talk over cake and coffee. Only a little more than a year later, on August 22nd, 1787, John Fitch's pioneer steamboat sailed the Delaware, its twelve mechanical oars speeding the craft along at twelve miles an hour. A fashion note of Mr. Colles' era recommended, for occasions such as this cake and coffee session, that a pea-green coat with white vest and nankeen smallclothes would be proper, plus white silk stockings and pumps with silver buckles; the smallclothes to be tied at the knee with double bows.

MR. COLLES preſents his Compliments to Mr Nich Low

and requeſts the favour of his company, at the Coffee-houſe, on Friday the 7th inſt. at 7 o'Clock in the evening, to meet a committee of the *Honorable Houſe* of ASSEMBLY, on the ſubject of the *Mohawk Navigation.*

NEW-YORK, *April* 5, 1786.

THE HONOR OF

Company is requested at a DINNER, to be given to the

Hon. R. R. LIVINGSTON,

late Minister at the Court of France, on Friday 6th inst.

at 4 o'clock, at the TONTINE COFFEE-HOUSE.

JOHN WATTS,
DANIEL LUDLOW,
JOHN R. MURRAY.

New-York, December 2, 1805.

The Tontine at Wall and Water Streets in New York City lasted from 1792 to 1816, and its assessed value of $7,000 was topped only by the $13,000 mansion of Peter Stuyvesant. Ex-Ambassador Livingston, returning from the Court of France, evidently caused the 4 o'clock dinner in his honor to be postponed from Friday the 6th to Saturday the 7th. Tontine was the name of a seventeenth-century Neapolitan banker who invented the idea of an annuity shared among a number of people; with the death of each beneficiary his share went to the survivors, the whole going to the last two or three. This New York Tontine was built by merchants, traders, and sailing masters who needed a place to eat, drink, and discuss business.

"The Good Quakers Bethought Themselves Of Temporal Luxuries..."

Taverns were plentiful in the quiet Quaker town of Philadelphia in the early eighteenth century, but as a Philadelphia historian notes, "they were frequented by the disorderly and the dissipated. Wililam Penn, Jun., and the young pleasure-loving Governor, John Evans, by their wild escapades, gave them a bad name. For the benefit then, of the graver and staider citizens, coffee houses . . . were opened."

And none had an aura of greater splendor than the Old London Coffee House pictured above, built close to Philadelphia's waterfront in 1702 by that "truly honest man, Charles Read." By the 1750's it had become famous. By its doors Captain Wise drank his bowl of punch while the crowd cheered him for having brought home the good news that the Stamp Act was repealed; and there, too, a Dr. Kearsley swallowed his in hot haste while the populace hooted and jeered him because of his Tory proclivities. Men met there to eat a chop or drink a glass of wine while they traded political gossip.

"GREAT INDUCEMENTS *for* MERCHANTS"

That is how George Brown put it when he announced the opening of his Coffee House at 71 Pearl Street, New York City, in the 1840's . . . "with very commodious rooms . . . celebrated for the dispatch with which refreshments are served up." He offered "oysters of the finest quality . . . at any time and the finest wines, ales, liquors and segars that can be found in the city." He boasted that his second floor dining room was "in summer one of the coolest in the city, the whole Slip being open before it and while a person is enjoying a good meal, he may also enjoy a refreshing breeze from the Bay." Breakfast was carefully timed for "the Eastern Boats" and the location, facing Coenties Slip, "presents good inducements for Merchants, Clerks and Others." Not far away, at 61 Whitehall Street, stood a warehouse which was to become the Eagle Hotel in 1856. The shell of that building, containing mahogany beams brought across the ocean as ballast in sailing ships, is part of the site chosen in 1963 for the enlarged New York Stock Exchange. Robert Fulton frequented Brown's Coffee House and often stayed at the Eagle, as did Jenny Lind, "the Swedish Nightingale," and P. T. Barnum, who supervised her spectacular concert tour in America.

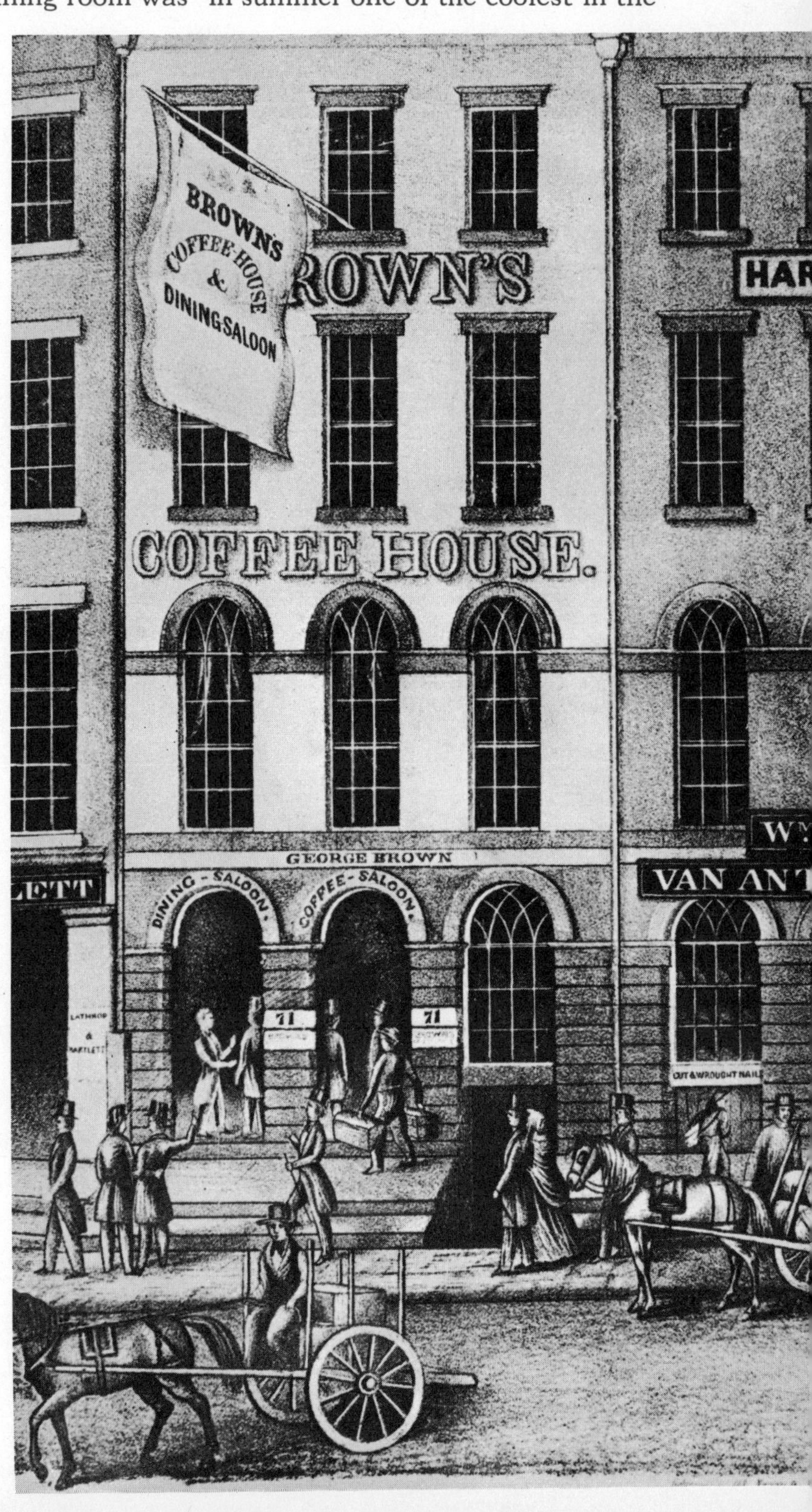

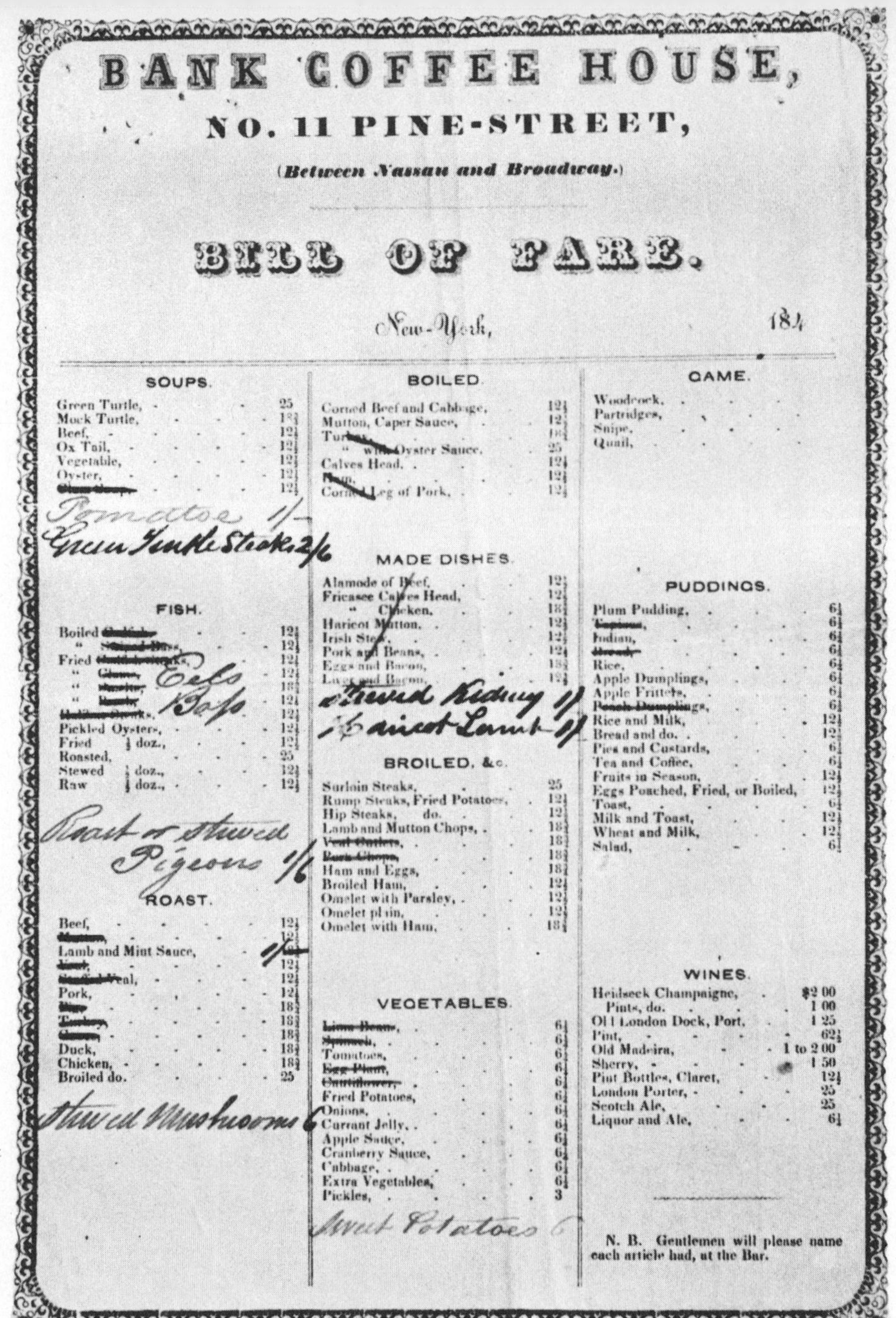

BANK COFFEE HOUSE,

NO. 11 PINE-STREET,

(*Between Nassau and Broadway.*)

BILL OF FARE.

New-York, 184

SOUPS.

Green Turtle,	25
Mock Turtle,	18¾
Beef,	12½
Ox Tail,	12½
Vegetable,	12½
Oyster,	12½
[illegible]	12½

Tomatoe 1/-
Green Turtle Steaks 2/6

FISH.

Boiled [illegible]	12½
" [illegible]	12½
Fried [illegible]	12½
" [illegible]	12½
" [illegible]	18¾
" [illegible]	12½
[illegible]	12½
Pickled Oysters,	12½
Fried ¼ doz.,	12½
Roasted,	25
Stewed ¼ doz.,	12½
Raw ¼ doz.,	12½

Eels
Bass

Roast or Stewed Pigeons 1/6

ROAST.

Beef,	12½
[illegible]	12½
Lamb and Mint Sauce,	1/-
[illegible]	12½
[illegible] Veal,	12½
Pork,	12½
[illegible]	18¾
[illegible]	18¾
[illegible]	18¾
Duck,	18¾
Chicken,	18¾
Broiled do.	25

Stewed Mushrooms 6

BOILED.

Corned Beef and Cabbage,	12½
Mutton, Caper Sauce,	12½
Turkey,	18¾
" with Oyster Sauce,	25
Calves Head,	12½
Ham,	12½
Corned Leg of Pork,	12½

MADE DISHES.

Alamode of Beef,	12½
Fricasee Calves Head,	12½
" Chicken,	18¾
Haricot Mutton,	12½
Irish Stew,	12½
Pork and Beans,	12½
Eggs and Bacon,	18¾
Liver and Bacon,	12½

Stewed Kidney 1/
Haricot Lamb 1/

BROILED, &c.

Surloin Steaks,	25
Rump Steaks, Fried Potatoes,	12½
Hip Steaks, do.	12½
Lamb and Mutton Chops,	18¾
Veal Cutlets,	18¾
Pork Chops,	18¾
Ham and Eggs,	18¾
Broiled Ham,	12½
Omelet with Parsley,	12½
Omelet plain,	12½
Omelet with Ham,	18¾

VEGETABLES.

Lima Beans,	6¼
Spinach,	6¼
Tomatoes,	6¼
Egg Plant,	6¼
Cauliflower,	6¼
Fried Potatoes,	6¼
Onions,	6¼
Currant Jelly,	6¼
Apple Sauce,	6¼
Cranberry Sauce,	6¼
Cabbage,	6¼
Extra Vegetables,	6¼
Pickles,	3

Sweet Potatoes 6

GAME.

Woodcock,
Partridges,
Snipe,
Quail,

PUDDINGS.

Plum Pudding,	6¼
Tapioca,	6¼
Indian,	6¼
Bread,	6¼
Rice,	6¼
Apple Dumplings,	6¼
Apple Fritters,	6¼
Peach Dumplings,	6¼
Rice and Milk,	12½
Bread and do.	12½
Pies and Custards,	6¼
Tea and Coffee,	6¼
Fruits in Season,	12½
Eggs Poached, Fried, or Boiled,	12½
Toast,	6¼
Milk and Toast,	12½
Wheat and Milk,	12½
Salad,	6¼

WINES.

Heidseck Champaigne,	$2 00
Pints, do.	1 00
Old London Dock, Port,	1 25
Pint,	62½
Old Madeira,	1 to 2 00
Sherry,	1 50
Pint Bottles, Claret,	12½
London Porter,	25
Scotch Ale,	25
Liquor and Ale,	6¼

N. B. Gentlemen will please name each article had, at the Bar.

Bread & Do.

"Do." was the abbreviation used on old menus to indicate "ditto," and in this case it refers to "milk." New Yorkers who lunched or dined at Bank's Coffee House in the 1830's and 40's doted on turtle soup and turtle steaks, a food fad that had begun fifty years earlier when groups of ladies and gentlemen would make excursions in pleasant weather to inns along the East River, where they held "turtle feasts, turkey shoots and the like." Shad, venison, and grouse were plentiful, and a favorite of that time and for many years to come was pickled oysters. Often a pint of Madeira went along with the meal—but note the memo at the end of the menu above.

N.B.—Gentlemen will please name each article had, at the bar.

"Such Independence of Manners..."

This is what that intrepid journalist, Mrs. Anne Royall, thought about New Yorkers when she arrived in the 1820's and "took up my lodgings" at a boardinghouse much like the one above.

"On entering a large room," she wrote, "I found an assembly of ladies and gentlemen sitting before a blazing fire (no unwelcome sight). The old men were smoking their pipes and the younger ones were amusing the ladies with anecdotes, perfectly regardless of the copious draughts of tobacco smoke. To diversify the picture, one of the young ladies sat down to her piano forte. Never did I witness such independence of manners, even in the land of Jackson; our western heroes when it comes to smoking, withdraw from the company of ladies."

. . . "a prolonged agony . . ."

At any rate, that's how the average American boardinghouse seemed to a writer named Dedell in 1869. Perhaps boardinghouses had changed for the worse, for seventy-five years earlier a visiting clothier from Wiltshire, England, one Henry Wansey, stayed at Mrs. Loring's boardinghouse near the Battery, and reported:

"This is one of the pleasantest situations imaginable. Our common sitting room was 50 ft. by thirty and 20 in height, with windows on 2 sides of it. As we sat at dinner, we could see the vessels on one side of the room, sailing out of the harbour, and on the other, the same turning up Hudson's River, apparently sailing around the house, within 50 yds. of us. At this house lodged Mr. Genet, the late French Ambassador."

By the 1850's, people were streaming into New York City in search of careers, adventure, or just plain jobs, and as they came a veritable epidemic of boardinghouses broke out. In the crowded downtown business section, boardinghouse signs popped up among the "dusky red stores" with their iron shutters and the names of their proprietors painted in white on a black ground. Thomas Butler, in his *The Physiology of New York Boarding Houses,* says that in 1857 "the sidewalks downtown are perpetually blockaded by bales, barrels, and boxes, where the pedestrian's progress is rendered perilous by the transit, on skids, of the unwieldy merchandise from cart to store or vice versa . . . where throughout the week wholesale traffic reigns and which on Sunday has a very funereal and dead-wall aspect." He picks out one seven-story building "bearing its designation in proportionate letters; it is at once a cheap hotel and boarding house."

In the small barroom at the front of this boardinghouse, Butler found "a fat German . . . reclining in an arm chair, half asleep yet with the instinctive vigilance of a landlord, keeping one eye open. He

TIT FOR TAT (*Harper's Bazar,* 1898)
Boarding House Mistress: "I want a week's board in advance so as to be sure of it."
New Boarder: "That's all right. Here's your money. Now I want a week's board in advance for the same reason."

..."swamps of squash & acres of collapsed cabbage..."

is wide awake enough of evenings and of all evenings, Saturday. Drop in then and you will find him the center of a busy scene and ready to take drinks to every member of a motley and miscellaneous crowd." On Saturdays, the customers paid their tabs for the week. Mr. Butler describes the general din, with men "sitting . . . drinking, spitting, smoking around the stove (if in winter), men bending over the bagatelle tables at one end of the room, men cursing, quarreling or striking the table at cards . . . a perfect Babel of clamor."

Most of the eighty boarders were laboring men. The rooms were plainly furnished and "indifferently supplied with water." The girls and women working there were, Mr. Butler notes, "mostly ugly, of squat figure, very good humored, slatternly and industrious."

The dinner bell brought a hungry rush to the tables, where everyone helped himself to everything in sight, and the average time for finishing a meal was ten minutes. Quantity was what they wanted and according to Mr. B., they got it . . . "joints of coarse meat already cut into slices, pyramids of potatoes, swamps of squash and acres of collapsed cabbage."

Veal was the favored meat for weekday dinners. On Sundays the "sumptuous banquets" featured "strongly scented ham and oyster soup," but the withered little oysters were "so few in number that you might imagine them swimming around the turreen in disconsolate search for one another." In spite of all this, he says that "the spare little landlady" was popular with everyone!

THE TABLE GIRL OF THE PERIOD
(*Harper's Bazar*, 1873)

Mistress of Boarding House: "Maria, you are too flashily dressed for a Table Girl."

Maria: "S'pose I'm a fool! S'pose I'm going to have a lot of unmarried young boarders around me and not make myself look pooty, eh?"

"THE RESULT OF AN OVERCROWDED CIVILIZATION"

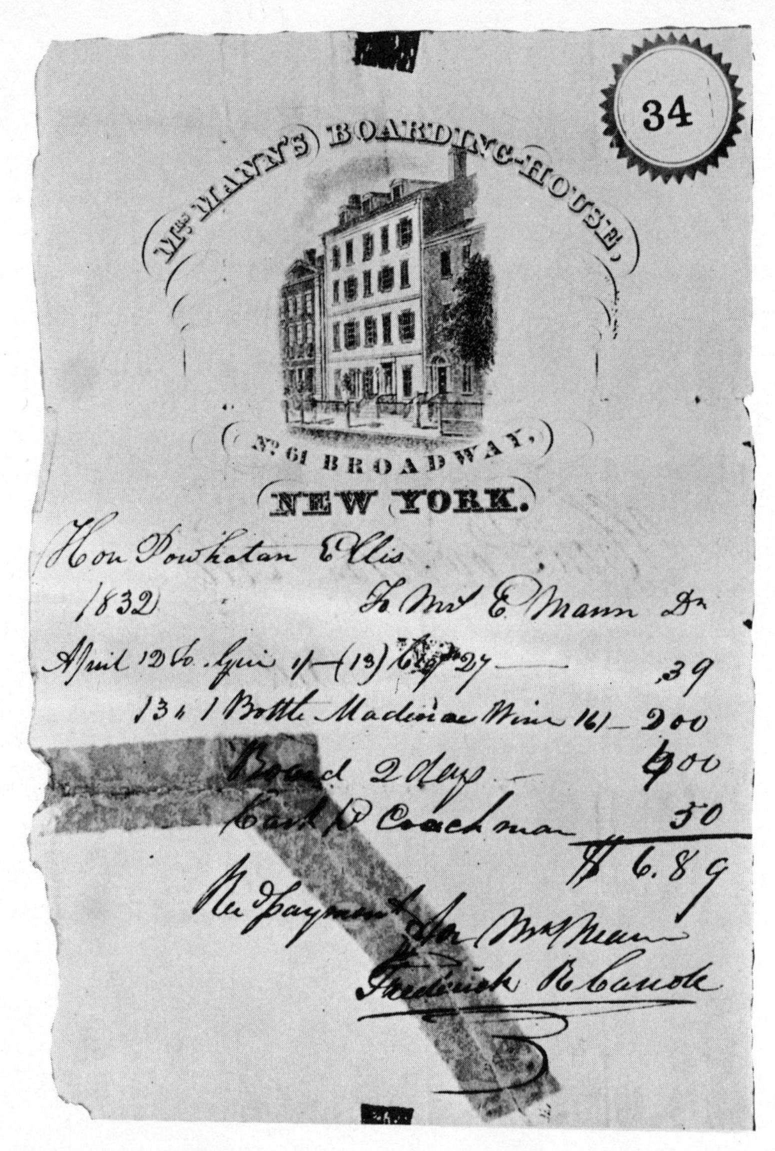

34

Mrs. MANN'S BOARDING-HOUSE,

No. 61 BROADWAY,

NEW YORK.

Hon Powhatan Ellis

1832 To Mrs E Mann Dr

April 12th Segars 1 — (13) — .39

13th 1 Bottle Madeira Wine 16/ — 2 00

Board 2 days — 4 00

Cash to Coachman 50

$ 6.89

Recd Payment for Mrs Mann

Frederick R Canoe

The above observation was made in 1869 by Junius Henri Browne, who believed that the ubiquitous New York boardinghouse was the direct result of this unhappy condition.

But boardinghouses had been with us for quite a time. This bill, made out to the Hon. Powatan Ellis on April 12, 1832, lists cigars at 39 cents, a bottle of Madeira, two dollars, board for two days, four dollars, and "cash to coachman, 50¢." Payment was received for Mrs. Mann, the boardinghouse mistress, by one Frederick R. Canoe, so evidently the good lady employed her own clerk.

The acid pen of Mr. Dedell addressed itself in the 1860's to the "cheap boardinghouse keeper . . . for that is her sex generally. She is resolved on buying much for little; and the quantity of leather steaks, highly perfumed butter, limed eggs, green fruit and unsavory vegetables she carries off!" He takes pity on any man "born above a boarding house who is still compelled to keep his body there with an appetite he cannot appease and through circumstance he cannot control."

PALACES & PLUSH for the POPULACE

BACKWARD in time from the boardinghouses and inns of the early nineteenth century, there occurs a date—1794—when something significant happened to the vocabulary of America and eventually to that of the world.

It was the word HOTEL.

Only a few years earlier, the New York City Directory told strangers where they could find food, drink, and a reasonable facsimile of a bed. In the whole list there is not a single hotel. There were:

121 taverns	1 lodging house & horse stabling
39 boardinghouses	1 oyster punch house
2 porter houses	1 tavern Elizabethan stage house

Most of the proprietors were men, but the Directory did list thirty-five females operating sundry establishments. If they'd lost a husband, they announced it to the world in such signs as The Widow Blake's, The Widow Blou's, The Widow Bailey's, The Widow Gale's. One was listed simply as Mrs. Bryan's.

These lodgings and taverns were in such fascinating and long-lost places as Market Stairs, Fly Market, Bowery Lane, Old Slip, Corporation Dock, and Anthony's Wharf.

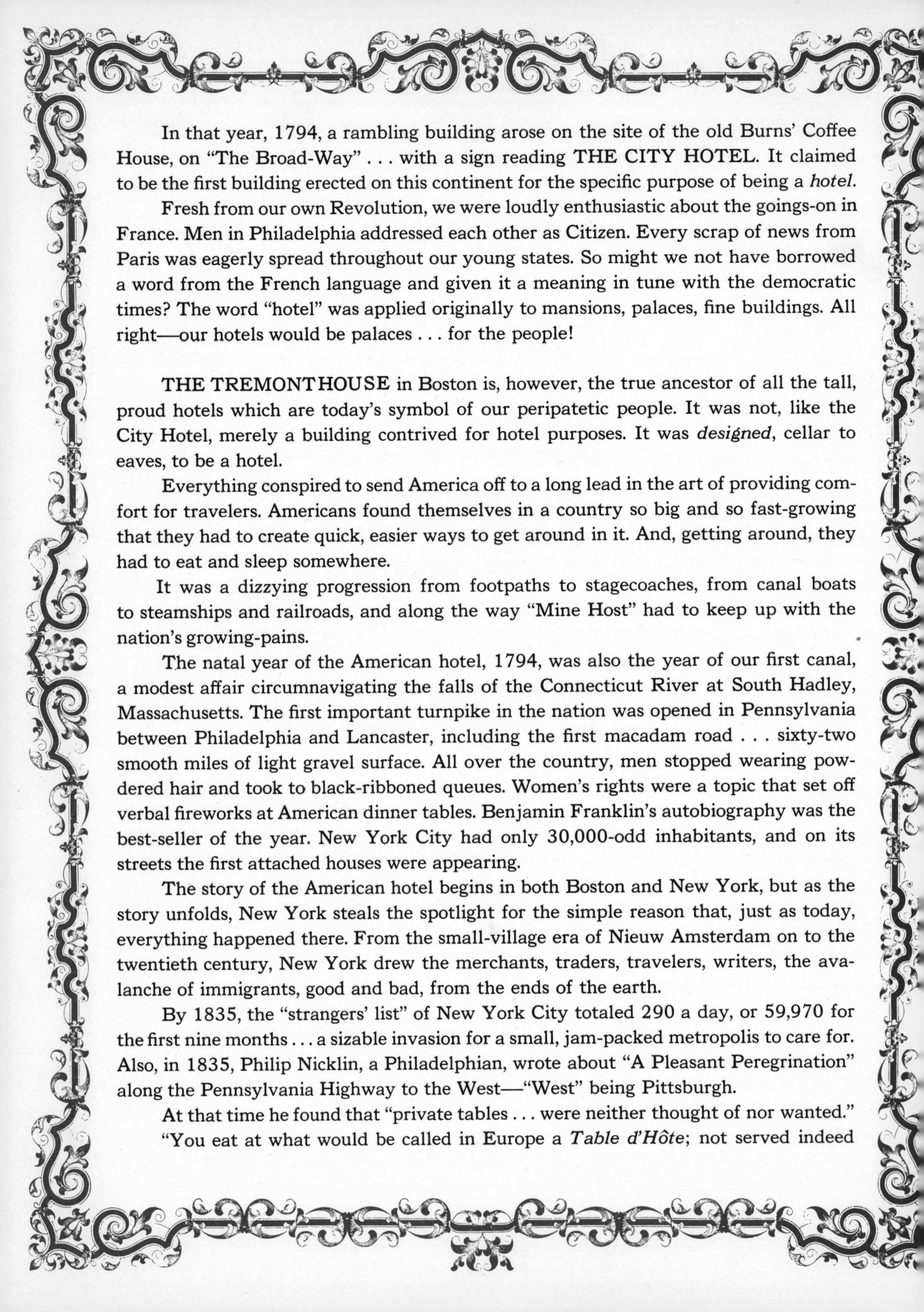

In that year, 1794, a rambling building arose on the site of the old Burns' Coffee House, on "The Broad-Way" . . . with a sign reading THE CITY HOTEL. It claimed to be the first building erected on this continent for the specific purpose of being a *hotel*.

Fresh from our own Revolution, we were loudly enthusiastic about the goings-on in France. Men in Philadelphia addressed each other as Citizen. Every scrap of news from Paris was eagerly spread throughout our young states. So might we not have borrowed a word from the French language and given it a meaning in tune with the democratic times? The word "hotel" was applied originally to mansions, palaces, fine buildings. All right—our hotels would be palaces . . . for the people!

THE TREMONT HOUSE in Boston is, however, the true ancestor of all the tall, proud hotels which are today's symbol of our peripatetic people. It was not, like the City Hotel, merely a building contrived for hotel purposes. It was *designed*, cellar to eaves, to be a hotel.

Everything conspired to send America off to a long lead in the art of providing comfort for travelers. Americans found themselves in a country so big and so fast-growing that they had to create quick, easier ways to get around in it. And, getting around, they had to eat and sleep somewhere.

It was a dizzying progression from footpaths to stagecoaches, from canal boats to steamships and railroads, and along the way "Mine Host" had to keep up with the nation's growing-pains.

The natal year of the American hotel, 1794, was also the year of our first canal, a modest affair circumnavigating the falls of the Connecticut River at South Hadley, Massachusetts. The first important turnpike in the nation was opened in Pennsylvania between Philadelphia and Lancaster, including the first macadam road . . . sixty-two smooth miles of light gravel surface. All over the country, men stopped wearing powdered hair and took to black-ribboned queues. Women's rights were a topic that set off verbal fireworks at American dinner tables. Benjamin Franklin's autobiography was the best-seller of the year. New York City had only 30,000-odd inhabitants, and on its streets the first attached houses were appearing.

The story of the American hotel begins in both Boston and New York, but as the story unfolds, New York steals the spotlight for the simple reason that, just as today, everything happened there. From the small-village era of Nieuw Amsterdam on to the twentieth century, New York drew the merchants, traders, travelers, writers, the avalanche of immigrants, good and bad, from the ends of the earth.

By 1835, the "strangers' list" of New York City totaled 290 a day, or 59,970 for the first nine months . . . a sizable invasion for a small, jam-packed metropolis to care for. Also, in 1835, Philip Nicklin, a Philadelphian, wrote about "A Pleasant Peregrination" along the Pennsylvania Highway to the West—"West" being Pittsburgh.

At that time he found that "private tables . . . were neither thought of nor wanted."

"You eat at what would be called in Europe a *Table d'Hôte*; not served indeed with so much ceremony, but furnished with more substantial fare . . . You can always get your meal in peace and plenty unless some unhappy prejudice sticks in your throat such as, that the vegetables can only be eaten with a silver fork; or the horror of eating peas with a knife."

Fifty or sixty dishes on the table at the same time was average in these days, and for special occasions the count could run to a hundred. There were plenty of special occasions, too, as the Americans seemed to have an urge to give a banquet on the slightest provocation.

It was about this time—the 1830's—that a few venturesome New York hotel proprietors tried out the European plan (first introduced in France) which eventually took over in practically every hotel in the country.

In 1837, a visiting New Englander reported three hotels in New York operating by this new system.

He called it "the European plan . . . or the English mode, of separating the two important concerns of bed and board. In taking the first you are under no obligation to take the last. You may eat at your landlord's if you please, and you may order what you please, but this has no connection with your bill for lodging, and you pay down on the nail for what you have eaten. The plan has only been introduced here within five or six years."

In the golden age of the American plan, landlords lured their patrons with four and five meals a day, and so much food that the tables did, literally, groan under the burden. The clang of the dinner bell brought a pushing, shoving crowd to the dining room doors, since meal hours were arbitrary. Breakfast at six, dinner at noon, tea at four, supper at six were usual, although in the five-meal-a-day marathon, hardy souls began with a hefty breakfast at seven, dinner at twelve, tea at five, supper at seven, and a late snack at nine or ten.

Thirty years after Mrs. Frances Trollope dipped her quill in vinegar to describe early nineteenth-century America *(Domestic Manners of the Americans, 1832)*, her son Anthony traveled across the United States and found himself astonished at that national phenomenon, the hotel (*North America,* 1862). He concluded that "everybody travels in the States" and added that "the first sign of an incipient settlement is an hotel five stories high, with an office, a bar, a cloak room, three gentlemen's parlors, two ladies' parlors, a ladies' entrance and two hundred bedrooms."

For an American hotel, "size and an imposing scale are the first requisites. Everything about them must be on a large scale." But he felt that the ladies' ordinaries and upstairs parlors were frequently chill and arid spots where nobody had any fun. "The intention is good, for they are established with the view to giving ladies at hotels the comforts of ordinary domestic life; but they fail in their efforts."

There was a lot of gilded furniture, Mr. Trollope observes, but "into these rooms no book is ever brought, no needlework is introduced; from them no clatter of many tongues is ever heard. On a marble table in the middle of the room always stands a large

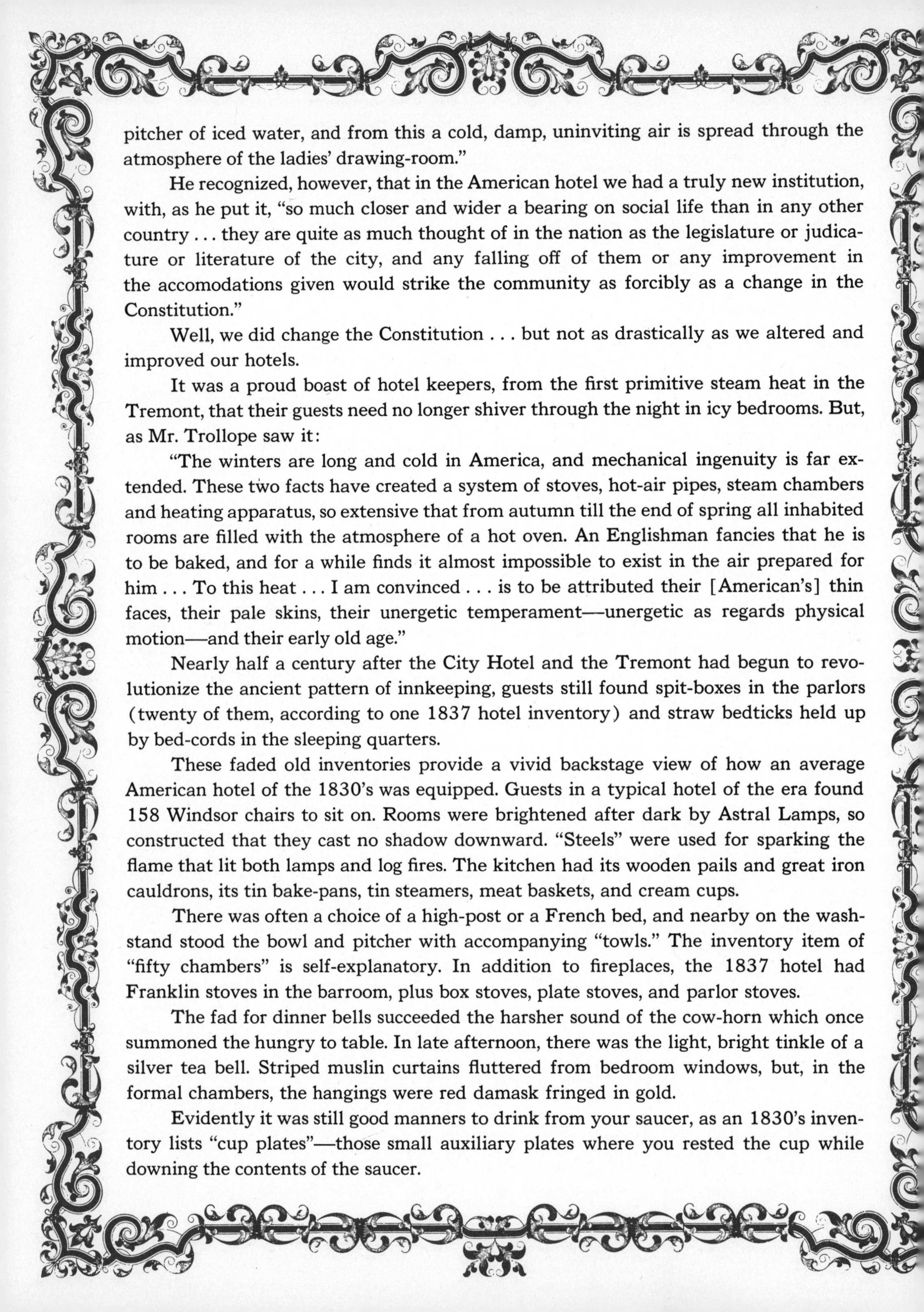

pitcher of iced water, and from this a cold, damp, uninviting air is spread through the atmosphere of the ladies' drawing-room."

He recognized, however, that in the American hotel we had a truly new institution, with, as he put it, "so much closer and wider a bearing on social life than in any other country . . . they are quite as much thought of in the nation as the legislature or judicature or literature of the city, and any falling off of them or any improvement in the accomodations given would strike the community as forcibly as a change in the Constitution."

Well, we did change the Constitution . . . but not as drastically as we altered and improved our hotels.

It was a proud boast of hotel keepers, from the first primitive steam heat in the Tremont, that their guests need no longer shiver through the night in icy bedrooms. But, as Mr. Trollope saw it:

"The winters are long and cold in America, and mechanical ingenuity is far extended. These two facts have created a system of stoves, hot-air pipes, steam chambers and heating apparatus, so extensive that from autumn till the end of spring all inhabited rooms are filled with the atmosphere of a hot oven. An Englishman fancies that he is to be baked, and for a while finds it almost impossible to exist in the air prepared for him . . . To this heat . . . I am convinced . . . is to be attributed their [American's] thin faces, their pale skins, their unergetic temperament—unergetic as regards physical motion—and their early old age."

Nearly half a century after the City Hotel and the Tremont had begun to revolutionize the ancient pattern of innkeeping, guests still found spit-boxes in the parlors (twenty of them, according to one 1837 hotel inventory) and straw bedticks held up by bed-cords in the sleeping quarters.

These faded old inventories provide a vivid backstage view of how an average American hotel of the 1830's was equipped. Guests in a typical hotel of the era found 158 Windsor chairs to sit on. Rooms were brightened after dark by Astral Lamps, so constructed that they cast no shadow downward. "Steels" were used for sparking the flame that lit both lamps and log fires. The kitchen had its wooden pails and great iron cauldrons, its tin bake-pans, tin steamers, meat baskets, and cream cups.

There was often a choice of a high-post or a French bed, and nearby on the washstand stood the bowl and pitcher with accompanying "towls." The inventory item of "fifty chambers" is self-explanatory. In addition to fireplaces, the 1837 hotel had Franklin stoves in the barroom, plus box stoves, plate stoves, and parlor stoves.

The fad for dinner bells succeeded the harsher sound of the cow-horn which once summoned the hungry to table. In late afternoon, there was the light, bright tinkle of a silver tea bell. Striped muslin curtains fluttered from bedroom windows, but, in the formal chambers, the hangings were red damask fringed in gold.

Evidently it was still good manners to drink from your saucer, as an 1830's inventory lists "cup plates"—those small auxiliary plates where you rested the cup while downing the contents of the saucer.

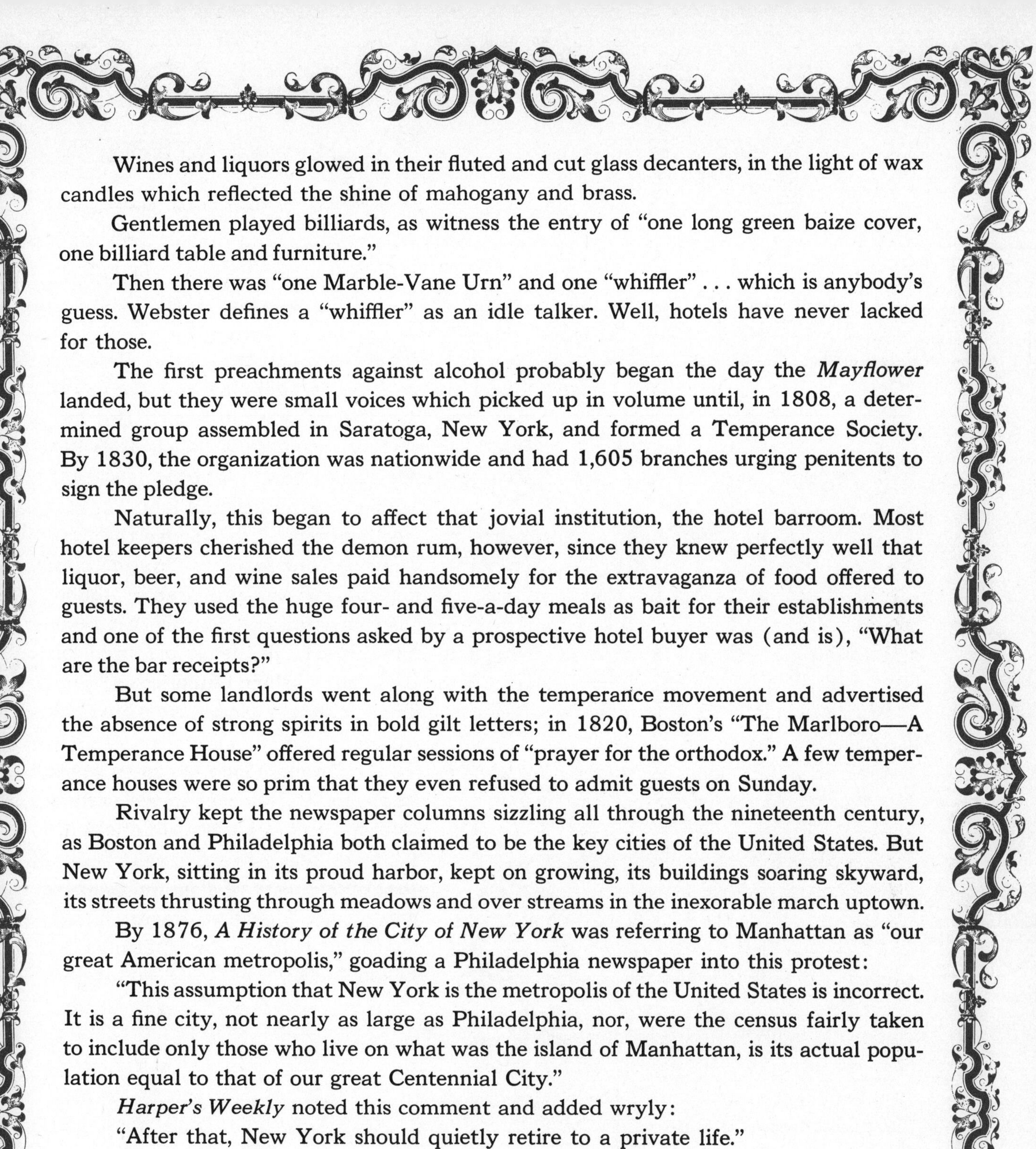

Wines and liquors glowed in their fluted and cut glass decanters, in the light of wax candles which reflected the shine of mahogany and brass.

Gentlemen played billiards, as witness the entry of "one long green baize cover, one billiard table and furniture."

Then there was "one Marble-Vane Urn" and one "whiffler" . . . which is anybody's guess. Webster defines a "whiffler" as an idle talker. Well, hotels have never lacked for those.

The first preachments against alcohol probably began the day the *Mayflower* landed, but they were small voices which picked up in volume until, in 1808, a determined group assembled in Saratoga, New York, and formed a Temperance Society. By 1830, the organization was nationwide and had 1,605 branches urging penitents to sign the pledge.

Naturally, this began to affect that jovial institution, the hotel barroom. Most hotel keepers cherished the demon rum, however, since they knew perfectly well that liquor, beer, and wine sales paid handsomely for the extravaganza of food offered to guests. They used the huge four- and five-a-day meals as bait for their establishments and one of the first questions asked by a prospective hotel buyer was (and is), "What are the bar receipts?"

But some landlords went along with the temperance movement and advertised the absence of strong spirits in bold gilt letters; in 1820, Boston's "The Marlboro—A Temperance House" offered regular sessions of "prayer for the orthodox." A few temperance houses were so prim that they even refused to admit guests on Sunday.

Rivalry kept the newspaper columns sizzling all through the nineteenth century, as Boston and Philadelphia both claimed to be the key cities of the United States. But New York, sitting in its proud harbor, kept on growing, its buildings soaring skyward, its streets thrusting through meadows and over streams in the inexorable march uptown.

By 1876, *A History of the City of New York* was referring to Manhattan as "our great American metropolis," goading a Philadelphia newspaper into this protest:

"This assumption that New York is the metropolis of the United States is incorrect. It is a fine city, not nearly as large as Philadelphia, nor, were the census fairly taken to include only those who live on what was the island of Manhattan, is its actual population equal to that of our great Centennial City."

Harper's Weekly noted this comment and added wryly:

"After that, New York should quietly retire to a private life."

The census complained about by the City of Brotherly Love showed, 1,046,252 persons for Philadelphia and 1,513,501 for the "great metropolis" . . . with Boston still scoring high in cultural achievement but down to a census of 446,507.

There has never been a year in New York's meteoric growth when people have not remarked wistfully that "you wouldn't recognize the city today." Back in 1851, the City Directory opened with the plaintive query—

"Where is Manahata—Where is Nieuw Amsterdam?"

1794 The CITY

...a boom town of

That's how bustling little New York looked to visitors in 1794, the year the City Hotel opened at 115 Broadway.

Operated for a time as Burns Coffee House, it was a hotbed of revolutionary conspiracy and later a military headquarters. Trees shaded the Broad-Way and the spire of Trinity Church rose against the sky close by the hostelry, which was also known as the Tontine City Hotel.

The City Hotel catered to the rich, the stylish, the leaders of New York's artistic, literary, and scientific circles. James Fenimore Cooper's famous Bread and Cheese Club met there, as did an informal group known simply as The Club and headed by Colonel Nick Saltus. In 1836, the Saltus followers organized the city's first private membership club with rooms of its own, the Union Club.

The City Hotel boasted seventy-three rooms and was the largest hotel in New York until 1813. It served breakfast at 8, dinner at 3, tea at 6, supper at 9, and for two dollars, room included. Landlord Chester Jennings moved the dinner hour from noon to 3 to conform with the then fashionable dining hour on the Continent.

HOTEL

thirty thousand

"Dangerous blue-blood habits . . . a menace to the foundations of the Republic . . . a threat to democracy," railed the press when the City Hotel introduced room service (in fine print at the bottom of its menu). It was popular with the packet boat captains who sailed twice monthly to Europe.

A minority report was filed on the City Hotel by a Lieutenant Fitzgerald of the British Royal Navy, who found it "immense, full of company, but a wretched place . . . the floors without carpets, the beds without curtains. There were neither glass nor cup and a miserable little rag was dignified with the name of towel."

The bar included a cage-shaped buffet where "an individual is engaged from morn to dewy eve in preparing and issuing forth strong drink and spices to strange-looking men who come to the house to read newspapers and talk politics."

The City Hotel, where gay young people had danced the rigadoon, the cotillon, and the minuet, took its last bow in 1849 and was replaced by a five-story business building.

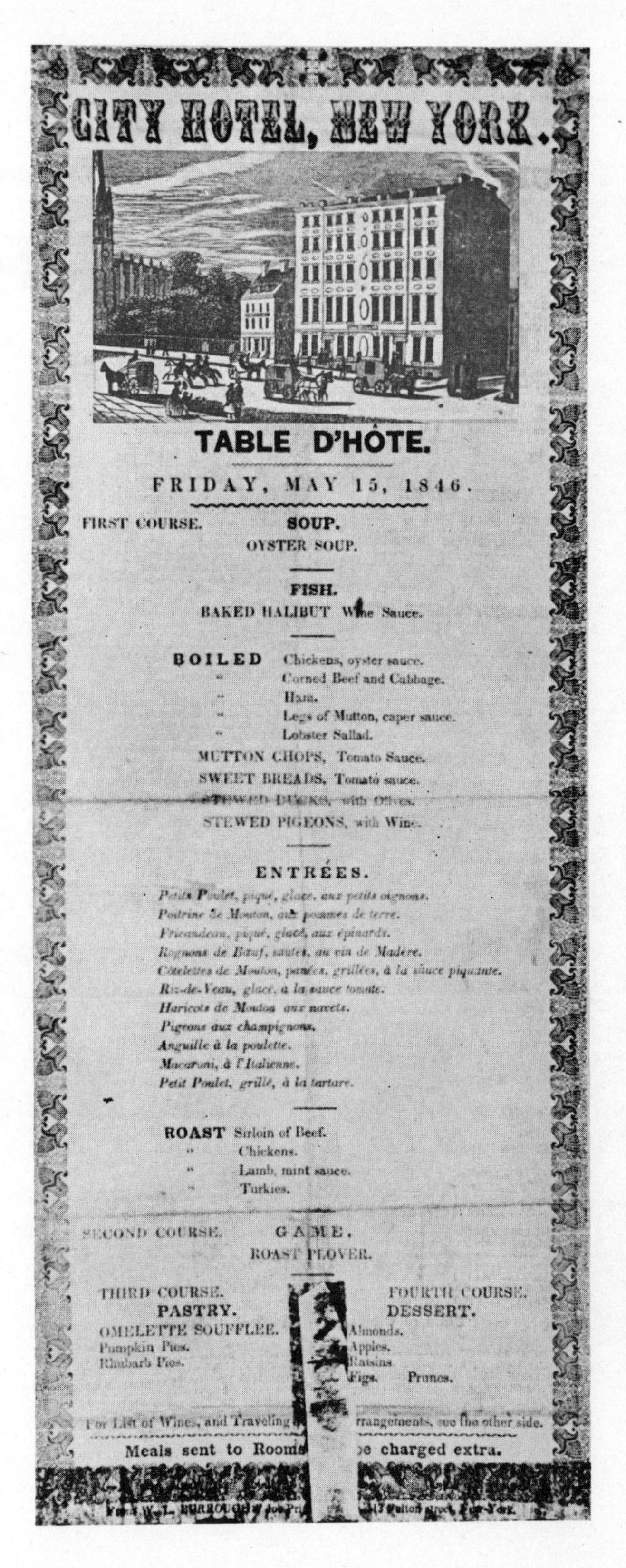

CITY HOTEL, NEW YORK.

TABLE D'HÔTE.

FRIDAY, MAY 15, 1846.

FIRST COURSE. **SOUP.**

OYSTER SOUP.

FISH.

BAKED HALIBUT Wine Sauce.

BOILED Chickens, oyster sauce.
" Corned Beef and Cabbage.
" Ham.
" Legs of Mutton, caper sauce.
" Lobster Sallad.

MUTTON CHOPS, Tomato Sauce.
SWEET BREADS, Tomato sauce.
STEWED DUCKS, with Olives.
STEWED PIGEONS, with Wine.

ENTRÉES.

Petits Poulet, piqué, glace, aux petits oignons.
Poitrine de Mouton, aux pommes de terre.
Fricandeau, piqué, glacé, aux épinards.
Rognons de Bœuf, sautés, au vin de Madere.
Côtelettes de Mouton, panées, grillées, à la sauce piquante.
Riz-de-Veau, glacé, à la sauce tomate.
Haricots de Mouton aux navets.
Pigeons aux champignons.
Anguille à la poulette.
Macaroni, à l'Italienne.
Petit Poulet, grillé, à la tartare.

ROAST Sirloin of Beef.
" Chickens.
" Lamb, mint sauce.
" Turkies.

SECOND COURSE. **GAME.**

ROAST PLOVER.

THIRD COURSE. **PASTRY.**	FOURTH COURSE. **DESSERT.**
OMELETTE SOUFFLEE.	Almonds.
Pumpkin Pies.	Apples.
Rhubarb Pies.	Raisins
	Figs. Prunes.

For List of Wines, and Traveling [illegible] rrangements, see the other side.

Meals sent to Rooms [illegible] be charged extra.

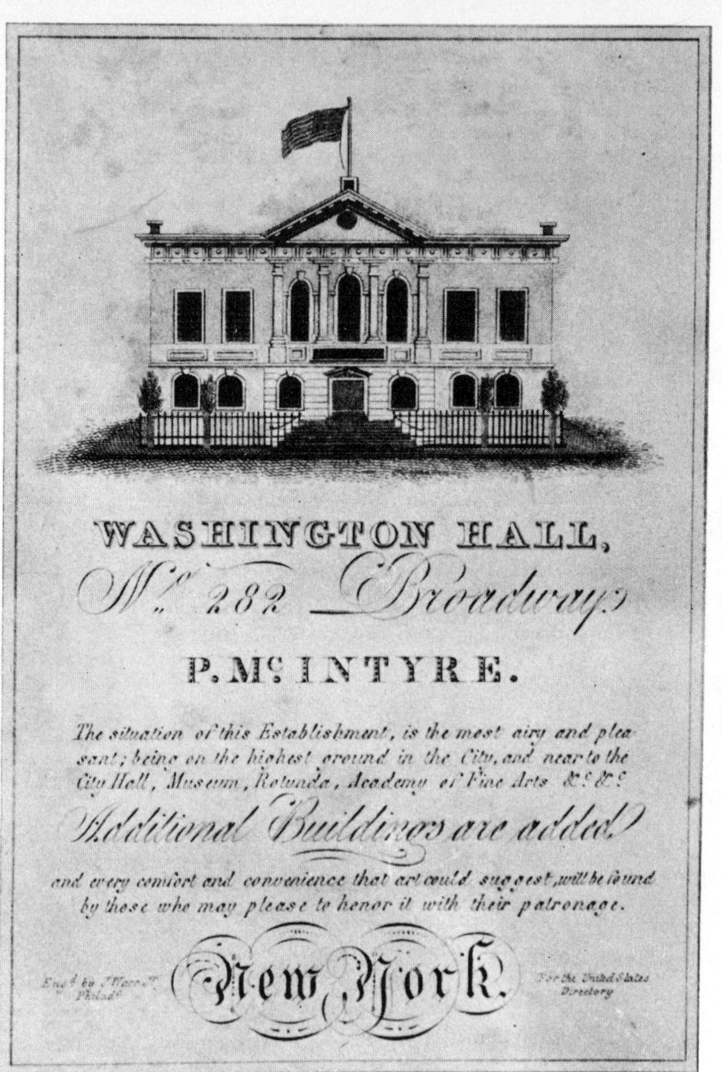

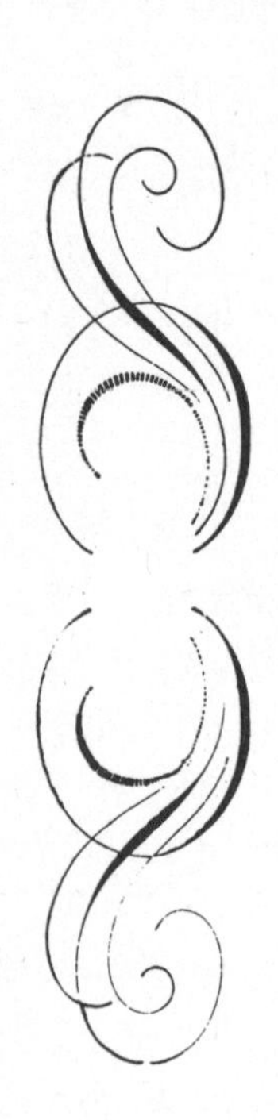
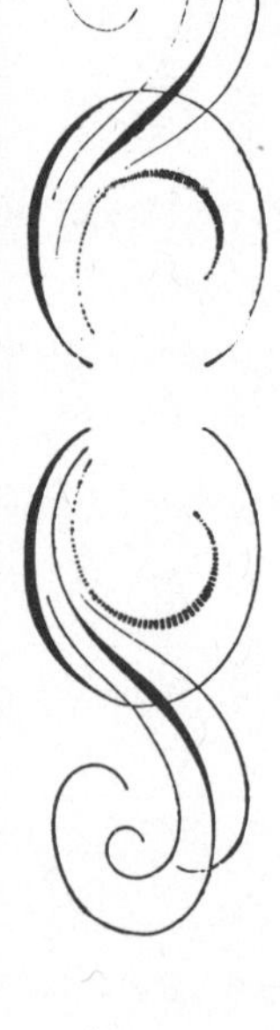

1809 WASHINGTON HALL

"...what is this new European plan?"

THE *New York Evening Post* of March 9, 1840, answered this question in an advertisement for Washington Hall:

"The establishment will be conducted on the much admired European Plan (namely) of letting the bedrooms, adequately furnished, at such terms as will square with the times—say from three to five dollars a week. . . .

"The situation is most pleasant and airy," noted the *U. S. Directory* shortly after the opening of the hotel in 1810 at 282 Broadway. It cost the lordly sum . . . for that time . . . of $140,000 and was located "on the highest ground in the city and near the City Hall, Museum, Rotunda, Academy of Fine Arts, etc. etc. . . . every comfort and convenience that art could suggest will be found by those pleased to honor it with their patronage." P. McIntyre was host of Washington Hall, which was the chief rival of the City Hotel for two decades.

1833 HOLT'S HOTEL

Mrs. Holt sews a fine stitch & Mr. Holt is sunk by a well.

At the exorbitant rate of $1.59 a day, guests could boast of stopping at the "largest and most magnificent building of its time"—1833—the new Holt's Hotel, on New York's Fulton Street between Pearl and Water. Mary, wife of Proprietor Stephen Holt, spent six years stitching the fifteen hundred towels, four hundred pairs of sheets, ruffled pillow cases to match, two hundred and fifty bedticks, and two hundred quilts of patchwork pieces as small as a twenty-shilling coin. Mr. Holt introduced a marvelous new gadget—a steam-powered lift. However, it lifted only the guests' luggage. The guests walked. The steam power was used for turning spits and for grinding food as well. Mr. Holt's most ambitious scheme was a well . . . and it sank him. The 599-foot deep artesian water supply was a wonderful idea in water-starved New York City, but it cost so much that the Holts went bankrupt in 1835 and the hotel was knocked down at auction for $175,000 . . . a bargain, considering its hundred-foot dining room with twenty-foot tall ceiling, its twenty-five parlors and one hundred sixty-five rooms. It bragged of being fireproof, too, with a cistern in the garret and connecting hoses to reach any part of the house. By the year of the Holt well disaster, New York had twenty-six hotels. Holt's could not keep up with the stylish Tremont's precedents. It had more the atmosphere of an old inn. Seafaring men adored it, though, and used to sit on the roof, railed in by a captain's walk, drinking juleps—probably New York's very first roof garden!

1836 PACIFIC HOTEL

"Be not disturbed by the noise & bustle of a thronged Street"

Oh, yes, even in 1836 poor little old New York was the target for jokes, snappish protests, and dire warnings about its dirt, noise, crowds, and traffic. Mr. Benjamin Jessups and Mr. R. C. Nichols made a formal announcement of the opening on July 1 of their "new and spacious building" at 162 Greenwich Street, New York. In addition to pointing out its quiet location, they noted that the "parlors, drawing and bed chambers are large, airy and well-lighted, and each one is furnished with a fireplace. Separate parlors and a dining room are fitted up for the convenience of the ladies." Finally, they pledged that "the proprietor will spare neither exertion nor expense to establish and preserve that internal order and regularity which will promote and secure quiet and comfort to the inmates and make it a pleasant and agreeable residence, who favor him with their patronage."

1836

The ASTOR HOUSE

BRODADWAY

Opposite The Park

NEW YORK'S FIRST PALACE FOR THE PEOPLE

ON the "fashionable side of the promenade" stood the Astor House, which opened in white and pristine beauty in the same year, 1836, that the *New York City Directory* published this rare print. As can be seen, the hotel, located on Broadway between Barclay and Vesey Streets, faced the tall trees and grass of City Hall Park. The *Directory's* door-by-door street guide identified only those establishments which paid the prescribed fee. The rest of the doorways were left blank. Opposite the Astor is glimpsed one paid-up subscriber who dealt in "Hair Wigs, Scarps, Curls & Fancy Articles."

The classic Greek style of the Astor was the work of architect Isaiah Rogers, who designed half a dozen magnificent hotels in the United States, beginning with the Tremont in Boston. The hotel stood on the site of the mansion of John Jacob Astor, who lived a dozen years after the opening. The Astor cost $400,000, blazed with lights fueled by its own gas plant, offered seventeen "bathing rooms" with hot water supplied by its own steam engine, and even had "patent locks" for its 309 rooms. It was luxurious, extravagant, and beloved by a moneyed clientele who seemed proof of the acidulous comment of that traveling Frenchman De Tocqueville:

"There is no lack of wealthy individuals in the United States. I know of no other country indeed where the love of money has taken a stronger hold than here on the affections of men."

All that nice money De Tocqueville commented on provided the Astor House with more parlor and bedroom suites than any other hotel. Designed by the architect who did Boston's Tremont, by order of Vincent Astor it had to outdo its predecessor, and so it was furnished from cellar to garret with fine black walnut, Brussels carpets . . . and, most wonderful of all, gaslights!

HARPER'S WEEKLY.

HOME AND FOREIGN GOSSIP.

A gentleman who was a guest at the Belmont House in Boston was recently found dead in his bed. The room was filled with gas, and it was still escaping from the burner. He had evidently blown out the gas on retiring.

"It Is a Handsome Light . . ."

At the Astor on opening night, gas ("a handsome light," according to the *New Yorker*) turned its white façade into a Christmas-tree glitter. But—

"This gas everybody is discussing . . . is here used in such quantity, being greater than common, that it gave out suddenly in the midst of a cotillion."

The report concluded that gas "is hardly calculated for the ordinary use of a family."

Disaster crowded the headlines in the 1840's when gaslight progressed from hotel public rooms to the bedrooms. In spite of warning signs, people went right on blowing out the light before retiring—and frequently blowing out themselves—out doors and windows, into hospitals and mortuaries.

The ebullient hotelier, Simeon Ford, said that suicidally inclined guests never inquired about the rates or fittings.

"Give them a good six-foot gas burner, about fifteen hundred feet of illuminating gas at $1.50 a thousand, and a few uninterrupted moments, and they are content."

As hotels grew higher in stature and in price, suicides by illuminating gas declined, according to Mr. Ford, because "When a guest is told the price of his room, it takes his breath away so he *can't* blow out the gas."

The Astor House parlor still retains some of its "unostentatious richness" in this picture, although the famous old hotel was in the social backwash as Manhattan marched steadily uptown. The parlor's gasoliers were now electrified . . . a modern convenience added when the outdated hotel closed its doors for renovations in 1875, trying desperately to defy the fate which caught up with all the once-fashionable spots below Twenty-third Street. The Astor installed private baths by fitting the parlors in its suites with plumbing. No doubt even the dignified parlor once reserved for Lincoln, with its white fireplace, Brussels carpet, mantel clock, and enormous gilt-framed pier glass, found itself equipped with tub, sink, and water closet!

Broadway, only four miles long when the Astor opened in 1836, was now zigzagging up Manhattan Island at a dizzying pace. No longer was the street in front of the Astor "distinguished for the fashionable, the gay and the idle," as reporter Anne Royall saw it in the mid-1800's, when "the broad windows" were "filled with china and glass ware, plate, millinery, fruit, confectionary" and when the hotel's bookshop was patronized by such as Walt Whitman, Herman Melville, Horace Greeley, and the like. Barnum's Museum was across the way, Brady's Daguerreotype Gallery nearby.

The parlor was evidently decked for some sort of do on this occasion, with smilax garlanding the gilt-framed pictures and ornate electrified lighting fixtures.

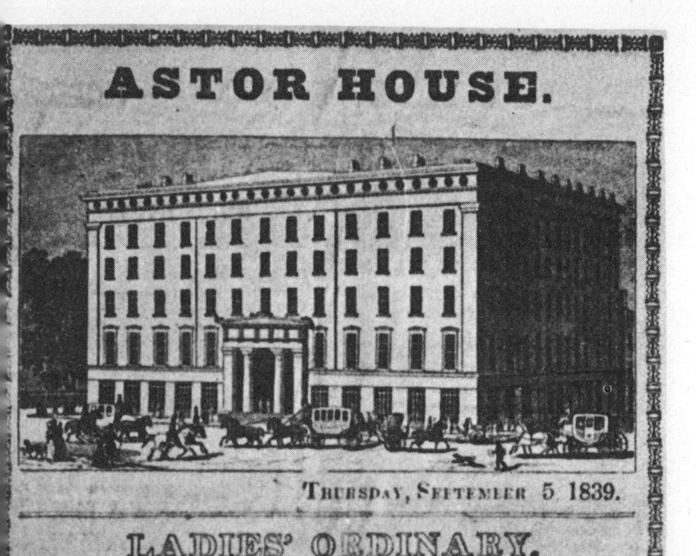

THURSDAY, SEPTEMBER 5 1839.

LADIES' ORDINARY.

SOUP.

Mock Turtle Soup.

FISH.

Boiled Bass, sauce à la maitre d'hotel,

BOILED

Ham,
Corned Beef,
Tongue,
Chicken and Pork,
Leg of Mutton,
Jole and Cabbage,

ENTREES.

Bifstecks aux pommes de terre,
Rolleau de veau sauce tomate,
Filets de volaille piqués à la financière,
Poitrine de mouton pannées à la maitre d'hotel,
Oreille de veau sauté à l'Italienne,
Epaule de mouton braizé sauce d'anchois,
Vol au vent garnie d'un blanquette de veau,
Cuisse de volaille pannées à l'Allemande,
Fricandeau à la purée de pommes de terre,
Canards poelés sauce espagnol,
Cervelle de veau frite,
Ragoût de mouton aux carrottes,
Tomates à l'espagnol,
Côtellettes de mouton sautées aux concombres,
Macaroni au gratin,
Aubergine frite,

ROAST.

Beef,
Veal,
Lamb, mint sauce,
Pork,
Ducks,
Chicken,
Goose, apple sauce.

PASTRY.

Apple Pie.
Custard Pudding,
Peach Pie,
Charlotte Russe.

DESSERT.

Peaches, Pears, Apples, Watermelons, Nutmeg-melons
Plums, Oranges,

Jared W. Bell, Printer 17 Ann-Street.

Ladies

EXTRA-ORDINARY

1839

The Ladies Ordinary of the Astor House was sacrosanct to feminine chatter and evidently to formidable feminine appetites as well. The Astor menus were produced daily on the hotel's own printing press and this one is clear evidence of the inroads being made by French cuisine.

The women who dined in the Ladies Ordinary were that rare breed who dared travel alone, or that far more numerous group, women who wished to enjoy a quiet meal away from the menfolk of their families. Having unpacked their nightgowns and nightcaps, cambric spencers (or jackets), corded petticoats and other garments, they were happy to relax in the Ordinary where this elaborate menu was offered them on the American Plan. In other words, they could eat all of it without extra charge. Beginning with mock turtle soup, a hungry and determined diner might have a bit of bass next, followed with "jole and cabbage," then a choice of the French entrees . . . "bifticks aux pommes de terre" with "Aubergine frite" . . . then perhaps a slice of pork, chicken, or goose, and for dessert a charlotte russe, a nutmeg melon, an exotic curacao sherbet or creamed fritters with vanilla sauce.

By 1864 the Astor was advertising that its "milk and vegetables are obtained from the Farm managed from the Hotel."

TO PLEASE THE EPICURE...

"Soft speaking marble," as a contemporary put it, lent its aura to the stately old dining room of the Astor House, pictured here in 1844. Its high ceilings, rising from carved Greek pillars, were a proper setting for the damask-covered tables where three hundred could sit down to dinner and be served, according to George Moore, Esq., of London, with "everything that could tempt the appetite or please the epicure."

Widgeons, meadow hens, and rail birds were among the appetite tempters on a menu which listed fifteen kinds of roast game, not to mention vegetables prepared in fourteen different ways. Astor wine waiters came equipped with card and pencil to record a guest's choice of Brigham's Imperial Pale—Very Delicate; Madeira—Thorndike—Very Old and Superior; wines aged "90 years in wood" as well as one labeled "Wedding Wine" and another called simply "An old family wine."

Another visitor from England in 1844 marveled at the service when he sat down to dine at 2 P.M. "The waiters are drilled like a regiment of soldiers," he said, "and we had the most sumptuous dinner, with literally all the delicacies of the season; what is more astounding . . . you are allowed to take your meals at any hour you please without extra charge; yet for board, lodging and attendance the price is only two dollars a day."

Colonel Charles A. Stetson had at this time become the popular and meticulous landlord of the Astor House. He was to gain fame for his patriotism during the difficult days of the Civil War when draft riots were staged in New York and many Southern sympathizers found the city friendly to their cause. Colonel Stetson supported the Union and announced that there would be no charge at the Astor House for "soldiers from Massachusetts."

Astor House.

New York, Thursday, October 11, 1849

WINE LIST

MOSELLE

Seltzers Water [illegible] per bottle [illegible]
Moselle, 1831 [illegible]

SAUTERNE

[illegible]
Sauterne Pints [illegible]
Sauterne [illegible]
[illegible]

HOCK

[illegible] Sparkling Hock [illegible]
[illegible] 1830 [illegible]
[illegible]
Sparkling Hock, [illegible] Brigham [illegible]
[illegible] 1834 [illegible]
[illegible] 1822 [illegible]
[illegible] Rothenberg 1831 [illegible]
Ausbrack Cabinet, Graffenburg, 1831 [illegible]
Johannisburger, 1834 [illegible]
Ausbruck Cabinet, Rothenberg, 1822 ... 4 [illegible]
Cabinet Schloss Johannisburger 1822 [illegible]
Prince Metternich Castle bottled, Yellow Seal, 1831 [illegible]
Metternich's Castle, bottled Red Seal 1822 [illegible]
Prince Metternich's celebrated Castle bottled, Gold Seal Johannisburger vintage 1822 [illegible]

CHAMPAGNE

Brigham's Grape Leaf ... 2 [illegible]
Bininger's Mumm ... 2 [illegible]
Sparkling Burgundy ... [illegible]
Sparkling Moselle ... [illegible]
Schreider ... [illegible]
Napoleon, Barsalou ... [illegible]
Moet ... 2 50
Cliquot ... 2 00
Heidsieck ... 2 00
Ruinart ... 2 00
Star ... 2 00
[illegible] Cabinet ... 2 00
Vin d'ay, Bloodgood's Superior ... 2 00
[illegible] ... 1 00
Pints ... 1 25
Moet Pints ... [illegible]

CLARET

Irish Claret, very superior ... $3 00
Claret ... [illegible]
Table Claret ... 0 75
St Julien in pint bottles [illegible] ... 0 75
Leoville do do ... 0 75
Pontet Canet do do ... 0 75
Latour do do ... 1 00
Pints of Barsalou ... 1 00
St Estephe, N. Barsalou ... 1 00
St Julien do ... 1 25
Leoville do ... 1 50
Pontet Canet do ... 1 50
St Julien, Barton & Guestier, pint bot's ... 0 75
St Julien, do do ... 1 25
Batailly do do 1834 ... [illegible]
Chateau Beychevelle, do 1841 ... [illegible]
Leoville do 1841 ... [illegible]
[illegible] do 1841 ... 2 50
Latour do 1841 ... 3 00
Chateau Lafitte do 1841 ... 3 00
Chateau Margeaux, do 1841 ... 3 00

BURGUNDY

Macon ... $1 [illegible]
Pouilly, White ... 1 [illegible]
Sparkling Burgundy ... 2 [illegible]
[illegible] ... 2 [illegible]
Chambertin ... [illegible]
Romanee ... 3 00
Vosne ... 3 00

PORT

Particular ... 2 [illegible]
Tower ... 2 00
Brazil ... 2 50

Bill of Fare.

SOUP.

Vegetable Soup

FISH.

Bass, Genoise sauce

ROAST.	BOILED.
Beef,	Jole and Cabbage
Turkeys,	Corned Beef
Chickens,	Beef Tongue,
Ham, Champagne sauce.	Duffield Hams

GAME--ROAST.

Venison, Currant Jelly sauce.

Black Ducks,	Mallard Ducks,
Lake Ducks,	Wood Ducks,
Teal,	Broad Bills,
Widgeons,	Gray Ducks,
Grouse	Meadow Hens,
Plover,	Short Neck Snipe,
Rail Birds,	Doe-Witches

GAME--BROILED.

English Snipe,	Robin Snipe,
Cedar Birds,	Surf Snipe

SIDE DISHES

Oysters Baked in the Shell,
Calf's Head, Brain sauce,
Curried Veal with Rice,
Frogs Fried in Butter,
Black Fish, Barbecued,
Broiled Pig's Feet,
Small Birds, Madeira sauce,
Macaroni with Cheese,
Stuffed Tomatoes, Baked,
Calf's Liver, Fried with Pork,
Rice Cakes flavored with Orange,
Sausages with Mashed Potatoes.

VEGETABLES.

Onions,	Boiled Rice,
Boiled Potatoes,	Cabbage,
Mashed Potatoes,	Sweet Potatoes,
Pickled Beets,	Raw Tomatoes,
Egg Plant,	Stewed Tomatoes,

Lima Beans, Squash, Spinach, Corn,

PASTRY.

Pumpkin Pies,	Cranberry Pies,
Rice Pudding,	Bread Pudding,
Charlotte Russe,	Almond Cakes,

DESSERT.

Ice Cream.

WINE LIST.

SHERRY.

Sherry, S. S. Rutheford, Drury & Co ... 1 5[illegible]
[illegible] pale, delicate ... 2 [illegible]
[illegible] Gold G ... 2 00
[illegible] Sayres, Gold ... 2 50
Do do Brown, extra, ... 2 [illegible]
Do do Amon[illegible] ... 3 [illegible]
[illegible] Sherry, imported [illegible] mild ... [illegible]
[illegible] Brigham's Imperial Pale, very delicate ... 2 50
[illegible] ... 3 00
Imperial pale, ... [illegible]
Brown imported in glass ... 4 00
[illegible] do very old ... 3 00
[illegible], pale very old, ... 3 00
[illegible] Brown F O, long bottled ... [illegible] 50
[illegible] Plus Ultra ... 4 00

MADEIRA

Madeira Oliveira ... 1 50
Symington's Reserve Madeira, (very fine and old ... 2 50
Symington's Tinta or Burgundy Madeira, (rich and delicate.) ... 2 00
Symington's Boal, (fruity, delicate, and high flavoured.) ... 2 50
Symington's Pure Juice, (fruity and very delicate, ... 2 00
Symington's Verdelho, (very high flavoured, ... 2 00
[illegible] Madeira ... 2 [illegible]
[illegible], South Side ... 2 00
Cruttenden's old Madeira, Eagle Tavern stock Albany, ... 3 00
[illegible] Reserve, do ... 2 50
Howard, March & Co's Madeira, imported for the Astor House, F ... 2 00
Newton, Gordon & Murdock's [illegible] M ... 2 00
Oliveiro's Reserve, 17 years old ... 2 50
[illegible] L. Leacock old, dry ... 2 50
South Side Madeira, delicious and very [illegible] ... 3 00
Leacock [illegible] L., imported, 1825, into New Orleans, ... 3 00
Henry Clay, imp. into Boston in 1825, ... 4 0[illegible]
[illegible] Yuille & Woodrope, M. Y., ... 3 00
[illegible] Seal, original N. G. M., delicate, ... 3 00
V. Sercial, very delicate ... 3 00
Brazil, V. I., very old, a favorite wine, ... 3 00
Brown Seal, old Monteiras, 'superior,' ... 3 [illegible]
Nabob, ... 3 50
Red Seal, old, bottled, East India, ... 3 00
Eclipse Madeira, ... 4 00
Rapid imported 1818, ... 4 00
Green Seal, Virginia Madeira, light & very delicate, ... 4 00
White Top, very old and delicate ... 4 00
Thorndike, very old and 'superior,' ... 4 50
Edward Tuckerman, Esquire, Scott, Laughnan, Penfold & Co's, imported 1820, P. M. ... 5 00
Gratz, yellow seal, 1806 ... 5 00
Do. green seal, 1806 ... 5 50
Do. black seal, 1806, ... 5 50
Gratz, red seal, bottled 1806 ... 5 00
Wanton, exceedingly delicate, 30 years in wood, W ... 5 00
John A. Gordon's Madeira, imported into Philadelphia 1798, ... 5 00
Caroline, an old family wine, ... 5 00
Gordon, Duff, Inglis & Co's, imported by H. G. Otis, and Edward Tuckerman, esq., 1811 ... 5 00
Stark's Madeira, bottled in Calcutta, imported 1825 ... 6 [illegible]
Hurd's Madeira, bottled 1822, Calcutta, ... 5 00
Essex, Jr., imported 1819 ... 7 [illegible]
Smith & Huggins, Dyker's White Top, bottled in 1800, in St. Eustatia, ... 7 00
Tuckerman's B, 1810, ... 8 00
Thorndike's A, 1809, ... 8 00
Wedding Wine, ... 8 00
Gov Philip's Wine, ... 9 00
Gov Kirby's original bottles ... 12 00

☞ EACH WAITER IS PROVIDED WITH WINE CARDS AND PENCIL ☜

...END OF THE MAUVE DECADE...

"The most distinctive of all American institutions, something which has to do with our liberties and the Constitution, is our Lunch-Room." *Harper's Weekly* of September 8, 1888, was thus describing the animated scene above, which was the famed Rotunda in the heart of the Astor House. The Rotunda, according to *King's Handbook,* "is a much frequented eating place for noonday meals. The two great circular lunch-counters, the big bar, and the side counters are always crowded, and here congregate at noon, hundreds of the best-known men of the town, politicians, and professional and business men."

"The railroad and the necessity of appeasing of hunger in the shortest possible time" were cited by *Harper's* as "being the parents" of the lunch-room phenomenon.

Harper's claims that, in the scene above, the artist "seizes the general contest . . . the whole battle." It goes on: "those who come to the lunch room are there to eat and not to talk or joke... there is the messenger boy who is carrying a bowl of soup to someone outside, who, pressed for time, must satisfy his hunger in his office." Bean porridge and soft clam scouse were favorite items on the Rotunda's noontime menu, as were roast, cut by "a carver . . . with a natural genius to get the proper amount of fat and lean in a hurry."

In its twilight years, the Astor House retained a musty dignity as an Astor estate taxpayer, but the loyal Rotunda House patrons still came at lunch time and still, at the end of the rush hour, came a skilled waiter who "with a flirt of a napkin and a rapid polish" prepared the Rotunda counter for celebrities who were soon to find newer and brighter spots uptown.

Gentlemen from Wall Street still came to the Astor dining room for a leisured lunch, and found the linen immaculate, the waiters attentive, the food abundant. But by the early 1900's there was clearly no hope for the once bright jewel of the hotel world. The gallant try at rejuvenation had failed in spite of installation of elevators and other extensive repairs. It was a long journey in time and a longer one in terms of the fantastic growth of New York from that sunny Independence Day in 1834 when John Jacob Astor presided at the corner-stone laying of the world's first modern palace hotel to the time of this photograph, May 29, 1913, when the Astor House locked its doors for the last time.

It stayed on, locked and forlorn, while that miracle of the industrial age, the Woolworth Tower, overshadowed its now grimy square bulk. Nobody bothered to glance at the tottering half remaining of a hotel which was once so cool and white an oasis in a tree-shaded block of old Broadway. The final demolition did not come until another skyscraper overtook it in the giddy postwar year of 1926. By then, long gone were the Rotunda Men who answered a bell within two minutes, the mustachioed and bearded politicians who smoked their Havanas and plotted their plots; gone were the treacherous gaslit chandeliers and the three-hour dinners... and gone, too, an elegant era of arrogant new millionaires and brash forays into the culture and cuisine of Europe. But the Astor had had its say, and much of what it said is still remembered.

...AND OF THE ASTOR HOUSE...

1851 METROPOLITAN HOTEL

...there were thirty-nine stars in the Flags...

... floating over the roof of the new Metropolitan Hotel at the corner of Broadway and Prince Street when it opened in 1851. In the heart of the Metropolitan was Niblo's Garden and Theater.

In the early years of the Metropolitan, gentlemen still cantered along Broadway on their sleek horses, accompanied by ladies riding sidesaddle. The national census of 1850 showed a population of 23,191,867 in the growing nation, immigrants totaling 364,980. It was the year when Henry Clay wrote a sentence for the history books: "I would rather be right than President." The year, too, when the Collins Line introduced to Americans the first trans-Atlantic steamer schedule: ten days, four and a half hours from New York to Liverpool.

A New York Guide Book described the Metropolitan as a "palatial brownstone" structure with "airy luxurious rooms accommodating 1,000 guests." Among those guests were visiting Californians (California had just been admitted as a state), who seemed to fancy the place. The brownstone look of the Metropolitan was relatively new; in general, New York was then "a city of red bricks faced with white marble and garnished with green blinds."

The hirsute gentlemen below were victims of a pre-Madison Avenue campaign staged by the various bathing establishments of New York in the 1860's when very few hotels offered proper cleansing facilities. No matter what was wrong with you, a bath would cure it . . . "the best medicine in the world to an invalid . . . refreshing to a healthy man" is the way one advertisement put it, while another stated its case in doggerel:

> "Go, in this changing weather, take a bath!
> It soothes the mind, the body gives relief;
> Comforts the system, drives away all wrath—
> A perfect antidote for toil and grief."

Simeon Ford, "wit" and famous hotel keeper, admitted that he dallied with "this luxury of the Orient" and added that, as a result, he "contracted a deep, sonorous cold which in all probability, will fondly nestle in my bosom till my ulster blooms again." For one dollar, bathers could go into a cooling room, where the temperature was a pleasant 98 degrees or directly into the disrobing room where the heat was considerably higher. There they were provided "a chair and a comb long past their prime." Then on to the "hot room . . . where a number of gentlemen were lolling about and perspiring affably and fluently." After sitting on a "seething chair until I came to a boil . . . I leaped from towel to towel in my efforts to keep my feet off the red-hot floor." As a finale, a muscular attendant flattened his digestive organs and generally disjointed him "limb from limb."

SCENE IN THE NEW RUSSIAN BATHS Nº 18 LA FAYETTE PLACE.

When President Pierce came to New York City in 1853 to open the World's Fair at the Crystal Palace, a door was cut through the hotel into Niblo's so that the big banquet in his honor could be held there. From then on, the room was used for banquets such as the one pictured here on April 10, 1856, the occasion of the eighth anniversary of the New York Dramatic Fund Association. *Frank Leslie's Illustrated Newspaper* noted that "the bill of fare was unusually large and included every luxury the market afforded. The tables were adorned with the following ornaments beautifully executed in sugar, viz:—*Shapespeare's House, Figure of Comedy, Merchant of Venice, Twelfth Night, The Irishman, 'Here's till yez,' The Globe Theater, Figure of Tragedy, The Yankee,*" and so on.

The dining room was described as "one hundred and three by fifty feet and thirty feet in height, frescoed and decorated." *Leslie's* went on to report that the hotel's proprietors, the Messrs.Leland, "have striven to eclipse themselves . . . We have never seen a feast in this city where everything was arranged more to the satisfaction of the guests." James T. Brady presided and there were notables from the theater, the publishing world, the judiciary, all pictured in *Leslie's* "exact engraving." The newspaper bragged that the "correct likenesses of Messrs. Brady, Blake, Brougham and many others . . . will be readily recognized by their friends . . . but whose names we do not publish as the parties may not wish to have public attention so pointedly directed at them."

"It Would Frighten Any One But a Millionaire . . ."

HEREWITH we present a representation of a portion of the silver plate designed and executed by Stebbins & Co., of New York, for Messrs. Leland Brothers of the Metropolitan Hotel, Broadway. The design is as singularly unique and tasteful as anything could well be imagined, and reflects the highest credit upon the skill of the enterprising house that originated it. The silver for the entire establishment—which has been ordered at a cost of fourteen thousand dollars—is to be finished after the same pattern and style. The proprietors of the Metropolitan, we learn, in the selection of the furniture for their entire establishment, have been equally lavish in expenditure, it being the determination to surpass in splendor and magnificence every other hotel in the world. Such expenditure, made upon prospective returns, would frighten any one but a millionaire. But the determination is to open an establishment which should be the focal point for travelers from every part of the globe; and as much so from its novelty, as its superior advantages. The task is herculean; but from what we hear of its progress, there is little doubt of its realization. How long the Lelands will maintain their superiority depends much upon the tact and skill with which they manage their mammoth establishment. Think of a thousand guests being elegantly accommodated in a single hotel!

Gleason's Pictorial—1852

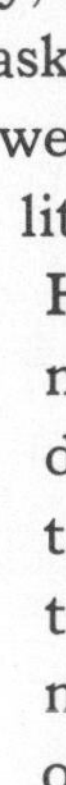

Niblo's Garden, "a picture of brightness . . . with its shrubbery, statuary, gas-lit arches and various belongings," was a pleasant oasis off busy Broadway, accessible from the street or from the Metropolitan itself. The Temple of Music glimpsed in the background lent the proper touch to culture-conscious patrons who came there to relax over good lager beer or more genteel wines and liqueurs. *Gleason's Pictorial* offered the comforting information that "the Broadway entrance and various rear exits . . . are spacious and available for the most excited crowds . . . in case of fire or accident." In the photograph below, facing away from the Temple of Music toward Broadway, could it be that the shadowy gentleman in the tall silk hat is Mr. Niblo himself? And perhaps a stagehand in shirtsleeves is in conference with him as the matinee hour approaches.

You are not seeing double in the photograph above. It was taken for the stereopticon views so popular at the time.

Hansom cabs and the grandfathers of the Keystone Cops dominated the scene in the gaudy postwar sixties when "The Black Crook" shocked some New Yorkers and delighted others. This naughty production at Niblo's Theater was the first to be publicly denounced as "lascivious," and it brought considerable fame and glamor to its daring *danseuse,* Maria Bonfanti. Niblo's Theater was remembered also for a "melancholy accident" on its boards in the 1850's, when, according to *Gleason's,* "One of the Ravels was dancing in her character of a sylphide, when in one of her pirouttes she approached too near to the foot-light. Her thin gauze dress became lighted at once and before it could be properly extinguished . . . the poor girl suffered sufficient injury to cause her death but a few days subsequent . . . However when there are so many delightful associations connected with any place, we must expect considerable of shade will creep into the picture of brightness." The theater, *Gleason's* went on, "has a light and graceful appearance, the interior columns and tier fronts being of iron . . . , it has a parquette which has become the favorite part of the house for gentlemen, and is much frequented by ladies."

1853 ST. NICHOLAS

The rumor that "fast persons affect it" added a fillip to the charms of the St. Nicholas Hotel, six stories of white marble elegance on the corner of Broadway and Spring Street. It was hinted that when a young female person accepted an assignation at the St. Nicholas, it was tantamount to an admission of lost innocence. That is, unless the young female happened to be a bride and lucky enough to get the hotel's Bridal Suite, described as "lined and ornamented throughout with the purest of white satin . . . an exquisite canopy of white satin gathered in heavy folds at each corner, falling over a bed of lace and white satin which is also surrounded with cushions of white satin."

The St. Nicholas was the first hotel to cost more than a million dollars. When it was enlarged in 1856 to total five hundred rooms, it became the biggest as well as the costliest . . . until 1859, when the Fifth Avenue Hotel opened with five hundred and thirty rooms.

In the summer of 1848, a young boy walked up Broadway with his immigrant parents, bound for the Erie Canal and eventually Allegheny, Pennsylvania. He was twelve years old and his name was Andrew Carnegie. Less than twenty years later he established his mother in the finest suite the St. Nicholas could offer.

HOTEL

..."the lordliest Caravansarai of them all".. says Charles Dickens

This was the era known as "The Feminine Fifties" because women had begun to dominate the once all-male American scene. Hotels such as the St. Nicholas catered to the fair ones in fittings of delicate rosewood, Flemish tapestries, gold-embroidered draperies at $1,000 per pair. But it paid off, as witness the printed reports of the hotel's $53,600 profits in 1854.

At least two of the fair ones managed a neat trick when they crossed the street to Tiffany's and asked to see sets of bracelets and necklaces. They just could not decide and Tiffany agreed to send over several of the jewels at about 6 P.M. The two ladies told the messenger that they were about to go to dinner, so they could not reach a decision for another hour or so. The Tiffany boy came back at the appointed hour and the necklace and bracelet sets awaited him, along with a polite note stating that the ladies would be along next day to make another selection. After three or four days of this on-again-off-again business, the ladies left the St. Nicholas without buying so much as a Tiffany sapphire. But that same day a gentleman came in to make a small purchase of some jewelry for his new bride. Shown a glittering necklace with bracelet to match, he noted that he had seen those jewels before. "Impossible," retorted Tiffany's man. "Well," he said with a thoughtful smile, "those were worn by a young lady at the St. Nicholas . . . she came to dinner three or four nights running and each time she wore a different set of dazzling gems . . . and any number of interesting gentlemen besieged her . . ." That was the St. Nicholas.

And here is Tiffany's

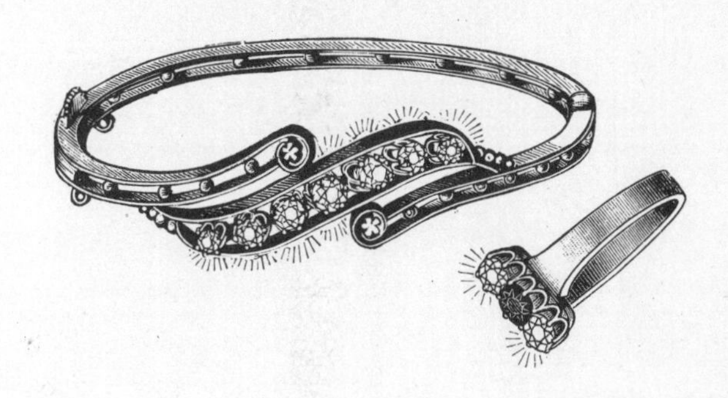

You are dining here... and
over there is your Menu...
It is January 19, 1876...

ST. NICHOLAS HOTEL,
S. HAWK & CO., PROPRIETORS.
BROADWAY, AT BROOME & SPRING STREETS, NEW YORK.

WINE LIST.

Champagnes.

	PTS.	QTS.
Moet & Chandon, Verzenay	....	$3 00
do. Green Seal	....	4 00
Verzenay, "G. H. Mumm & Co."	....	3 00
Heidsieck, Piper & Co	....	3 00
Chas. Heidsieck		3 00
V. Clicquot, Ponsardin	....	4 00
St. Marceaux, Red Lac	....	4 00
L. Roederer's Imperial	....	4 00
L. Roederer's Cabinet	....	3 50
Krug & Co	....	3 50
Geo. Goulet, Dry	....	3 00
J. Goerg & Co., Carte Blanche (Extra Dry)		3 50
J. Goerg, La Perle de la Cuvée	....	4 00
Dry Monopole	....	4 00
Delmonico, (half pints)	....	4 00

PINTS OF THE ABOVE.

American Wines.

Pleasant Valley Great Western	1 50	2 50
Still Catawba	....	1 50
California Hock. Los Angelos vintage	....	1 50
do. Angelica	....	1 50
do Port	....	2 00
Amer. Wine Co. Imperial, (St. Louis)	1 50	2 50

Claret.

IMPORTED BY ADOLPHUS OECHS, FROM THE HOUSE OF BRANDENBURG FRERES, IN BORDEAUX.

St. Estèphe	75	1 00
St. Julien	75	1 25
St. Emilion, 1st quality	....	2 00
Margaux	....	2 00
Château Leoville	1 50	3 00
Château La Rose	1 75	3 50
Château Mouton	....	4 00
Château Margaux	3 00	6 00
Château Lafite	3 00	6 00

FROM BARTON & GUESTIER.

Floirac	75	1 25
St. Julien, 1st quality	1 00	1 75
Pontet Canet	1 25	2 50
Mouton, 1851	....	4 50
Château Margaux	3 00	6 00
Latour, 1857	....	6 00
Old Médoc Key brand, imported by Spotts & Hawk	....	2 00

Hock.

IMPORTED BY ADOLPHUS OECHS, FROM THE HOUSE OF HENKELL & CO., IN MAYENCE.

Deidesheimer	1 25	2 00
Ruedesheimer	....	3 00
Do. Berg	....	4 00
Marcobrunner	....	3 00
Johannisberger	....	5 00
Steinberg Cabinet		5 00
Sparkling Hochheimer	2 25	4 00
Do. Moselle Muscatel	2 25	4 00
Marcobrunner, Ausbruch, finest production	....	4 00

Port.

FROM GIL. DAVIS.

George Sandeman's fine old Port	....	4 00
Do. Do. Old White Port	....	4 50

FROM J. & R. OSBORN.

Old Port, superior	....	3 00
London Dock, pale and mellow	....	4 00
Queen's Port	....	4 50

Sherry

	PTS.	QTS.
Table, pale, from wood	$1 00	$2 00
Table, brown, from wood	1 00	2 00
Haurie	....	3 00
Cabinet, full and delicate	1 25	2 50
Beickbeder Brown	....	3 00
Topaz, very full and delicate	1 50	3 00
Imperial, pale	1 75	3 50
Vino de Pasto, pale and delicate	2 00	4 00
Amontillado, Pemartin, pale and old	....	4 00
Old Royal William Brown Sherry, 1820	....	4 00
Peter Domecq's Competition	....	5 00
Royal Pale Sherry, fine and old	....	6 00

IMPORTED BY SPOTTS & HAWK.

Single Diamond	1 25	2 50
Villegas, light, dry, golden	1 50	3 00
Agredo	1 75	3 50
Portilla, fine old pale	1 50	3 00
Double Star, full bodied	2 25	4 50
Double Crown, very old choice	....	6 00

Madeira.

Scott, pale and delicate	2 50
Newton, Gordon & Murdock's old, full, delicate and high flavored	3 50
Monteiro's very old, pale and delicate	5 00

FROM GIL. DAVIS.

Victoria Royal, pale and delicate	4 00
Howard, March & Co	5 00

IMPORTED FROM WELSH BROTHERS, MADEIRA, BY TREDWELL, ACKER & CO.

Favorite Vintage, 1842	5 00
Old Reserve do., 1815	7 00

White Wines.

IMPORTED BY ADOLPHUS OECHS, FROM THE HOUSE OF BRANDENBURG FRERES, IN BORDEAUX.

Sauternes	1 00	1 50
Château Sauternes	1 50	2 50
Latour Blanche	....	3 00
Chablis, white	....	4 00
Château Latour Blanche	....	3 50
Château Yquem	....	6 00

Burgundy.

FROM R. BRUNINGHAUS, NUITS, IMPORTED BY ADOLPHUS OECHS.

Nuits	2 25	4 00
Chambertin	....	5 00
Romanee Conti	....	6 00
Clos de Vougeot	....	6 00
Old Pomard, Key brand, imported by Spotts & Hawk	....	3 50

Brandies, etc.

Old choice Brandy, Key Brand, imported by Spotts & Hawk, vintage of 1843	5 00
V. O. P. Brandy, Vassal & Co	6 00
Otard, Dupuy & Co., Pale Brandy,	5 00
Pale Hennessy Brandy	3 50
Dark Hennessy Brandy	3 50
Fine Old Crow Whiskey	2 50
Monongahela Rye Whiskey	2 00
Old Bourbon Whiskey	2 00
Old Grenada Rum	2 00
Old Jamaica Rum, from London	2 50
Old Jamaica Rum, very fine	4 00

Ales and Porter.

Scotch Ale, (R. Younger's.)	40	....
India Pale Ale, (Bass's.)	40	....
London Porter	40	....
Champagne Cider	50	0 75

Liqueurs, Cordials, &c.

☞ EACH WAITER IS PROVIDED WITH WINE CARDS AND PENCIL. ☜

St. Nicholas Hotel.

Wednesday, January 19, 1876.

FIVE O'CLOCK DINNER.

Soups

Mock Turtle — Consommé au Riz

Fish

Boiled Striped Bass, Anchovy sauce
Broiled Bluefish, à la Maître d'Hôtel

Boiled

Corned Beef and Cabbage — Jole and Spinach — Leg of Mutton and Capers
Beef Tongue, Tomato sauce — Cobb Ham — Turkey, Oyster sauce
Beef à la Mode — Capon and Pork

Roast

Saddle of South Down Mutton, Currant jelly — Spring Duck — Leg of Mutton
Buck's County Chicken — Turkey stuffed, Cranberry sauce — Loin of Pork
Ham glacé, Champagne sauce — Ribs of Prize Beef

Cold Dishes

Boned Turkey, with Jelly — Beef Tongue — Beef — Terrine de Foie-Gras
Cold Pressed Corned Beef — Chicken — Plain Lobster — Ham — Mutton — Chicken Salad

Entrees

Chicken Pot Pie, à l'Américaine
Salmi of Grouse, aux olives
Fricandeau of Veal larded, sauce tomate
Soft Shell Crabs fried in crumbs, à l'Anglaise
Ragoût of Ox Tail, with small turnips
Apple Charlotte, aux croûtons glacés
Macaroni à la Milanaise
Mutton Cutlets breaded, sauce piquante

RELISHES

Assorted Pickles — Chowchow — Olives — Horseradish — Celery — Pickled Beets
Apple sauce — Cranberry sauce

Vegetables

Stewed Tomatoes — Lima Beans — Boiled, Baked and Mashed Potatoes
Saco Corn — Boiled Rice — Turnips — Hominy
Squash — Onions — Fried Oyster Plant — Stewed Parsnips — Beets — Spinach

Game

Roast Partridge, Celery sauce — Roast Red-Head Duck, Currant Jelly
Roast Mallard Duck, Game sauce

Pastry

Apple Dumpling, Cream sauce
Sliced Apple Pie — Rhubarb Pie — Cocoanut Pie — Biscuit Glacé, à la Vanille
Sauterne Jelly — Coffee Caramels — Gâteaux au Punch

Dessert

Oranges — Apples — Raisins — Almonds
Filberts — Brazil Nuts — Hickory Nuts — Walnuts — Pecan Nuts
Lemon Ice Cream — New Figs — Pop Corn — Coffee

No Seats Reserved after 5¼ o'clock.

ST. NICHOLAS HOTEL.

S. HAWK & CO., PROPRIETORS.

HOURS FOR MEALS.

BREAKFAST, .	FROM 6	TO 11	O'CLOCK.
DINNER, . . .	" 1½	" 3½	"
	" 5	" 7½	"
TEA, . .	" 6	" 8½	"
SUPPER, . . .	" 9	" 12	"

FOR CHILDREN AND NURSES.

BREAKFAST, . . .	FROM 7	TO 9	O'CLOCK
DINNER, ...	" 1	" 3	"
TEA, . . .		AT 6	"

CHILDREN OCCUPYING SEATS AT THE PUBLIC TABLE WILL BE CHARGED FULL PRICE.

Meals sent to rooms charged extra.

January 19, 1856

Dear Sister Anne:

There is a Cooking School opened in New York and I think it is high time. You can get there easily from this hotel, since it is right over on St. Mark's Place and is operated by one Juliet Carson.

This hotel is said to have cost a million dollars and I do not doubt it, since all the rooms are warmed by hot air registers. The dining room is delightfully mirrored and you see yourself in myriad reflections which challenges you to wear your prettiest gowns. The plates are kept warm by spirit lamps and there is a great deal of gold embroidered brocade. It has been called the St. Nicholas, I mean, "the lordliest caravansarie in the world" and I believe it. To the right of our entrance is a marvelous place called Phalon's Hair Dressing Establishment for gentlemen only, of course and I have learned that the mirror in there cost $5,000 and the furniture $16,000. It has a marble floor and the shaving chairs cost $100 each. The advertisement claims that "Phalon's is as great a lion in its way as St. Mark's in Venice." It has baths on the lower floor, as well.

They say the bridal chamber here is really splendid. I know there is a grand piano worth $1,500 and all the public rooms are panelled in mahogany and walnut.

In that New York newspaper, The Tribune, I read that my hotel is the "ne plus ultra of expense, of richness, of luxury." The newspaper account adds that it is no longer sufficient for a hotel to offer quiet comfort, neatness and an adequate table. They must compete in terms of grandeur, pier glasses and Brussels carpets and fancy chandeliers and lots of gilt paint.

But sister dear, we have baths at the St. Nicholas and mine is boxed in with carved walnut, very splendid but rather like a coffin. The bathroom walls are wood-panelled, too... all in all a most elegant room and equally as large as the drawing room of a modest dwelling.

The Tribune reports that it is an awful toll on human legs to reach the top-floor rooms, which are six stories above the street, but I am on the fourth floor and I do not find it unduly fatiguing to arrive at my room.

I think I must tell you about the sommier elastique, a most marvelous new aid to sleeping. It is a mattress put upon springs, which gives a joyous buoyancy when one lies down to sleep.

I read that the gaslight here is made from resin and costs only $924 a month, whereas if the hotel bought it from the gas companies it would cost over $2,500 for the same period. Yet it does brightly illuminate all the rooms and for those who understand its workings, is no menace at all.

Well here is something for you! I copy it from a magazine here called Ballou's Pictorial and it is by a lady writer who is describing an event having to do with the male patrons of the St. Nicholas. She says:

"I saw something go into the St. Nicholas the other day. What do you think it was? It was the most splendid mirror I ever beheld, large as the side of a house and cost some $1,400... I thought of course it was designed for the ladies' saloon; but no! it went into the bar-room, and there sit the Adonises before it drinking cobblers and smashes and admiring themselves between drinks."

Dear Sister, I think you must know that I am having a most amusing time in New York City at the St. Nicholas.

My fondest wishes to you,

Your devoted sister,

Jennie

1859 THE FIFTH

..."for those desirous of sparing their ambulators any extra trouble"

"No single hotel in the world has ever entertained so many distinguished people as the Fifth Avenue," commented *King's Handbook of New York* in 1892.

"Presidents of the United States, Senators, Congressmen, Governors, Generals, Admirals, Emperors, Princes, foreign Ambassadors . . . the list would fill a volume."

When the Fifth Avenue Hotel, fronting on leafy Madison Square at the junction of Broadway and Fifth Avenue, opened its doors in 1859, it had as proprietor Paran Stevens, formerly of Boston's Revere House. He was an innovator, as witness the "perpendicular railway" he installed, which is credited as being the first hotel passenger elevator in the world. It was designed "for those desirous of *sparing their ambulators* any extra trouble."

The Fifth Avenue Hotel soon took its place among those New York hotels chosen as informal meeting places for political leaders. A certain pair of plush-covered benches near the bar became famous as "The Amen Corner," where anyone from the President of the United States down to . . . or up to . . . Boss Tom Platt could be found plotting strategy.

AVENUE HOTEL

The corridor of the Fifth Avenue was magnificent in polished woods, marble and crystal, and the bright flicker of gaslights for twenty-one years of its existence. Then, in 1890, it came of age in a blaze of Mr. Edison's incandescents, although in this picture the gasoliers still linger on forlornly below the clustered bulbs. The Fifth Avenue's renowned bar was well to the rear, with porters posted at discreet vantage points on the way so as to fend off any except "gentlemen in first-rate condition." "Everybody who wishes to keep in touch with the men of the day," noted *King's Handbook*, "must frequent its corridors." The roster of the famous included the Emperor of Brazil, the Crown Prince of Siam, Prince Augustine de Iturbide of Mexico, the Marquis of Lorne, and the whole entourage of the Chinese Embassy. The Prince of Wales, later King Edward VII, endured one of New York's more riotous welcomes to royalty during which his barouche was mobbed and nearly overturned. Several nights later, partially recovered, it is said that he slipped out of his hotel window and happily went forth to discover whether or not the city's night life lived up to its reputation.

CENTENNIAL FOURTH!

Seventeen years after the opening of the Fifth Avenue, New York staged an ebullient celebration of the Glorious Centennial and, as can be seen above in the goings-on in Madison Square, it was a case of "anything goes." While celebrant gentlemen hung on lampposts and rockets sprayed the night sky, the Fifth Avenue ballroom was the scene of more restrained but quite elaborate salutes to 1776. Centennial gowns, created at enormous cost, were described in detail in society columns. One was white satin embroidered in water lilies, topped by a tulle headdress and a diamond tiara; there was a Centennial model of pink satin arranged with tiny shells of tulle and boasting a chatelaine of Gueder roses and pearls, and a train of pink damask brocade.

The hotel attracted luminaries on this gala holiday, as indeed it did during its entire span of nearly half a century. With its five hundred and thirty well-appointed rooms, it remained one of the great hotels for fifteen years, and, even after losing that accolade, it remained "the" place to stay for people who felt they "mattered."

The muted hush of a library was notably missing from the Fifth's Avenue's Reading Room. The atmosphere was Republican and lively; as a newspaper of the time commented, "it was considered little less than treason for a man to patronize any public place outside his own 'political hotel.' "

It was an uninhibited era and political campaigns in the 1870's and 80's were sizzling and often slanderous. Loyal followers of James G. Blaine held a council of war in the Reading Room to counter the campaign propaganda of the Democrats against their man:

"Blaine, Blaine, James G. Blaine,
Continental liar from the State of Maine."

They openly circulated a cartoon of rival candidate Cleveland, showing an unidentified "lady" wheeling a baby carriage from which came a wail: "Ma, Ma, where's my Pa?" and the answer, "Gone to the White House—Ha, Ha, Ha!"

But Cleveland won in 1884, and Republican strategists blamed it on a speech made at the Fifth Avenue by a Reverend Stephen D. Burchard denouncing the Democrats as the party of "Rum, Romanism and Rebellion" . . . a slogan which backfired and helped put Cleveland in the White House.

On the melancholy occasion of the last dinner served at the Fifth Avenue Hotel on April 4, 1908, the menu offered classic American cuisine, for the most part, but exquisitely prepared: clear green turtle soup after Blue Point oysters or Little Neck clams, boiled red snapper for the fish course, corned beef and cabbage, followed by Philadelphia capon, then Maryland's terrapin. The dinner went on to cold courses, salads, vegetables, pastries, other desserts and cheese.

The high-ceilinged dining room with its pillars and frescoes had been the scene of many auspicious entertainments, including the Peabody dinner of 1867 when the campaign for Grant's nomination was born. A glittering entertainment was given, also, for Charlotte Cushman by the Arcadian Club when she retired from the theater. But "the most noted assembly of distinguished Americans ever brought together," according to the *London Times,* was at the Fifth Avenue in 1885, after Grant's funeral.

"A sort of clearing-house for the city, the Nation and the world," the account concluded.

A gentleman who lived and dined there for forty years estimated on closing day that he had spent close to a million dollars for the pleasures afforded him by New York's gracious Fifth Avenue Hotel.

Want to try a Fifth Avenue Hotel *Specialite*? Here are three from *Demorest's* of 1878.

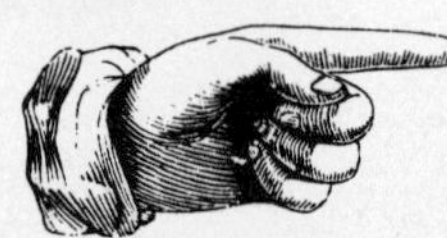

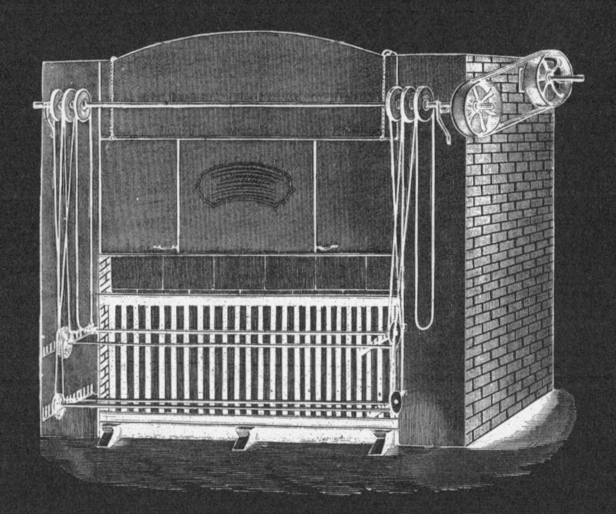

FIFTH AVENUE HOTEL ENGLISH MUFFINS—One and a quarter pounds of flour, one pint warm milk, one half pint yeast; mix well together and allow to rise; work over again, add a little salt, and two eggs. Bake on a hot griddle in rings.

FIFTH AVENUE HOTEL CODFISH CAKES—One quart of picked fish (soaked), two potatoes, two eggs. Boil fish and potatoes together until the potatoes are cooked, mash both together with eggs and a little butter, and white pepper. Dip up with a spoon, and fry in hot butter.

FIFTH AVENUE HOTEL OYSTERS BAKED IN THE SHELL—Make a thick batter of flour, milk, and butter, and cook it well in a saucepan; scald a few small oysters and wash them afterward in cold water; drain off the water and mix the oysters with the batter. Season with nutmeg, pepper, and salt and put in clam shells. Sprinkle them with bread crumbs, put a small piece of butter on them and bake until brown.

The HOFFMAN HOUSE 1864

..."the finest collection of barroom art to be found"...

The Hoffman House was to gain world renown for its collection of paintings and statuary, but when it first opened in New York City in the fall of 1864, it was noteworthy principally because of its dashing Boniface, Captain Dan Howard.

Standing on the corner of Broadway and Twenty-fifth Street and occupying nearly the whole block, the Hoffman House, according to *King's Handbook,* "has a sightly and beautiful location overlooking Madison Square and the broad plaza where busy Broadway and exclusive Fifth Avenue converge."

Known as a perfectionist in the business of building and operating hotels, Captain Howard, who had brought luster to his Howard Hotel and subsequently to the Irving House, now saw to it that his finest and final venture did not lack in carved woodwork, gold leaf, damask, and massive mirrors, and that the Hoffman House cuisine won "the approval of the most fastidious epicures." The establishment was run under the proprietorship of Read, Wall and Company, Captain Dan being the "and Company."

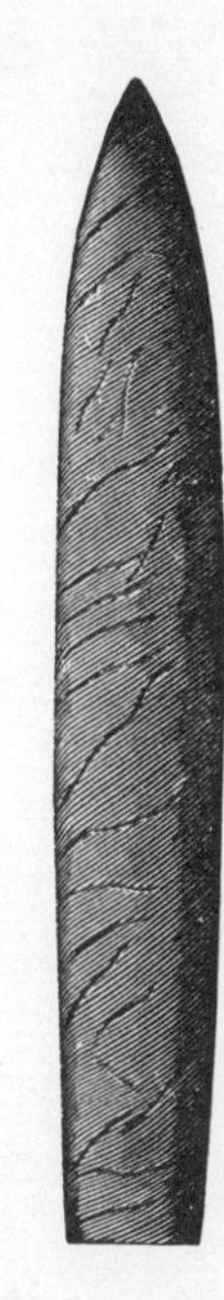

Toward the back, Billy Edwards standing beside a magnificent Stetson beneath which is the Honorable William F. Cody (Buffalo Bill). With them is the Honorable Thomas W. Palmer, president of the World Columbian Exposition. In the front, the Honorable Grover Cleveland talks to the Honorable Chauncey M. Depew. Slightly to right of center and in background is Tony Pastor, and then forward, Mr. M. Hilson, Detective Jacobs, Professor Herrman, and Nat Goodwin.

The gentlemen whose names and pictures adorned the lid of Hoffman House Banquet Cigars attested to the prestige of the hostelry which quickly became known as "a rendezvous for men who are prominent in financial and political circles." The Banquet Cigars sold at five cents each, but there was also a favored Hoffman House Perfecto at "ten cents straight."

Almost from its opening day the Hoffman House was knee-deep in politics. Boss Tweed made it a sort of unofficial annex to Tammany Hall, meeting there with his henchmen to plan campaign strategy and organize the torchlight parades in which his followers wore brilliant red shirts and displayed the Tammany tiger. At the height of his notorious career, Tweed was the favorite target for the devastating pen of Cartoonist Thomas Nast. The cartoons were instrumental in Tweed's downfall and made his face so familiar around the world that when he escaped from debtor's prison to Spain, he was recognized immediately and returned to the United States, to die in jail in 1878.

The Hoffman House had earlier been headquarters for Generals Winfield Scott and Benjamin F. Butler when they were sent to New York in 1864 to help put down the bloody draft riots which threatened to sweep Manhattan into the arms of the Confederacy. That same year saw Lincoln renominated and Grant named Commander in Chief of the Northern Armies.

"Out of the splendor of his Oriental experience," a Mr. Greiff of Constantinople undertook the decor of the Hoffman House public rooms when an eight-story fireproof addition was erected on Twenty-fifth Street in 1882, to double the original 212-room capacity.

Theater parties and small social groups loved the private dining rooms which Mr. Greiff offered in an effusion of motifs, ranging from "Oriental, Moorish and Persian" to "Orange, Chinese and Blue Satin."

Remodeling of a Popular Caravansery (*Frank Leslie's*, Feb. 11, 1882)

One parlor described by *Harper's Weekly* was done in "splendid Chinese style," had embroidered satin walls and a cocobolo trellis which "represents a piazza through the lattice railing of which a lawn shows below, and above, the sky."

Judging by these pictures, Mr. Greiff favored ferns and palms and general greenery in the larger rooms. His room for billiards, a fashionable pastime for men of the period, was geared to simpler masculine tastes.

The broad high corridors leading from the entrances provided easy access for guests to the waiting lines of hansom cabs as well as to the half a dozen lines of public transportation which came to the doors of the hotel.

..."I've been looking all the World over for that creek"...

A popular cartoon bore the above caption and showed a shabby hobo gazing wistfully at the most famous painting in the Hoffman House collection, Bouguereau's billowy nudes seducing a satyr. "The Nymphs and Satyr" was reproduced on the box top of Hoffman House Perfecto Cigars.

The hotel's art gallery was purchased by Edward S. Stokes, the redoubtable fellow who was sent to Sing Sing for the fatal shooting of Jim Fisk. When he was pardoned by President Cleveland, Stokes came to the Hoffman House as proprietor and proceeded to amass such canvasses as Correggio's "Narcissus," "The Russian Mail Carrier" by Chelmiński, and Demenceaux's "The Holy Mother." These, along with life-size statues of Nubian slaves bearing baskets of fruit on their heads, a marble figure of Eve, and a huge bronze by Schlessinger, "Pan and Bacchante," were displayed throughout the seventy-foot-long bar (shown above) where "Joints at 2 P.M." were a lunchtime favorite, and there were also baked chicken with oyster sauce at a dollar, Widgeon Salmi, eighty cents, Red Head Duck, two dollars, and Canton ginger, twenty cents.

A drink fancied by gentlemen who had been up too late the night before was a "Corpse Reviver": equal parts of noyau, maraschino, and yellow chartreuse, "one on top of the other without mixing . . . to be taken off at one draught."

"Handsomely decorated and elaborately furnished" was an understatement when it came to the Hoffman House Banquet Hall. Gilded, carved, and painted, the sixty-foot-square room had a ceiling done in gold, silver, and copper, and a series of allegorical paintings "upon a broad cove which takes the place of a cornice." The room was divided by two massive arcades with three arches each.

By 1883 the head chef of the Hoffman House, Eugene Lapperque, had been lured away from the Rothschilds in London by a salary of $300 a month. Many the five-hour banquet he planned and many the bird-and-bottle supper attended by the reigning musical comedy stars, who expected and usually got a diamond trinket or a hundred-dollar bill tucked into the gaudy floral tributes presented by their hosts while the orchestra, cued in advance, played the hit songs from their Broadway shows.

But it was not a woman's world. As late as July, 1907, Mrs. Harriet Blatch sued the Hoffman House for refusing to serve her in the roof garden because she came unescorted. She lost, the jury holding that the hotel had a right to refuse a lone woman service in any public room, provided it offered to serve her elsewhere. As "Jennie June" put it in *Demorest's Magazine* a few years earlier, "It is a rather curious fact that in a republic alone, of all forms of government, no place of trust, honor or responsibility has been permitted to women."

Broadway police were not averse to escorting attractive ladies to the horsecar when, as frequently occurred, the street was awash with rain, slush or general debris. Here the Hoffman House sign glints in the background as a horsecar bound for a rival hotel waits to take on passengers.

The lumbering omnibus was introduced to New York in 1831 by the enterprising Abraham Brower who borrowed the idea from a retired French officer named Baudry. Baudry, who ran a coach from Nantes to Richsbourg, one day noticed a sign over a store run by a M. Omnes. It read "Omnes Omnibus," or "Omnes for All." He promptly borrowed the notion and christened his coach an "omnibus."

Street railways had operated in New York since November, 1832, when a celebratory dinner at City Hall signaled the opening of a line running down Fourth Avenue and the

A Broadway scene in an early February thaw. *Harper's Weekly*, 1872

Bowery to Walker Street. The cars had seats upholstered in flowered plush, three compartments with brightly painted decorations, and accommodations for thirty-two passengers. But conservative Fifth Avenue kept its horse-drawn omnibuses, named after national heroes, until the year 1905. Riding them, according to the *New York Herald,* amounted to "modern martyrdom . . . the driver quarrels with the passengers, the passengers quarrel with the driver. It is . . . a perfect Bedlam on wheels."

Gentlemen whose arrival at the Hoffman House was reported in the newspapers were apt to find in their morning mail a discreet engraved notice from "The Seven Sisters" indicating that they would be welcome at the seven adjoining "parlor houses" close by on Twenty-seventh Street, where the female welcoming committee always wore evening dress and diamonds. Named for a long-run musical comedy, "The Seven Sisters" was the most luxurious and high-priced brothel in the city.

The NEW FANGLED LIGHT!

Harper's Weekly, 1882

Madison Square, the "front yard" of the Hoffman House, burst into luminous beauty after dark with the installation of this curious lighting fixture in 1882. *Harper's Weekly* described the mast as being 160 feet high with two poles at the top from which "shine down the great electric lights . . . a very beautiful effect in the Square . . . it can be seen plainly from Orange Mountain fifteen or sixteen miles away."

Gas still lighted most of the city in 1882, although Edison's incandescent lamps were available and one hotel, the Everett down on Park Row, had startled rival innkeepers by installing one hundred and one of the newfangled lights in its dining room, lobby, reading room, and public parlors.

Even more newsworthy than electricity had been the announcement twelve years earlier of the opening of a new brokerage firm in Parlors 25 and 26 of the Hoffman House by "two pretty and fashionable lady partners," thirty-one-year-old Victoria Woodhull and her sister, Tennessee Claflin. They were ardent woman's rights crusaders and in 1872 the People's Party nominated Victoria for President of the United States.

The suffragette movement was still going strong in March of 1915 when the Hoffman House, Nymphs and all, vanished from the metropolitan scene.

1871
GILSEY HOUSE

John F. Tracy of Chicago was the first name on the register when the Gilsey House opened in New York City in April of 1871. On the same site, Broadway at 29th Street, there had stood until the preceding year a white cottage surrounded by flower beds. Now the Gilsey's snowy white walls rose to a corniced mansard roof crowned by a clock tower. Urns of flowers flanked the handsome ground-floor restaurant and the Gentlemen's Cafe. Two days before the first guest signed in, the Gilsey House had a grand preview by invitation. The hotel blazed with light as every gas jet was turned on, and, by eight o'clock on the evening of April 15th, more than 2500 guests were surging through the rooms. An orchestra played from one of the stairwells and in the restaurants a "bounteous collation" was served, complete with the best imported wines and champagne. The guests were a distinguished lot, but a thirsty group as well. They had nearly exhausted the supply of champagne long before midnight. When informed of this impending crisis, the senior Mr. Gilsey snapped at his manager, "Send out and borrow some. Let them swim in it." A contemporary account added, "And verily I suspect some heads did swim."

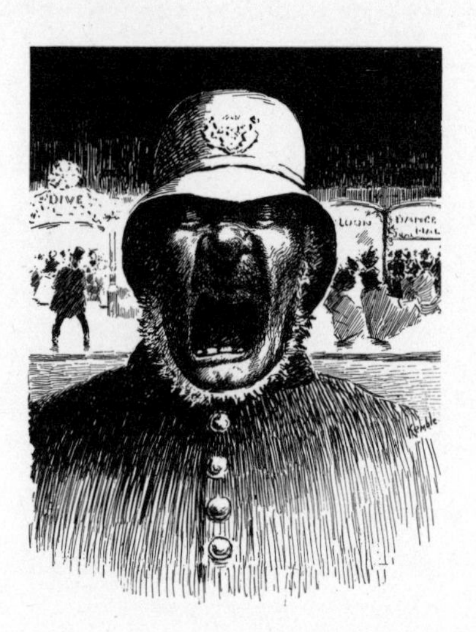

"Everything Wide Open . . ."

The Gilsey enjoyed a somewhat riotous reputation. Just west and north of it was the notorious district known as Tenderloin. Legend has it that a city policeman newly assigned there said with a wide grin, "Well, I've been living on scrag ends a long time; now I'll be living on tenderloin." The district grew progressively worse, and, by the time the Gilsey was thirty-five years old, New York's Police Commissioner William McAdoo was denouncing the graft and corruption among his men in the Tenderloin, noting that "high officers grow rich on the blood and tear-stained money of this army of wretched unfortunates, degenerates and criminals."

The Gilsey's urbane manager, Colonel James H. Breslin, created a mild furor when he decided to put his staff in livery. Newspapers noted that the "boys" didn't care much for the gold braid and buttons. But, within the year, practically all fashionable New York hotels had liveried attendants.

A HOT SUMMER'S DAY ON BROADWAY

The clock in the Gilsey House tower stood at 11:15 on this sunny July morning in 1901. Along Broadway strolled the Gibson girls twirling their parasols, and the perspiring males mopping their faces under straw boaters while overwarm and overtired children burst into tears as children have in hot weather since time immemorial.

Refuge from the heat of the day was at hand, within the white marble and iron walls of the Gilsey House, whose builder, Peter Gilsey, was responsible for New York's first iron building (1856, Broadway and Cortlandt Street). Corinthian columns and balconies graced the white façade and striped awnings shaded the windows of cafes and restaurants on the street floor. The original lessee, Robert Coleman of the Coleman House, shied away when he saw the hotel attaining proportions which to him seemed extravagant; James Breslin was a happy substitute, selling out his interest in the St. James and joining forces with Peter Gardner, another hotel keeper, and the owner's son, Henry Gilsey. It proved a felicitous combination.

The city's foremost decorator, Garibaldi, was called in to see that the 200-odd rooms offered everything in comfort and elegance. Evidently he succeeded, for after the somewhat riotous opening the hotel's register showed eighty-five arrivals on the first day of business and a full house by the end of the first week.

Broadway at night was exuberant, slightly naughty, and brimming with infinite entertainment in the 90's.

The Gilsey's restaurant was rated "one of perhaps half a dozen which are considered as standing abreast of Delmonico's . . . famous for its excellence, it has been approved by many lovers of good living." Army and Navy officers liked its proximity to the theaters, while railroad magnates and coal operators met there to eat, drink and hatch schemes of reorganization and development.

Harper's Weekly was charging, perhaps with reason, that American women were becoming addicted to hotel life "at the expense of domestic virtue and happiness," while their duties were taken over by "gay cooks and merry chambermaids."

For over a quarter of a century righteous New Yorkers had been bemoaning the night life that centered around Broadway, and such institutions as the "Midnight Mission for the Rescue of Fallen Women" had been aided by "Christian men" who scoured the streets "with cards of invitation and religious tracts, trying by kind words to persuade these poor despised ones to forsake their evil ways."

But nighttime Broadway flourished and reached ever farther uptown, leaving Shanley's, the famous lobster palace, Wallack's Theater, Toney's and everything else in the picture below, even the Gilsey, to settle into drab old age . . . the Gilsey "a sad spectacle of its former elegance, jammed with lofts and offices, its Tower clock stopped forever."

MIDNIGHT AT THE GILSEY

A MUSEUM PIECE...

No historic importance attaches to this little hotel. It is a curio. But it lasted nearly half a century, attracting to its bizarre public rooms such patrons as knew the proprietor, Mr. Thomas Riley, or wanted a change from the standard barrooms of the time. The Fifth Ward Museum Hotel, at West Broadway and Franklin Street in New York City, opened in 1826, when its 174-foot flagpole (glimpsed at far right, above) was a landmark on New York's modest skyline.

The *Times*, reporting the demolition of the amusing hostelry in 1868, noted that "in connection with the hotel, Mr. Riley founded a museum consisting of Revolutionary relics, pictures, specimens of natural history, *objects de vertu* and an assortment of old coins. In 1852 Mr. Riley retired with a fortune of nearly $100,000, and resided in Varick street until his death in 1858."

1873 *The* WINDSOR

"LARGELY PATRONIZED BY FOREIGNERS..."

Banners fluttered high above Fifth Avenue and four-in-hands, landaus and hackneys clattered past the porticoed entrance when the Windsor Hotel opened in New York City in 1873, occupying the block between Forty-sixth and Forty-seventh streets on Fifth Avenue where once "the gay youth of both sexes had disported themselves on real ice."

The Windsor opened in the middle of a panic and depression which saw some 5000 businesses closed. Nevertheless success attended the Windsor from the start. The press soon noted the prevalence of distinguished foreign names on its register and the hotel itself advertised "Largely Patronized by Foreigners."

People were still talking about a brash experiment which ended the same year the Windsor opened . . . the first New York City subway. This contraption, a cylindrical car seating twenty people, ran by compressed air through a tunnel 312 feet long, still in existence under Broadway from Warren to Murray streets. The fare was twenty-five cents and the inventor, Alfred Ely Beach, had an impassioned belief in underground transportation for the burgeoning city, although it is doubtful that even he foresaw the grisly subway rush hours which were to try New York nerves and dispositions in the years to come.

HOTEL

Fifth Avenue was still largely a street of brownstones and stately mansions in the uptown area of the Windsor, and the old Gould family fortress across Forty-seventh Street was holding its own among encroaching commercialism. The curious, dismounting from hansom or omnibus in front of the Windsor, could hope for a look at one or two Goulds as they came and went from the mansion just next door. Two blocks up the Avenue stood St. Patrick's Cathedral, even then an architectural "Gothic Tale" that attracted native New Yorkers and visitors alike.

High tea was one means of pampering visitors from abroad and the Windsor served it in "English fashion," the table centered with an epergne of fruit and flowers surrounded by silver baskets of cake and a dish of jelly or charlotte russe, then platters of ham, turkey, chicken and tongue, with biscuits, jam, sardines and the like on the side.

The Windsor's opening year also saw the country's first free mail delivery (limited to cities with 20,000 or more population), and the first penny postcards, of lamented memory, issued for quick, economical communication.

In time, the Windsor's corner was taken over by a sedate and proper firm of furniture purveyors, but as the personality of the Avenue changed irrevocably, this, too, gave way to a garish, crowded discount house.

Men in silk hats and derbies had plenty of room in the spacious lobby of the Windsor to gather in the marble-floored area with its gas fixtures encircling the stately columns. They also . . . apparently . . . wore their hats indoors with complete indifference, as witness the dignified patrons of the Windsor's billiard room below. Such premises were, however, never invaded by a lady in whose presence doffing of the hat was required. Billiard rooms were for relaxation, shirt-sleeved if the weather called for it, and informal enough to allow taking your draft of ale from the bottle.

No hint of tragedy tinged the bright air of St. Patrick's Day, March 17, 1899, when gay holiday crowds gathered at the doors and windows of the Windsor Hotel to watch the parade come down Fifth Avenue.

Nobody knows how it happened. Suddenly the hotel was a holocaust of flame and smoke. The screams of trapped men, women and children, the crash of falling masonry, the clang of the city's fire-fighting equipment engaged in brave but futile battle . . . these combined to make news stories and pictures that horrified the nation. Floods of water poured over the flaming building, but the ruins were too hot to permit an immediate search for the entombed victims. A fortunate few were rescued by extension ladders before the walls fell in. But next morning a photograph showed somber groups huddled under umbrellas in the rain as the death toll mounted.

Headlines in the *New York Herald* on Sunday, March 19, read:

Loss of Life and Money at Windsor Fire . . . Dead 16; Injured 57 and Missing 45 . . . Many Bodies Are Under Ruins . . . Jewels Valued at Half a Million Missing . . .

Police nabbed looters, including one man who said the $8,000 worth of jewels he carried in a bundle were the property of his employer and he was simply taking them off for safekeeping! An untold fortune in valuables vanished; no trace was ever found of the hotel clerk and the wine steward. So the grim story unfolded until the death toll had mounted to forty-five . . . the worst hotel fire in New York's history.

WHAT GOOD HOTEL IS NEAR THE DEPOT

THE GRAND UNION HOTEL

Directly opposite the

Grand Central Depot,

42d Street and Park Avenue,

NEW YORK.

Offers every inducement to the traveler seeking a comfortable and convenient hotel. Every street-car transfers past its door. Fine Cafe and Restaurant. European plan. We attend to your baggage.

Rates, $1 a day and upwards

PHOTO PLATE CO. N.Y.

1874

GRAND UNION HOTEL

"HAIR CURLERS, HOT HOUSE ROSES & HAND-PAINTED PIANOS"

Simeon Ford, ebullient proprietor of New York City's Grand Union Hotel, located on Park Avenue, only a walk away from Grand Central Station, listed the above items as indicative of the details which had to be considered by anyone hoping to run a successful hotel.

The first Grand Central Station was opened in 1871, but it is seen here in its remodeled version of 1899, with the old Harlem Railroad tunnel visible in the center of Park Avenue, running from Forty-second Street to its terminal at Thirty-third. Long before this, there had been a New York Central Depot at Forty-second, and on the site of the Grand Union had stood a modest family hotel called Robinson's, succeeded after the Civil War by another unpretentious hostelry, the Reunion Hotel.

Simeon Ford's establishment was considerably more elaborate and was specifically designed to accommodate a public which became increasingly travel-minded as the nineteenth century neared its close.

The emphasis was on quality at economy prices. The cafe, lunchroom, restaurants and wine rooms offered "the best" but at prices carefully quoted below New York's luxury hotels. A special inducement at the Grand Union was: "Toilet and baggage rooms for ladies and gents where coats, valises and parcels can be left free."

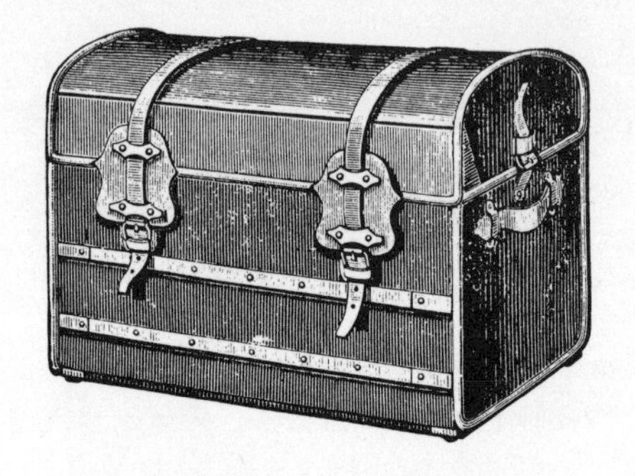

"GUESTS' BAGGAGE TAKEN TO AND FROM DEPOT FREE"

This young matron with her two children is typical of the hundreds of families who hurried to the nearby Grand Union Hotel when they arrived in New York on their way to the Centennial Exposition in Philadelphia. Her trim-waisted traveling dress has an overskirt for extra warmth as the time of year is evidently toward the close of the Quaker city's gala Fair in November of 1876. The Grand Union, in addition to its free porter service to and from trains, also supplied in its lobby and public rooms complete information, including time tables, for traveling via train or boat to the Centennial City.

The hotel also provided unusual facilities for "freshening up" after a journey that was bound in those open-window days to be pretty dusty. Traveling ladies were advised by *Demorest's* magazine to take with them "mask vails to bring out the brightness of the eyes, the rose of the complexion and the carmine of the lips."

A more discreet addition to her wardrobe might have been "the new Zephyr Bosom Pads . . . a novel invention for increasing the size of the bust . . . soft, flexible, yielding to the touch like the natural bosom . . . expanded with air."

About the time of the Grand Union's heyday, buildings were rising so high in New York that *Harper's Weekly* in 1881 reported four hundred elevators, "each of which carry an average of seven hundred persons a day to an average height of sixty feet. . . . Should the tall buildings multiply . . . as they have done for the last few years, the streets will be found too narrow to accommodate the multitudes of human beings who must use them. . . . This will lead to underground passageways or to elevated sidewalks. . . ."

The Grand Union, "fitted up at an expense of $1,000,000," advertised, about this time, that its 450 rooms were "reduced to one dollar and upwards a day."

Among new notions with which Mr. Simeon Ford was toying were twin beds, which were being colorfully promoted at the time as having supplanted "the old fashioned double bed among the better classes in England . . . The change being largely due to the advice of scientific men and physicians that 'It is poison to breathe again the human breath.' "

By the time the Grand Union had been renovated there was a stream of commuters from Westchester and Connecticut pouring in daily to Grand Central, and the businessman's breakfast was being featured on Grand Union menus, which conveniently carried railroad timetables on the back of the bill of fare. Proprietor Ford observed: "I see by the papers that a scientist has discovered that the average man eats one thousand times his own weight in food during a lifetime. Some of my boarders try to do that trick in two weeks."

In another of his famous after-dinner speeches, Simeon Ford defended the clerks of his and all other hotels as being "the most good-natured and accommodating of mortals." He added that if said clerk were "not of a serene and placid nature he would long since have decorated a cemetery. He is expected to remember everybody, and to give everybody the best room in the house; to laugh at every humorous anecdote related to him, no matter how antique; and to lend a sympathetic ear to every traveler who is in distress, or imagines he is."

Arranged for the guests of the Grand Union was a giant version of the stereopticon viewer so popular in Victorian parlors all over the country.

Simeon Ford decided in 1914 to close the doors of the Grand Union and put everything up for sale. The photographer recorded the time, 10:45 A.M., on closing day, May 3, 1914, when he focused on the abandoned Oyster Bar with its prints of popular comedians, its polished counter and iron grille. On the same day the Horseshoe or Amen Corner below stood equally sad and empty; its carved chairs, paintings, electric fixtures and even the mounted heads of buffalo and moose awaited the auctioneer's hammer which on Tuesday, May 12, was to signal the end of yet another of New York's notable Victorian hotels.

Automobiles were scurrying along Park Avenue when the Grand Union finally closed its doors in 1914. The "new America of Henry Ford" was dawning and Mr. Ford's promise to build "a motor car for the multitude . . . one which any man with a good salary can afford" came to fruition in that year as more than a quarter million of the famous black "flivvers" rolled off a primitive assembly line.

In 1913, the last full year for the Grand Union, most people in the United States were still naïvely optimistic about their futures in the best of possible worlds. But in Europe the season had a certain desperate gaiety. Our Minister to Copenhagen, Maurice Francis Egan, reported that "all decorum had fled from society" and that at one fasionable party the young

people "had sat on the floor of the dining-room surrounded by a ring of champagne bottles." The political skies were murky and ominous and when the Egans announced plans to spend the Christmas holidays in Berlin, a German diplomat told them:

"No—you'd better stay away. The Germany of your fancy does not exist. There are cannons even on the Christmas trees."

And so the beautiful years, *La Belle Epoque* as the French called the era coinciding with the last of the Victorian and the brief span of the Edwardian reign, came to an end in 1914 for a stricken Europe. For the United States there was a little time left, but only a little. It was probably a proper year for the demise of a hotel such as the Grand Union where gentlemen long ago spent pleasant twilights sitting in armchairs out of doors waiting for their favorite minstrel to turn up with his banjo and sing them sad Southern songs.

The

"IN THE VERY HEART OF THE GAY AND SOCIAL METROPOLIS"

"The most complete and elegant family hotel in the world," announced the Buckingham in an elaborate brochure when it opened in January of the centennial year, 1876.

The nation may have been celebrating the one hundredth year of its independence from England, but the Buckingham of New York City, rising eight floors above Fifth Avenue at the corner of Fiftieth Street, was feudal and baronial in style, and its management, Fuller and Gage, felt certain it would remind its guests of "Warwick Castle, Blenheim or Chatsworth."

Although the old aristocracy of the 80's and 90's quickly took the Buckingham to its heart, it also had its share of visiting royalty, including one nervous ex-president of Guatemala who was rumored to have a trunkful of gold tucked away in his suite of parlor and bedrooms. The genial old gentleman who was ousted as emperor of Brazil, "Dom Pedro the Magnanimous," also came to stay at the Buckingham, whose Fiftieth Street entrance looked across to the newest marvel of Fifth Avenue, St. Patrick's Cathedral.

The hotel's brochure, not modest even by comparison with today's press agentry, noted that this "most conspicuous ornament of Fifth Avenue . . . looks up and down the great promenade of America, one of the most magnificent streets in civilization." The Ladies Parlor shown here was distinguished by its "chastity of tone and harmony of colors and proportions, as rigidly observed in the style of Louis XVI . . . in white, French gray and gold. It is a reproduction of the famous Salle de Glaces in the Grand Trianon at Versailles."

The charming little bridge leading to the Breakfast Room of the hotel was a miniature conservatory with plants and flowers flourishing under its arched glass roof.

All the bedrooms had open fireplaces and most were in suites—parlor, bedchamber, bathroom and toilet room, these latter entirely separate to guard against "the escape of noxious gases." The rates were not for those of modest budget. The most elaborate of the suites began at sixty-five dollars a week, although a parlor and bedroom furnished in "Eastlake style" could be had for forty-five.

Entering the imposing Buckingham, which was built of Baltimore brick, guests came into a marble-floored lobby shimmering with the varicolored light from stained glass windows. A skylight eight stories above the main lobby gave a spectacular feel of height.

The Grand Dining Room of the Buckingham was a glorious mixture of fourteenth-century "baronial" plus the "refinement and elegance of the nineteenth century." It, too, had a great open fireplace with polished brass dog irons. Its walls were done in imitation stamped leather, its ceiling in heavy oak. But the *pièce de résistance* was the enormous antique sideboard of carved ash with black decorations.

The dinner served on the hotel's opening night was supervised by the former *chef de cuisine* of the Union Club, Domenico Piretti, and the *New York Herald* reported that the "six hundred astonished guests were served a superb supper, the table decorations representing an Erie Railroad train, the Centennial Bell, *a Troupee de Musique*, a Swiss cottage and a Temple of Liberty!"

In contrast to the carved, frescoed, stained glass splendor of the rest of the hotel . . . which, incidentally, had in the lobby a gilt statue of its namesake, the Duke of Buckingham, plumed hat and all . . . the hotel's breakfast room was simple and charming. The "coffee and roll habit" decried in *Harper's Bazar* in the nineties, had not blighted the morning fare at the Buckingham, where there was a choice of fruit *au naturel,* fresh breads, broiled steaks, chops or chicken and a variety of eggs.

In general, the Buckingham promised that "people will not find here the red-plush chairs and sofas, the gorgeous china vases, the marble centre tables and other monstrosities of outfit to which they may be partial," but rather the grace and elegance of "the London private hotel" after which it was modeled.

The Buckingham lived to quiet middle age. In June of 1922 it signed finis to an era which saw many great hotels foundering on the "Ararat of Prohibition." In its fashionable shadow rose an equally chic and famous specialty shop.

"THE BUCKINGHAM PRIDES ITSELF AND WITH ADEQUATE REASON, ON IT'S CUISINE"

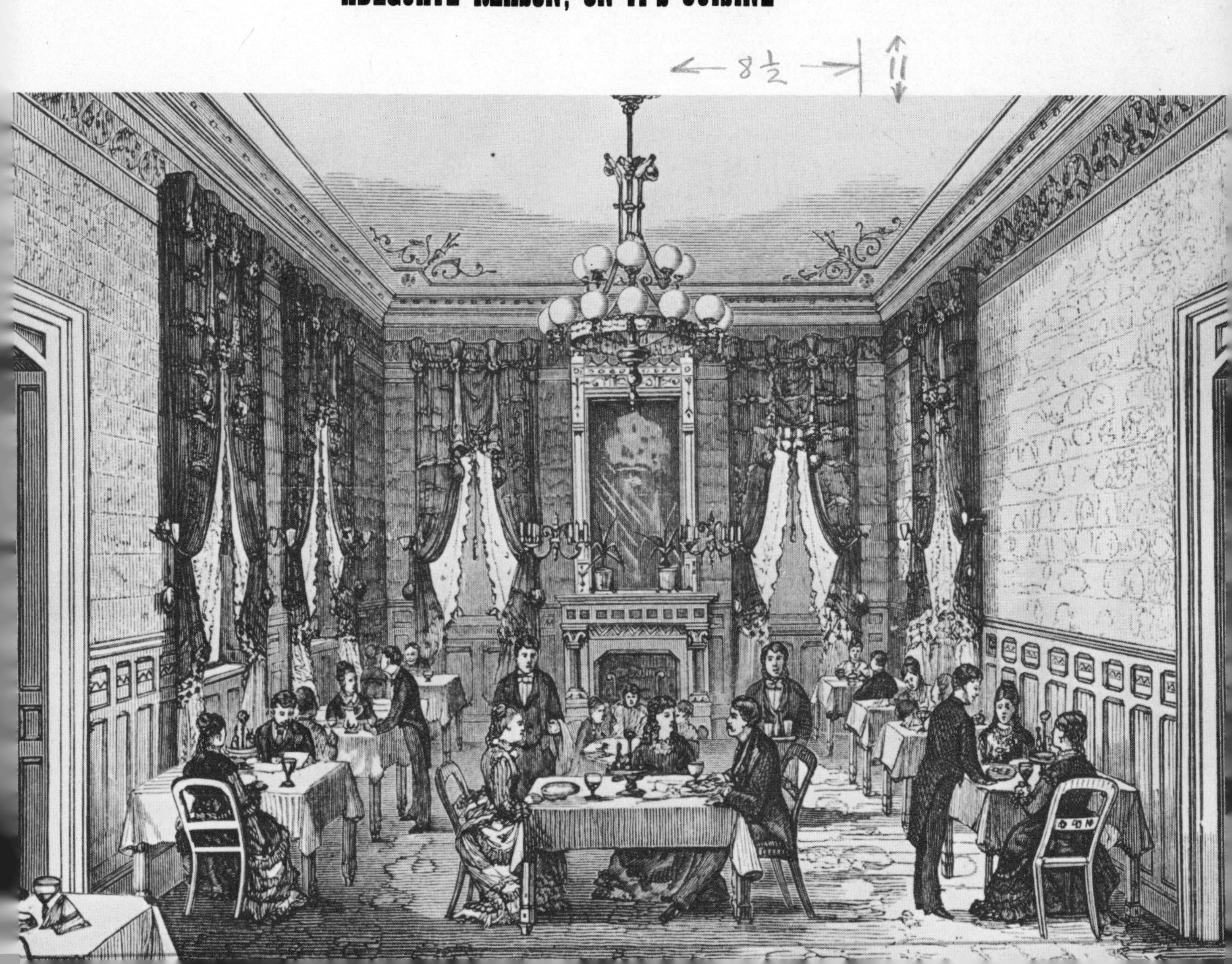

APRIL 13, 1878.]

WOMEN'S HOTEL,

Fourth Ave., 32d & 33d Sts.

MRS. ALEXANDER T. STEWART takes pleasure in announcing that this Hotel WILL BE OPEN for the reception of Boarders on WEDNESDAY, APRIL 3,1878.

The BUILDING erected by Mr. STEWART has been completed in accordance with his plans and purposes, as a HOME FOR WOMEN who SUPPORT THEMSELVES by DAILY LABOR. All such, to the extent of its capacity, are invited to participate in its benefits.

ITS REGULATIONS will be such as govern first-class hotels, except that all applying for Board will be required to present a satisfactory written certificate of good character and conduct from their employers or other persons known to the Hotel Managers.

EIGHT LARGE RECEPTION ROOMS are provided for visitors; but the Dining-Rooms, Parlors, and Library will be exclusively for the use of Boarders.

THE LIBRARY contains over twenty-five hundred volumes of selected literary works, to which Boarders have free access, with the use of writing materials at all times.

STEAM ELEVATORS convey passengers to every floor, and the building being fire-proof throughout, each floor is thus made equally desirable and convenient.

THE SLEEPING ROOMS, over Five Hundred in number, are furnished uniform in quality, and equally well ventilated and adapted to the comfort and convenience of the occupant. They are of various sizes, and the prices for each have been graduated accordingly, depending upon their being occupied by one or more persons; but the

Board and Lodging for Each Person will be at the Rate of Six Dollars Per Week,

That being the lowest sum which it is calculated will be the cost of the meals, lodging, attendance, &c., of each Boarder.

BATHS are located on every floor, for which a nominal charge for attendance, &c., will be made.

AN EXTENSIVE LAUNDRY is provided on the premises, where the washing, ironing, &c., for Boarders will be done at rates intended to cover the mere cost of labor and materials used.

The KITCHEN AND CULINARY DEPARTMENT will be under the personal management of cooks of the first class.

A LIMITED NUMBER OF ROOMS will be set apart for the use of ladies visiting the city on business. In such cases the Manager must have previous notice of the intended arrival, and the rooms must be engaged in advance.

APPLICATION FOR BOARD may be made by letter, addressed to "THE MANAGER OF THE WOMEN'S HOTEL," and will be notified, and accepted (when satisfactory) in the order received.

NEW YORK, *March*, 1878.

THE FOURTH AVENUE FRONT.

THE WOMEN'S HOTEL.—From Sketches by Theo. R. Davis and Photographs by G. W. Pach.—[See Page 294.]

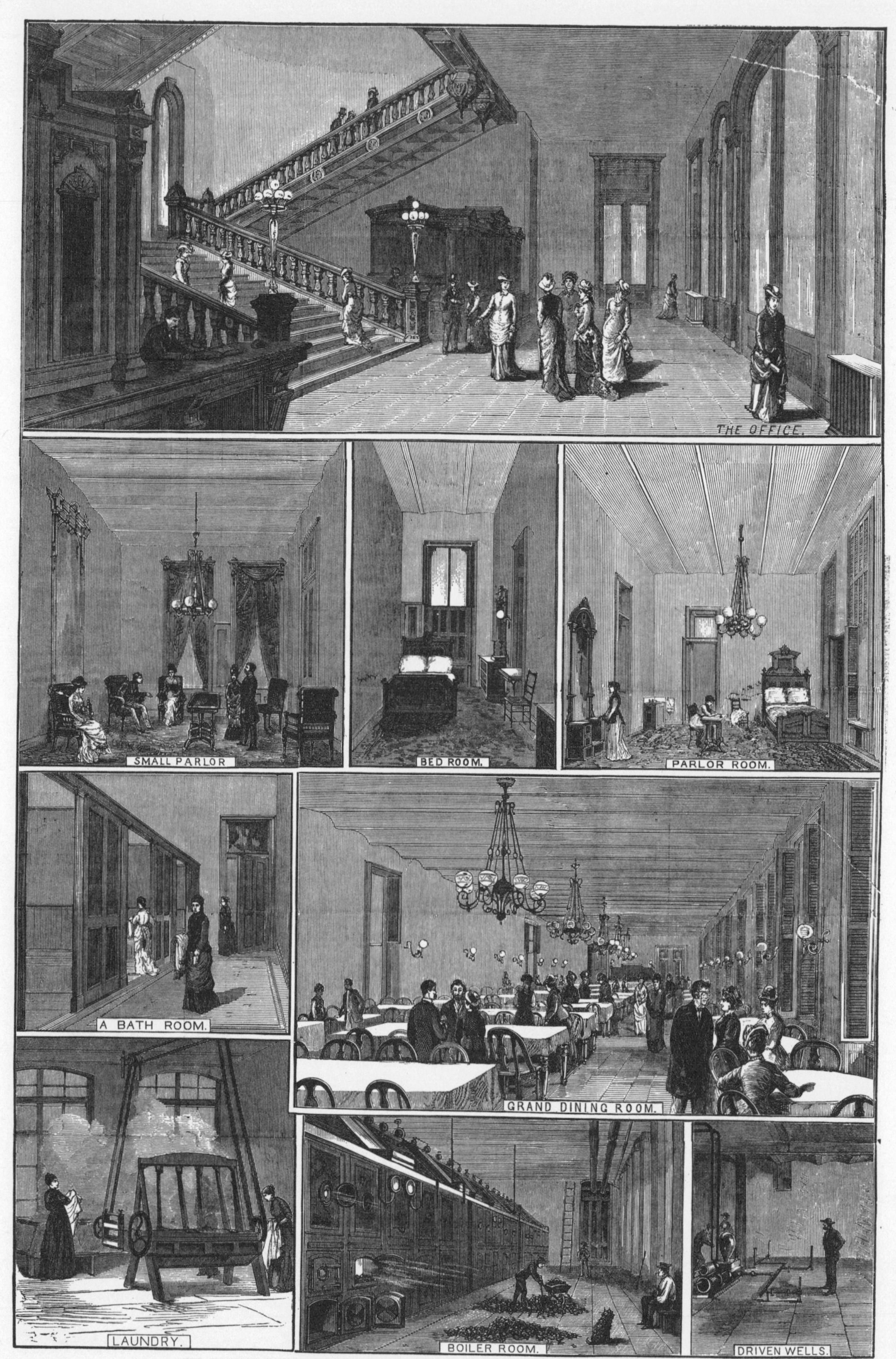

THE WOMEN'S HOTEL.—FROM SKETCHES BY THEO. R. DAVIS AND PHOTOGRAPHS BY G. W. PACH.—[SEE PAGE 294.]

THE GRAND PARLOR.

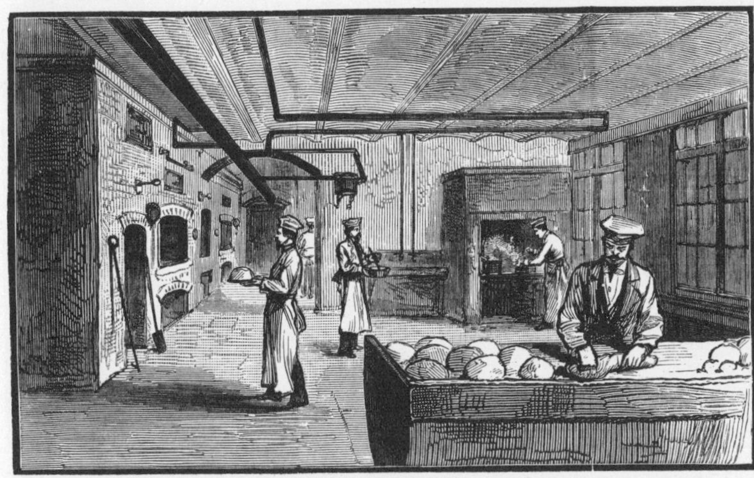

THE COLUMBIA OVENS.

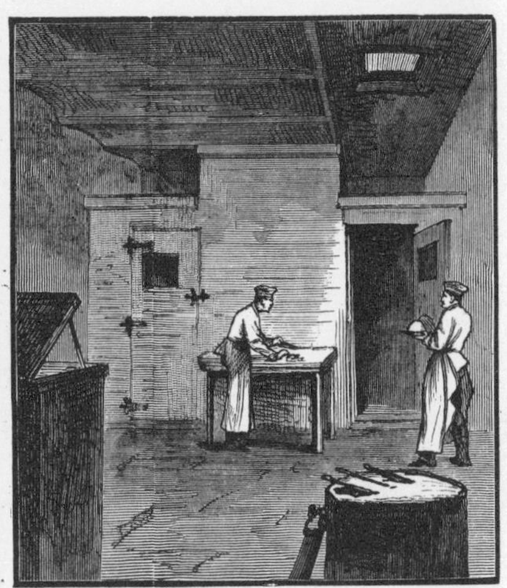

REFRIGERATORS.

THE KITCHEN.

THE WOMEN'S HOTEL.—FROM SKETCHES BY THEO. R. DAVIS AND PHOTOGRAPHS BY G. W. PACH.—[SEE PAGE 259.]

THE GREAT OBSTACLE IN THE WAY OF STEWART'S HOTEL.

in accordance
vart, and open-
he success anticipated by Mrs. Stewart. Consequently it is to be abandoned as a special hotel for women, and early in June will be opened to the general public, under the name of the Stewart Hotel. The number of boarders who availed themselves of the advantages offered in the Women's Hotel was too small to admit of the extensive and costly arrangements being continued for them. With five hundred or a thousand guests the hotel would have been self-supporting, but with fifty it was impracticable. Numerous "reasons" have been assigned for this failure: that an isolation of one thousand women is impossible; that there was a lack of home feeling in consequence of the fixed regulations; that there was a burdensome system of espionage; that the prices, though reasonable enough for what was furnished, were beyond the means of the class for whom the hotel was designed; that working-women preferred more independence and less luxuriousness; and many others of similar nature. Perhaps by combining all, the true explanation may be reached; or it may be that if the test time had been twelve months instead of two, a different result would have been seen. But it is understood that alterations are now going on to fit the building for a general hotel.

June 15, 1878

A SKETCH AT STEWART'S HOTEL.

GENTLEMANLY CLERK. "Excuse me, madam, but you know our Rule—no Pets allowed in the House."

...AND SO IN... 1878 ...IT BECAME...

New York had a more than liberal representation of buildings erected by the famous merchant A. T. Stewart, the Women's Hotel of New York City among them. And they all, according to a Western journalist, were "great pale palatial structures so coldly solid by day and so etherally picturesque when illuminated by night."

But Mr. Stewart was dead before his pet project, the Women's Hotel, became a reality. Mrs. Stewart supervised the opening of the eight-story hotel which rose around a central garden court on Park Avenue between Thirty-second and Thirty-third streets. More than 20,000 people jammed the hotel on opening night, April 2, 1878, most of them wearing street or business costumes in deference to the character of the establishment.

Harper's Weekly in June, 1878, described it as "by far the finest structure of the kind in New York City . . . No millionaire for one hundred dollars a week would be better served." Yet, the editorial went on, "its prices, while very moderate . . . places it beyond the means of working girls." So, apparently, did the long list of rules and regulations laid down by Mr. Steward to safeguard the morals of the girls, for, quite simply, they stayed away in droves. In despair, the management closed the doors, made considerable renovations, and opened the place as the Park Avenue Hotel, complete with "the inspired brain of a *cordon bleu,* Professor Edward Schelcher, former chef of the Grand Union in Saratoga."

What could be more enchanting on a summer's day than to choose a table on the Dining Verandah of the Park Avenue Hotel with gaily striped awnings keeping off the sun and a garden vista of fountain, trees and flowers spread across the spacious court? New Yorkers adored it for tête-à-tête luncheons and even more for dinner when the shaded candles gleamed above crystal goblets, linen and silver while a Hungarian band played in the courtyard.

The Park Avenue continued on its sedate and well-mannered way, the pride of Murray Hill, until the year 1925.

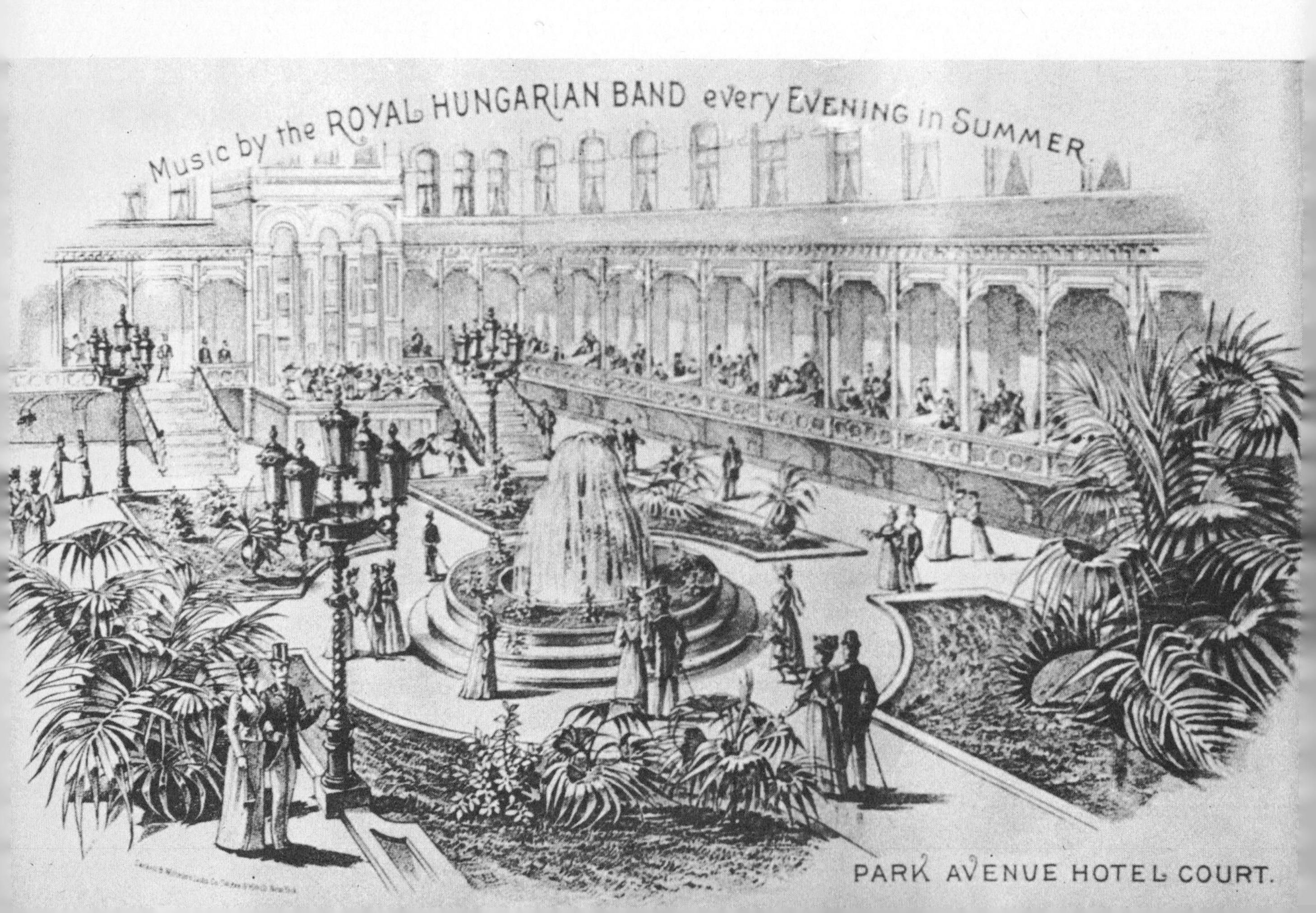

1889 *The* HOTEL VENDOME

OPENING DAY ON THE GAY WHITE WAY...

The bright lights of New York cafes and theaters circled the Hotel Vendome at Forty-first Street and Broadway. The new bar is shown here on opening day, October 1, 1889. Center front is Mr. W. Johnson Quinn, then manager of the Vendome . . . whose name had been associated by the authors of this book only with a treasure-trove of pictures, menus and information gathered over the years with the idea of putting it into a history of the American hotel. Having found Mr. Quinn, we here salute him, with the hope that we have made good use of his collection since he did not live to do so himself. We think he would have fancied this advertisement for Vinous Rubber Grapes, which could be carried in a discreet opera glass case by a lady desiring a spot of stimulation during a matinee or musicale. The Philadelphia firm manufacturing this little monstrosity explained:

"These Vinous Rubber Grapes are pure rubber capsules filled and expanded to the capacity of a small pony glassful of choice selected wines and liquors for medical use, and put up in handsomely decorated metal boxes containing fifteen grapes or drinks of either Whisky, Brandy or Gin, or eighteen smaller grapes filled with the most popular wines, such as Port, Madeira, Sherry, etc. . . . When putting in the mouth, press the lips tightly together, bend the head forward slightly, then crush the grape between the teeth, or insert a pin or toothpick between the lips and penetrate the grape. After swallowing the contents eject the skin." Cost was seventy-five cents a box for whisky, a dollar for brandy, fifty cents for wine.

No such subterfuge as a Vinous Grape was called for when the Vendome spread its bounteous New Year's Day collation on January 1, 1889. Garlanded tables bore the elaborate *confiserie* and *grande pièces* dear to the hearts of chefs of the period . . . galantines of ham and chicken, airy spun-sugar "fountains," even a festive Ferris wheel in sugar. Pheasant in full plumage, a sugar-sculpted Neptune with trident, flag-decked poles . . . and the whole extravaganza was by courtesy of Mine Host, including brimming bowls of eggnog.

1893

1897

STRICTLY FOR THE CARRIAGE TRADE

"Replete in a lavish degree" reported *King's Handbook* in the summer of 1892, describing an imposing building of brick and terra cotta that was rising ten stories above Fifth Avenue. New York's gilt-edged society leaders still looked on aghast as a corner once sacred to the Astor family surrendered to the world of commerce. They had not recovered from William Waldorf Astor's announcement two years earlier that he was leaving his native land forever, embittered at the voters' rejection of his bid for Congress.

But by the time the Waldorf Hotel opened on March 14, 1893, on the site of his mansion at Thirty-third Street and Fifth Avenue, society had been won over by the beguiling George C. Boldt of Philadelphia's Hotel Bellevue and now also proprietor of the Waldorf. It was Mr. Boldt who influenced the formidable Mrs. William K. Vanderbilt to arrange a benefit concert at the hotel on its opening night, for her favorite charity, St. Mary's Free Hospital for Children. A young conductor named Walter Damrosch directed an evening of classical music and more than 1500 guests from New York, Philadelphia, and Boston defied rain and sleet to attend. The rococo carriage entrance shown above was jammed as twinkling lights caught the sparkle of jewels, the shimmer of satin, the starched shirt fronts, and shiny top hats. It was a triumph for Mr. Boldt and for Mrs. Vanderbilt, too, since she was the first to openly flaunt the unwritten law that the "right people" must entertain at home, never in public.

Although it opened in the financial panic of 1893, the Waldorf was a glittering success from the start. Above the entrance to the South Palm Garden shone a stained glass picture of the Astor home in the German town of Waldorf. Nearly in the front yard of the Waldorf stood the Mansion of the late William B. Astor. His son, Colonel John Jacob Astor, eyed the establishment with distaste and even threatened to raze his house and put up a stable. Mr. Boldt not only dissuaded him from this spiteful venture, but proposed that he build

Colonel John Jacob Astor in his automobile—*Harper's Bazar*, 1899

a hotel even grander than the Waldorf and that the family betake themselves to the quiet upper reaches of Fifth Avenue. So it was that another Astor town house vanished and in its place, towered the Astoria. Designed by the same architect who did the Waldorf, Henry J. Hardenbergh, it, too, dipped into family history and took its name from the town of Astoria in Oregon, founded in 1811 by John Jacob Astor I. The Astoria Hotel opened with due fanfare on November 1, 1897. Colonel Astor consented to a passage linking the two hotels, but with the proviso that it could be shut off if the partnership did not prove to his liking.

The linked hotels were a treasure house of paintings, tapestries, antique furniture, and sculpture. The two goddesses adorning the first page of this story were executed by Giovanni Maria Benzoni of Rome (1829-1873) and are still being admired in the lobby of the present Waldorf-Astoria.

...and came the Hyphen

A thousand bedrooms, more than 750 private baths, suites ablaze with tapestries, embroidered portieres, Italian carved screens, rosewood, walnut, and mahogany . . . that was the Waldorf-Astoria, with an array of public rooms which included a State Banquet Hall where Proprietor Boldt permitted his $35,000 set of Sèvres china, part of his private collection, to be viewed by visitors. Within days after the opening of the new hotel with its passageway leading to the old, knowing New Yorkers were telling their friends: "Meet me at the Hyphen."

"A fine outlook on this great avenue of American fashion," was promised by an advertisement of the time for those who arrived at the main entrance of the Astoria, to be deposited inside an imposing colonnade.

"No such façade was ever planned, certainly none such was ever built, either in ancient, medieval, or modern times," reported the ordinarily conservative *Scientific American* just before the completion of the Astoria. Since the hotel reached the improbable height of sixteen stories, the builders had to adopt a new technique of incorporating steel trusses above the ceilings of the lower floors to support the walls they carried above. Within the combined hotels could be found, the magazine continued, "every pleasure and convenience of

metropolitan life . . . a grand ballroom, a theater, a banqueting hall, a full suite of rooms for wedding celebrations, lecture rooms, clubrooms and even a hall furnished specially for meetings of secret societies."

Around the Waldorf-Astoria a spate of chic shops opened, and on the premises themselves were the hotel's bank, brokers' offices, a photographic gallery, Turkish and Russian baths, hairdressing salons for both ladies and gentlemen, as well as "trunk packers" for those who did not bring their own servants. The billiard room boasted "one English and five American tables."

The Astoria's roof garden was "a literal German spa where all the best mineral waters of the world can be obtained."

A WORLD OF WORTH

Mrs. John Jacob Astor—1899

By abolishing the Ladies Entrance, Mr. Boldt endeared himself to the hearts of the influential female coterie upon whose patronage he depended, understandably, for the many social functions they sponsored at his hostelry. So he spared no expense when it came to fitting out the lounge or "retiring room" shown here, with its domed ceiling, delicately painted, its deep-carpeted floor, velvet and damask draperies, and ample room for chatting, primping, or discussing their views of the new fashions being created by Worth of Paris.

The Waldorf's chosen clientele of fashionable women were, for their era, catholic in their tastes, and such august patronesses as Mrs. Edwin Palmer and Mrs. Mace Moulton joined J. Pierpont Morgan, Chauncey M. Depew, and the Russian Consul General, Baron Schlippenbach, in putting on a Dramatic and Musical Recital with Miss Anna Held entertaining, and a potpourri of featured acts which took in child impersonations by a Mrs. Hardin Burnley, "The Ballad of Judas Iscariot," musical setting included, by Mr. Edmund

Russell; and Miss Zelda Sears in Comedy Monologues, all decorously presented in the Astor Gallery. The Gallery was modeled after the Palais Soubise in Paris and its walls presented, in the words of the hotel's own publicity release, "sixteen magnificent allegorical paintings, of the twelve months and the four seasons . . . by Simmons."

Visitors were provided guides free of charge to show them the rosy cloud ceiling in the Marie Antoinette Room where Edwin H. Blashfield had painted "The Birth of Venus," and the murals done by Will H. Low collaborating with two other artists, Edward Simmons and Charles Y. Turner.

On the occasion of the Astoria opening, Mr. Boldt had again invoked the presiding *grande dames* to lend their names to a fete which began in the afternoon, continued on to an early concert, and climaxed in a presentation of the second act of "Rosemary" in the Grand Ballroom, starring Maude Adams and John Drew. There followed a "most recherché supper" in the Sun Room, a large hall with an arched glass roof, furnished with Wakefield rattan and shaded by palms and hanging curtains.

This is believed to be the first long-distance telephone booth, and one like it graced the Waldorf-Astoria at the turn of the century. It had curtains, carpets, upholstered seats, and was delightfully comfortable for those venturesome souls willing to wait for the operator to put through a call.

Wall Street's Famous Uptown Branch . . . (left to right) T. S. Taylor, A. A. Houseman, James R. Williston, James R. Keene, Jacob Field, William Stow, H. Content, William Oliver, J. W. Gates, Jesse Wasserman.

"BULLS & BEARS"

A reporter from *Harper's* viewed the "Bulls and Bears" with something less than awe. Between the hours of five to seven in the evening such bigwigs as the men pictured here could be found in lively discussion around the cafe tables. Said the weekly, ". . . any unusual disturbance, such as a panic in the Street, or a rumored war with England, brings them from their clubs in shoals to discuss the situation, or to listen to Colonel Storm from Texas, who proposes to enlist a battalion of Waldorf volunteers, which he cheerfully consents to command during the few weeks which, he thinks, will suffice for the utter annihilation of the British Empire." The men assembled daily in the cafe were also ticked off by a newspaper of the time as "personages whose names are known all over the world and whose financial resources aggregate many hundreds of millions."

One of the group above, John W. (Bet-A-Million) Gates, maintained a suite at the hotel where poker was played for astronomical stakes.

& FASHION PLATES!

The gentleman so impeccably attired is from a tailor's fashion plate of the period, drawn with an exquisite eye to detail. His counterpart strolled the marble lobbies of the Waldorf-Astoria daily. Although *King's Handbook* proclaimed that the patrons of the hotel "may enjoy life at wonderfully moderate cost," a bill of 1901 would not indicate that the establishment was geared to a moderate middle-class budget. The total rendered by Mr. Boldt to Mr. Franklin MacVeagh for a ten-day stay was $206.50. This included maid's board and an express charge of eighty cents.

The menu for the gentleman's cafe included an unexplained but fascinating item, *La Financière,* which seems a misnomer in that small world of masculine conniving.

The cafe clique did not get off lightly if they fancied a Waldorf canvasback duck, priced in 1902 at four dollars, with a serving of beets offered at forty cents and a dish of broiled tomatoes at half a dollar. Hothouse grapes came at a dollar per serving, although there was a twenty-five cent compromise dessert on the bill of fare, "Religieux Cake."

The cafe patrons took sides when Proprietor Boldt decided that chin whiskers and mustaches were unsanitary when worn by waiters. Boldt arbitrarily banned any such hirsute adornments for all Waldorf-Astoria staff members. Governor Flower of New York took offense, since he had risen from the ranks and had always worn whiskers; he held that the Boldt edict was not in the spirit of the republic. Be that as it may, a clean-shaven staff materialized at the Waldorf-Astoria and as with all things decreed by Boldt, hotels around the nation followed suit.

BANQUETS & PRIVATE PARTIES

Room 1452

with compliments of Mr Oscar

Date ____________ Signed ____________

. . . A Byword Among Epicures

Another "Horatio Alger" boy to find fame at the Waldorf was a genial and gifted Swiss, Oscar Tschirky, who, like George Boldt, came to America very young and very broke and stayed as the legendary *maître d'hôtel* of the old Waldorf from its opening to its closing day. Oscar himself almost forgot his last name. He had achieved such high acclaim simply as "Oscar" that once he confessed he'd hardly know who was being referred to should anyone address him as "Mr. Tschirky."

Oscar remembered the only visit ever made to the Waldorf by the man who built it . . . then Viscount William Waldorf Astor. It was in 1893, and Oscar recalled that he "escorted him through the corridors to whose frescoes, murals, and luxurious furnishings he seemed to pay no heed. Hands behind his back and head down, that tall, distinguished gentleman walked along, slightly bent, and looking neither to the right nor left . . ."

But Oscar looked to both right and left as he gathered in the millionaires, the theatrical greats, the visiting dignitaries from abroad. Some people say that Oscar invented chop suey upon the occasion of the visit in 1896 of the Viceroy of China, Li Hung-chang . . . a pleasant notion, even if unsubstantiated by fact, especially since the Viceroy's party included three of his own cooks. Oscar, however, does report that the "mantle of Oriental inscrutability and austerity dropped when I presented my two small sons . . . it was flattering to see a broad and kindly grin light his face."

Oscar of the Waldorf was part of the fabric of New York at the turn of the century, an era he referred to wistfully as "the halcyon days when dining was an art . . . the menu, the wines, everything perfect!"

This menu for a late Sunday breakfast was handwritten by Oscar for each of the guests and the card was embossed in gold. It was the sort of meal Oscar himself liked, deceptively simple, exquisitely prepared. Yet never in his long career, which included half a century with the Waldorf, had Oscar been either a chef or a cook. He always admitted this cheerfully and when taxed with the responsibility for at least one all-American dish, he countered with, "Waldorf Salad? Oh yes, I did invent that, but that's not cooking."

Oscar liked to tell how he landed his job with the Waldorf. He was taking a Sunday stroll with his father and at Fifth Avenue and Thirty-third Street the elder Tschirky stopped to examine an excavation.

"What are they doing there?" he asked Oscar.

"A hotel is to be built."

"A hotel . . . that might be a good place for you."

And that is how Oscar went to see Mr. Boldt, armed with a letter of reference, which he described as "ten foolscap pages long with some of the most famous signatures of the 90's." These were names of men who had known and admired him at the Hoffman House and Delmonico's. They were such as the elder J. Pierpont Morgan who would have no one but Oscar supervise a meal when he came to the Waldorf; Sir Thomas Lipton, of tea and yachting fame, who declared that he had never been better cared for than in the hands of Oscar; Mark Hanna and others equally prominent, all insisting that Oscar attend to their culinary wishes.

WHERE TOO MANY COOKS DIDN'T SPOIL THE BROTH!

Oscar was proud of the roll of chefs at the hotel, describing them as "the world's finest cooks; the French predominate, but we also have Germans, Swiss, Italians and, of course, native Americans. We . . . are trying to symbolize the international nature of American cooking."

Shortly after the Astoria opened, the hyphenated hotel employed, according to *Mirror and Farmer*, "an army of 1,400 employees . . . a monthly payroll of $50,000 . . . housing for between 1,200 and 1,400 people. Every employee is fed on vegetables as fresh as those furnished to guests, and there is plenty. At the lowest estimate, management furnishes 3,600 hardy meals a day for 1,314,000 every year and there is a special dining room for the waiters. The yearly meat bill at the Waldorf-Astoria probably amounts to $100,000. 150 lbs. of coffee a day, 200 lbs. of tomatoes a day. In the dullest times, the kitchen employs 75 . . . There are 19 freight and passenger elevators, 30,000 incandescent lights."

Oscar regarded chicken and turkey as typical American dishes, explaining that "we broil them, we roast them, we boil and fry them . . . Heaven knows what we don't do to them. But it doesn't matter. In the very simplicity of the food and its treatment is our right to acclaim ourselves as a nation of good eaters."

The intricate basements and subbasements of the Waldorf-Astoria included the "Segar Company" with humidors storing choice cigars "from all the leading factories on the Island of Cuba." The temperature was maintained as a constant the year round and the value of the tobacco was estimated at between $300,000 and $400,000. Another important section was the "Importation Company" and its wine cellars, supplied by "foreign agents all over the world . . . who pick up choice lots of old and rare vintages."

In the great days of Oscar, Mr. Boldt and the old Waldorf-Astoria, much care attended the setting of a table, whether for a formal banquet or a dinner *intime*. The present banquet manager graciously reproduced a table setting of the time, complete with the gold flatware bearing the Waldorf monogram, the wine and water glasses etched in gold, the elaborate tablecloth and the handsome gold-fired china, plus the old-fashioned roses and shaded candles which were *de rigeur* at the time. The hotel still has enough of this gold service to serve five hundred.

"The art of dining," Oscar once said, "is certainly one of the half-dozen outstanding contributions to man's rise from prehistoric barbarism to modern civilization."

Menus were created by Oscar for every United States President of his time as well as for the Crown Prince of Siam, Prince Henry of Russia, the King and Queen of Belgium, Carol of Rumania. On a subfreezing February night, Oscar watched the delighted face of Randolph Guggenheimer when waiters brought on a course of blue raspberries! The banquet hall had been transformed for the occasion into a summery bower of singing birds, arbors of ripe grapes, masses of orchids, roses, and lilies.

High Above the Avenues

On the same historic corner where New Yorkers and out-of-towners alike are awed by the dazzle of the city as seen from the top of the Empire State Building, New Yorkers and out-of-towners of fifty years ago were equally awed at being whisked high above Fifth Avenue to the Waldorf-Astoria roof garden.

The decor, according to the *Scientific American*, 1897, was in "a modified classic style . . . painted in Pompeiian red . . . with trellised vines, palms, evergreens and flowers." Greek columns upheld a glass-roofed pergola, fountains splashed about, and over all flew the American flag.

On the floor below guests with a more relaxed attitude toward life could enjoy the arched and glass-roofed sun parlor, furnished in fashionable rattan and shaded by palms and hanging curtains. Still another rooftop meeting place was "a literal German spa where all the best known mineral waters of the world" could be obtained, and where the city could be viewed from a broad promenade. On the fourteenth floor "a lecture room with a stage, featured a range and stove for use in lectures on cooking."

FIT FOR A KING

And kings frequently stayed in such a suite as this. The King Henry IV of France Drawing Room (above) was furnished with original pieces of the period, although the Flemish tapestries "illustrated the history and prosperity of Rome . . . and unfortunately had to be cut to fit the various spaces." The painting of Henry's wife, Margaret de Valois, was by Denman, the carved screen was Italian. In the François I Bedroom, described as being "after the Musee de Cluny," the famous bedstead was carved in the United States . . . but the "exquisite *prie-dieu* was an original Italian work of art."

EVENING at the WALDORF

The Palm Room took on a theatrical glamor in the early evening hours as performers from the season's tragedies, comedies, and light operas hurried to finish a favorite Waldorf dessert and get to their dressing rooms on time. *Harper's Bazar* describes such a scene in 1896:

". . . as they hurry off in cabs and hansoms . . . some of the people who are to form a part of their audience later on are seating themselves at the tables under the palms. Busy waiters lean to catch the orders and bustle about to arrange the tables, and the Hungarian band, stationed near an open window on the main stairway, tunes up and commences its programme.

"Soon the Palm Court is filled and Oscar, the dictator of that much-desired dining place, stands at the door and explains to insistent guests his utter inability to provide more tables in a place already overcrowded. The

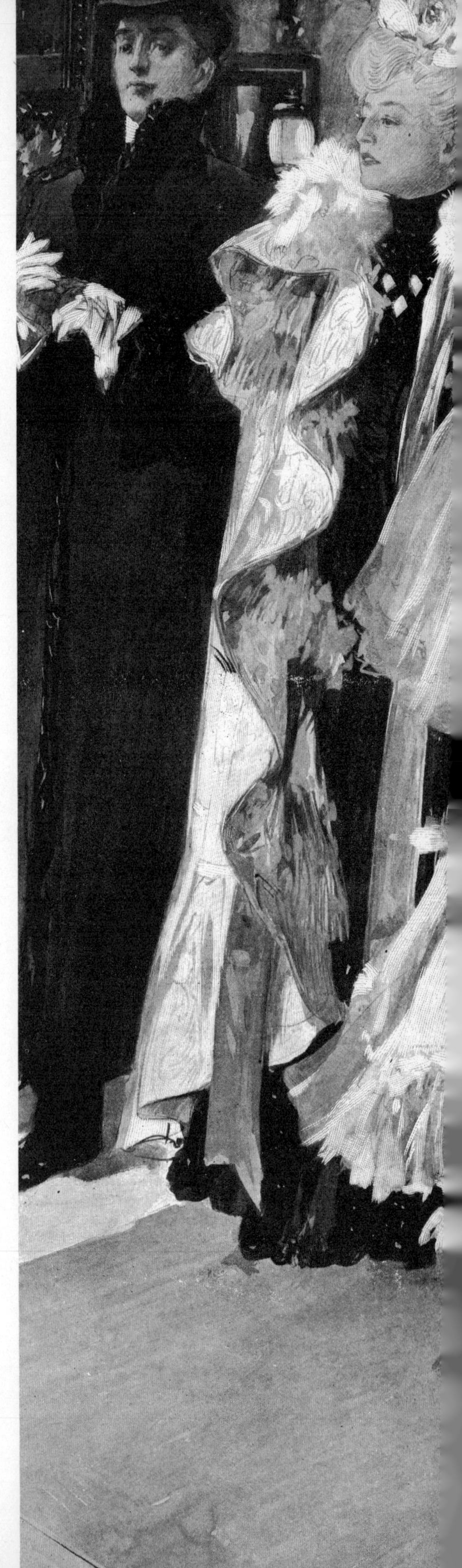

After the theater . . . stopping at the Waldorf-Astoria for supper.
Harper's Weekly, 1901

After the Horse Show Ball

Hungarian band makes vigorous but unsuccessful efforts to dominate the ever-increasing hum of conversation that fills the room; the waiters, driven to their utmost capacity, rush about with anxious and distracted faces, and the sound of corks popping in every direction proclaims the gay scene at its height. Soon little blue wreaths of smoke ascend here and there towards the dark glass dome from some of the tables where the men are taking hurried puffs at their cigars, and then there is an exodus for the theatres, in which nearly half the diners join, leaving the room so much quieter that the band stops playing Wagner, and revels through a czardas in sheer delight at having the chance of being heard."

Even before the Astoria joined it, the Waldorf was the chosen gathering place of New York society. An account in the 1890's describes the silk-stocking crowds assembled during the annual Horse Show Week.

"The Rockaway and Westchester sets overflow into the adjoining gentlemen's cafe, which is brightened for the time by the unfamiliar spectacle of bonnets and flowers and gay silk wraps within its walls."

The dinner menu on the night of the Horse Show Ball was a la carte and very horsy, with dishes named for ribbon-winning hunters, ponies, and five-gaited champions. Filet of Sole "Buddy" cost ninety cents, Sweetbread Croquettes "Quicksand," seventy-five cents. There was a Pudding "Lady Dilham" at half a dollar, a *Glacé* "Marksman" at sixty cents, and "Ices in Horse Show Souvenirs," one dollar.

The cuisine, the decor, and the service at the Waldorf were geared to please even such pace-setting matrons as Mrs. Stuyvesant Fish, who was among the first of the fashionable hostesses to give a small luncheon party there . . . and thereby to launch a revolutionary fad of ladies entertaining at public restaurants. Oscar planned menus of elaborate length but delicate flavor . . . Eggs Tivoli, broiled squab chicken or guinea hen, beets in butter, cucumber and escarole, hothouse grapes, Religieux Cake, frozen peaches, and after-dinner coffee.

Table especially set at the Waldorf for *Harper's Bazar*, 1899. An elaborate decoration of chrysanthemums and candles, showing the new idea of placing one tall candelabrum in front of the hostess' seat.

Through the mirrored walls and gleaming marble of Peacock Alley proceeded such august personages as Mrs. Ogden Mills, Mrs. Oliver H. P. Belmont, Mrs. John Jacob Astor, Mrs. Ogden Goelet.

The Waldorf-Astoria table settings were famous, and pictures such as this one changed the look of America's dinner tables as the "little woman" hastened to create flower arrangements, stir up a Waldorf Salad, and serve her guests by candlelight. Perhaps she, too, would dine some day at the Waldorf, admiring Turner's murals in the Astoria Restaurant or, even better, in the lordly Astor dining room, located over the old Astor mansion where the electric lights sparkled from hammered brass chandeliers and the carved mantel, draperies, paintings, ceiling, and woodwork had all been preserved from the original family dining room. There they discovered the joys of game and venison, of soufflés and ices and exotic fruits, and a privileged few might even hear Oscar quoting a favorite bit of Byron, "Albeit all human history attests that happiness for man . . . the hungry sinner . . . since Eve ate apples, much depends on dinner!"

At extreme left Mrs. John Jacob Astor, in white; Mrs. Astor in black on the arm of Mr. Elisha Dyer, Jr. *Harper's Weekly,* 1902.

NABOBS

"The greatest social event of the season," enthused society editors in reporting the first Assembly Ball, held at the Waldorf-Astoria in 1902, noting that Mrs. John Jacob Astor and Mrs. Lloyd Bryce headed the receiving line while Mr. Elisha Dyer, Jr., led the cotillon.

The talk of the town a few years earlier, in 1897, had been the Bradley Martin Ball. Everything about it made headlines . . . the names (Vanderbilt, Morgan, Cutting, Van Rensselaer, Burden, Mackay, Oerlich, Sloane, Livingston, Beekman); the Louis XIV theme, flaunted by Miss Anne Morgan who came as Pocahontas, R. W. G. Welling as an Algonquin Indian complete with scalps dangling from his belt, and the hostess herself as Mary Queen of Scots, but plus an authentic Marie Antoinette necklace of rubies. Three orchestras played, there was a supper of terrapin and canvasback duck and vintage champagne . . . and breakfast at dawn. So much was printed about the extravagant cost of the affair (some estimated $116.28 per plate) that the Bradley Martins joined the expatriate William Waldorf Astor in Europe. As a parting gesture they gave a small bon voyage dinner for thirty-odd guests and *this* time the tab came to $250 per person.

Prince Henry of Prussia, brother of Kaiser Wilhelm, was honored at an impressive banquet in the Grand Ballroom in 1902. One hundred feet square, its walls were tiered with double rows of boxes and the forty-foot-high ceiling was adorned with a painting by Blashfield, believed at the time to be the largest single canvas in the world. The decor was Louis XV and the portable stage could be installed at short notice for musicales and concerts.

One of the first eminent conductors there was Anton Seidl, who introduced Wagnerian opera to New York. John McCormack sang there, as did Galli-Curci, Rosa Ponselle, and Schumann-Heink, at evening concerts of the Rubinstein Club. Memory did indeed, as one distinguished guest put it, weave "a mystic veil . . . around the Ballroom of the dear old Waldorf-Astoria." The Charity Ball was always a glittering occasion for the turnout of the "Four Hundred," as were the Old Guard Ball and the festivities of the Palestine Commandery.

A procession of notables came and went as the hotel attained giddy heights of prestige. During its gilded years, the ballroom was the scene of brilliant affairs honoring Theodore Roosevelt as newly elected Governor, John Hay as new Secretary of State, Field Marshal Viscount Kitchener as honor guest of the Pilgrims of the United States.

& NOBILITY

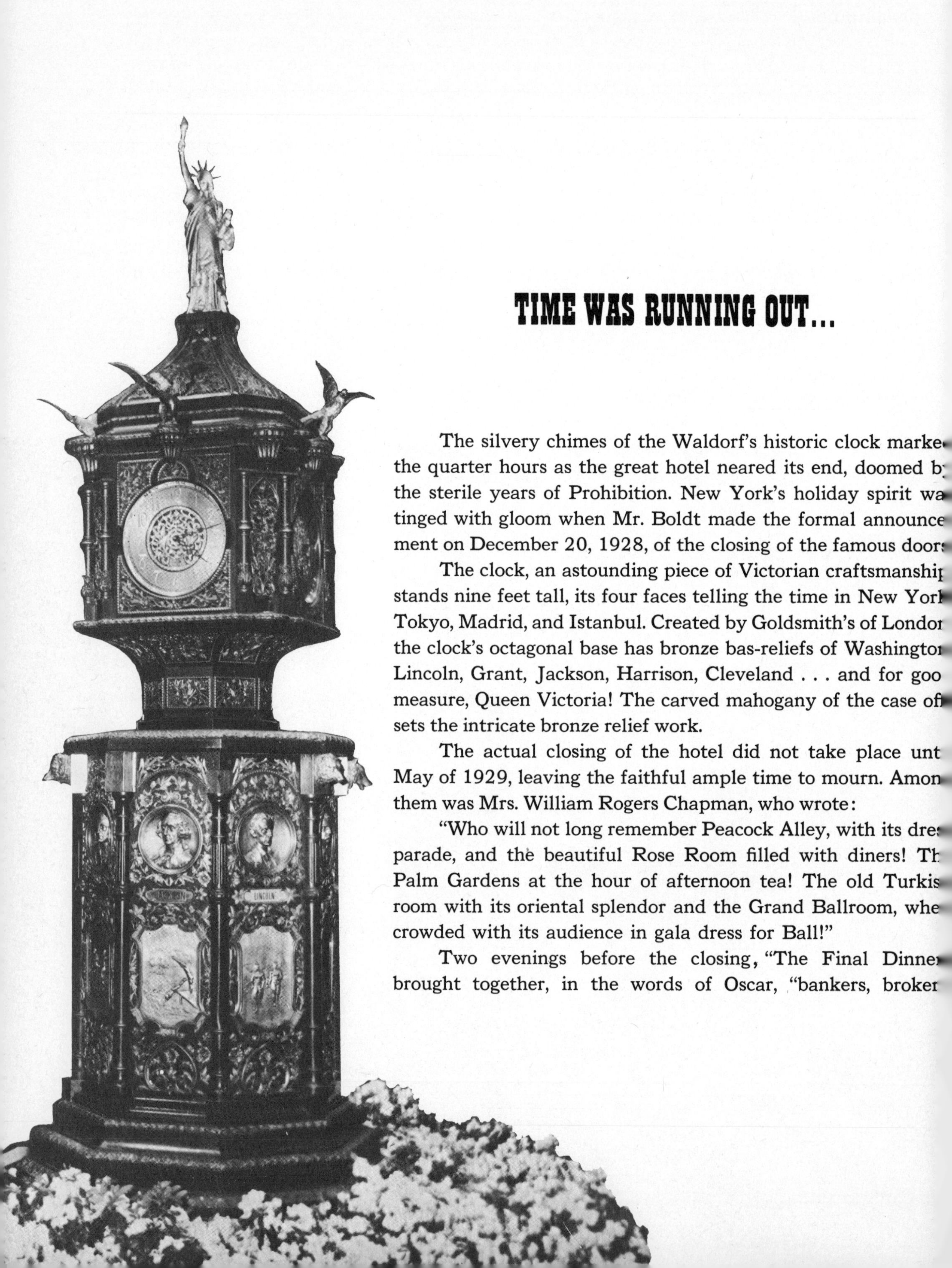

TIME WAS RUNNING OUT...

The silvery chimes of the Waldorf's historic clock marke the quarter hours as the great hotel neared its end, doomed b the sterile years of Prohibition. New York's holiday spirit wa tinged with gloom when Mr. Boldt made the formal announce ment on December 20, 1928, of the closing of the famous door

The clock, an astounding piece of Victorian craftsmanshi stands nine feet tall, its four faces telling the time in New Yor Tokyo, Madrid, and Istanbul. Created by Goldsmith's of Londo the clock's octagonal base has bronze bas-reliefs of Washingto Lincoln, Grant, Jackson, Harrison, Cleveland . . . and for goo measure, Queen Victoria! The carved mahogany of the case of sets the intricate bronze relief work.

The actual closing of the hotel did not take place unt May of 1929, leaving the faithful ample time to mourn. Amon them was Mrs. William Rogers Chapman, who wrote:

"Who will not long remember Peacock Alley, with its dre parade, and the beautiful Rose Room filled with diners! Th Palm Gardens at the hour of afternoon tea! The old Turkis room with its oriental splendor and the Grand Ballroom, whe crowded with its audience in gala dress for Ball!"

Two evenings before the closing, "The Final Dinne brought together, in the words of Oscar, "bankers, broker philanthropists, politicians, newspapermen, writers, churchmen, big business men, military men, university men . . . the greatest of all tributes to the old hotel . . . and yet it was sad, too."

Even though plans for a towering new Waldorf-Astoria were announced almost at once, the mood was one of a time gone by, something of which is captured in a description in *Harper's Bazar*:

"When the late suppers are finished, and the people from the opera have re-entered their carriages, the room soon empties and the tired waiters no longer suggest additional orders, but look wearily and reproachfully at the few groups that linger at one or two of the tables, until they too take their departure. The gorgeous Turk in his lavishly embroidered costume and red fez has long since deserted his brass coffee-pots in the Oriental room, and the turnstile creaks wearily as the last departing guest from the cafe pushes his way out and hails a night-hawk, and then the chairs are piled on top of the tables, the waiters hurry home, the scrubwomen bring in their brooms and pails, and the evening at the Waldorf is finished."

As were all evenings at the Waldorf from 1929 through the remaining dreary years of prohibition and depression until the uptown opening of the great new namesake hotel on Park Avenue, October 1, 1931.

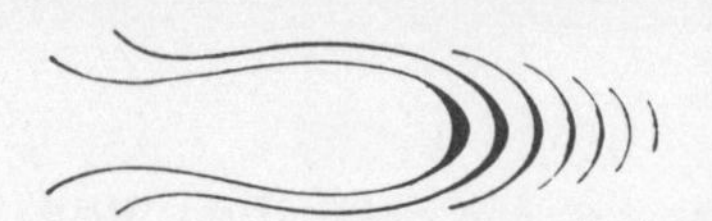

RELISH

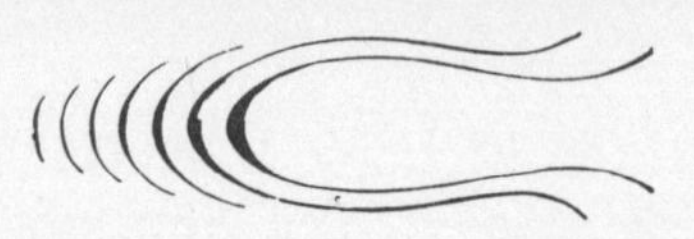

SUMMER EXODUS TO FOREIGN PARTS

"The annual spring and summer exodus to Europe has already commenced. Many travellers have made the passage so frequently that experience has taught them the various little ways of adding materially to the comfort of an ocean voyage," noted a news account in the 1870's. But it was still marvelously exciting "When the great black hulk of the steamer slowly slides out of the dock, while you stand behind the rope, even while you wave your handkerchiefs and your umbrellas and the voyagers wave back their handkerchiefs and their hats and their bunches of roses while the pilot boats put their heads together and push and make more fuss than the huge steamship will do in open sea . . . the faces along the side seem to put on . . . a look of those who go into some vast unknown experience. . . .

"It is all a festive scene to-day, with bright morning, gay cries and flags and flowers, with hope of wonders to be seen; with excitement and sense of prayers for safety, and joy over opportunity."

Americans were becoming increasingly sophisticated about going abroad since the *Savannah,* an American sailing vessel with steam auxiliary, crossed the Atlantic to

Liverpool in 1819. The voyage took twenty-six days and was headline news, although a British ship, *Rising Sun*, actually made the first steam crossing the preceding year, to South America.

For many decades of the nineteenth century steam was combined with sail to speed passengers across the ocean. The White Star Line, of which the *Oceanic* (shown here) was a part, continued to whittle down the sailing time . . . seven days in the 1870's, six in the next decade, and in 1894 a record five days, nine hours, six minutes, Queenstown to New York.

"The (White Star) steamers are palaces," *Demorest's* magazine advised the traveling public in the 1880's. The voyage "is safe, easy, speedy and pleasurable . . . daily comfort is provided as fully as in the finest private home . . ."

Demorest's carried a series of letters by a lady correspondent, urging American women to pack up their Gainsborough hats, habits of indigo-blue summer serge, plus, perhaps, a box of Demorest's "Lily Bloom" for the complexion, and set forth alone for the Continent.

She even counseled economical third-class accommodations on European railways . . . "It is very entertaining to watch the ways of the peasant, providing one is not over-dainty regarding smoke. Always carry a candle in your bag," she added, "and never go to the Continent without also having a piece of soap, for this is never seen in even the most expensive hotels."

The program she outlined began with serious reading at home, of histories and guidebooks. In Spain, she warned that "sweet potatoes are cooked as preserves and served as a dessert, cauliflower is dipped in butter and fried like oysters and celery is always served stewed in hot butter."

As for Paris . . . "And Oh! American girls, do not pine for Paris life, for with it might possibly come a Parisian husband, which of all things is the most terrible fate that could befall you!"

Wines and liqueurs in abundance, elaborate courses, and congenial groups in the Main Saloon, rendezvous and flirtations on the Promenade Deck . . . all were to be found in that "little world of fears and joys" embodied in a great ocean liner like this White Star steamer *Germanic*.

...A little world of fears and joys...

Steamship dining was en masse, judging by the 1880 sketches below. The so-called Social Hall was rather austere, and heaven knows what a female was doing in the sanctum of the Smoking Room.

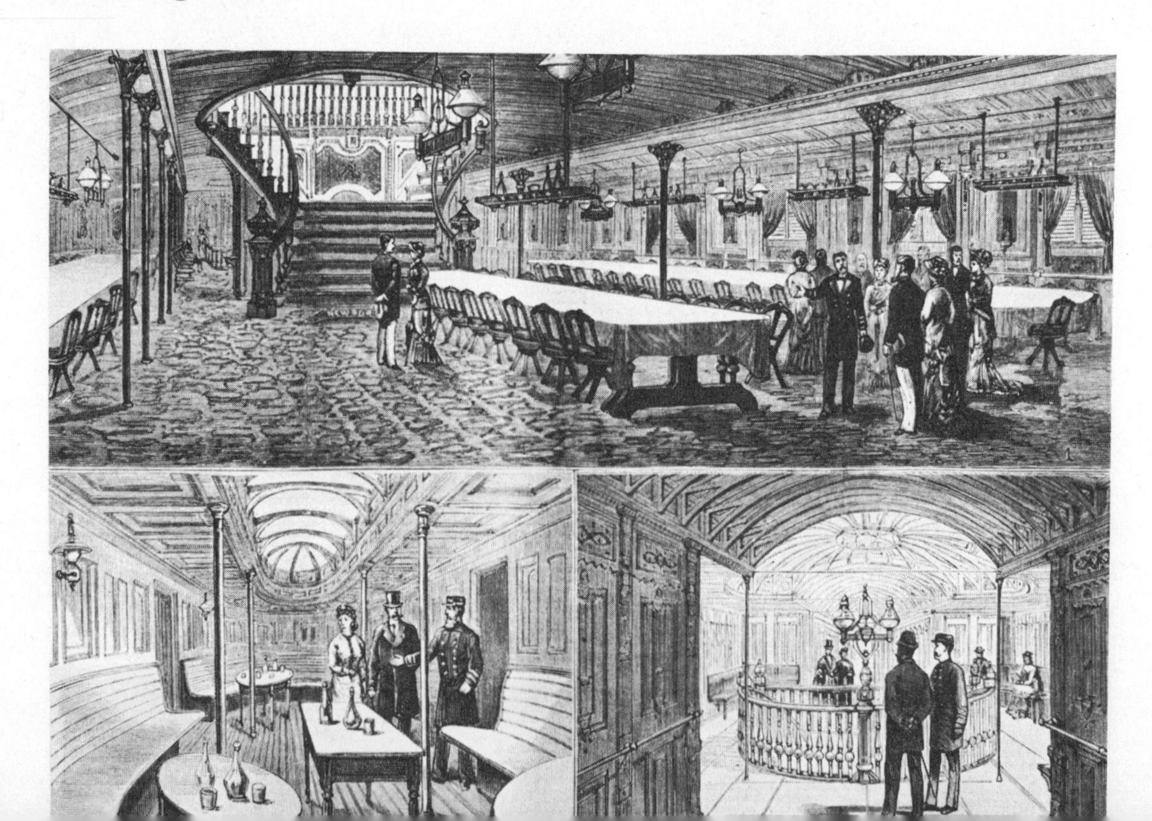

"A Japanese Kimono and a Large Himalayan Shawl"

The above items were recommended by *Harper's Bazar* as "desirable additions to the voyager's outfit" when undertaking a trip to Europe in the 1880's, along with a Japanese hand-stove and rolls of tinder, one or two rubber hot-water bottles, and a canvas clothes-bag for rugs, pillows, bed shoes "and even those little white papier-mache basins which *may* be needed." Another item noted gloomily that "no drug has yet been discovered which is a specific for seasickness," but advised that "by regulating the act of breathing to correspond with the rolling of the vessel, seasickness may be prevented; that is, to draw in the breath as the ship rises, and expel the breath as she falls."

The White Star Line was described by *Harper's* in 1880 as "probably the best and completest line in the world. The steamers are palaces . . . the ship's companies and officers are polite, efficient, prompt; ladies are attended with zealous kindness."

Tickets first class from New York to London cost between ninety and a hundred dollars, according to *Demorest's Monthly Magazine* of June, 1881. The same article advised ladies to "wear on the steamer underclothing that you are willing to throw over for the mermaids when you need to change, that you may go on shore fresh and trim, and without having to ask for the service of a laundress one of the first things you do."

"As to the expense of living abroad," added *Demorest's,* "six dollars a week will suffice, if the small items are carefully watched."

1907 *The* PLAZA

FLOWER of PUBLIC PALACES

..."CONSONANT WITH THE DIGNITY OF ITS LOCATION"...

It was typical of the burgeoning new century that the old Plaza which at its opening in 1890 had been hailed as "palatial . . . luxuriously furnished . . . one of the grandest hotels in the world" was considered hopelessly outmoded within a decade. Yet on a pleasant day in May, 1890, the old hotel, glimpsed at right (above), had a certain serenity and the scene a rather continental air with white-capped nursemaids wheeling prams and coaches, victorias, coupes, and dogcarts trundling by. The eight-story red brick Plaza cost $3,000,000 and its site at Fifty-ninth Street and Fifth Avenue was compared to Hyde Park corner in London. It was furbished with polished brass and carved mahogany. Stained glass windows glowed in its dining room,where the ceiling rose thirty feet and was fretted in gold.

Life was running full tide for the gilded rich when in the fall of 1907 they took to their hearts a sumptuous new hotel built on the site of the old one, facing the leafy sweep of Central Park and looking down upon the Vanderbilt mansion and the upper promenade of Fifth Avenue. The new Plaza cost a breath-taking $12,500,000, resembled an oversize Renaissance chateâu, and measured eighteen stories from its carriage entrance to its heavy mansard roof. It was destined from opening day to be the darling of society.

The first names on the register on October 1, 1907, indicated that the Plaza was prepared to live up to the predictions of the press that it would "make millionaires' lives easy."

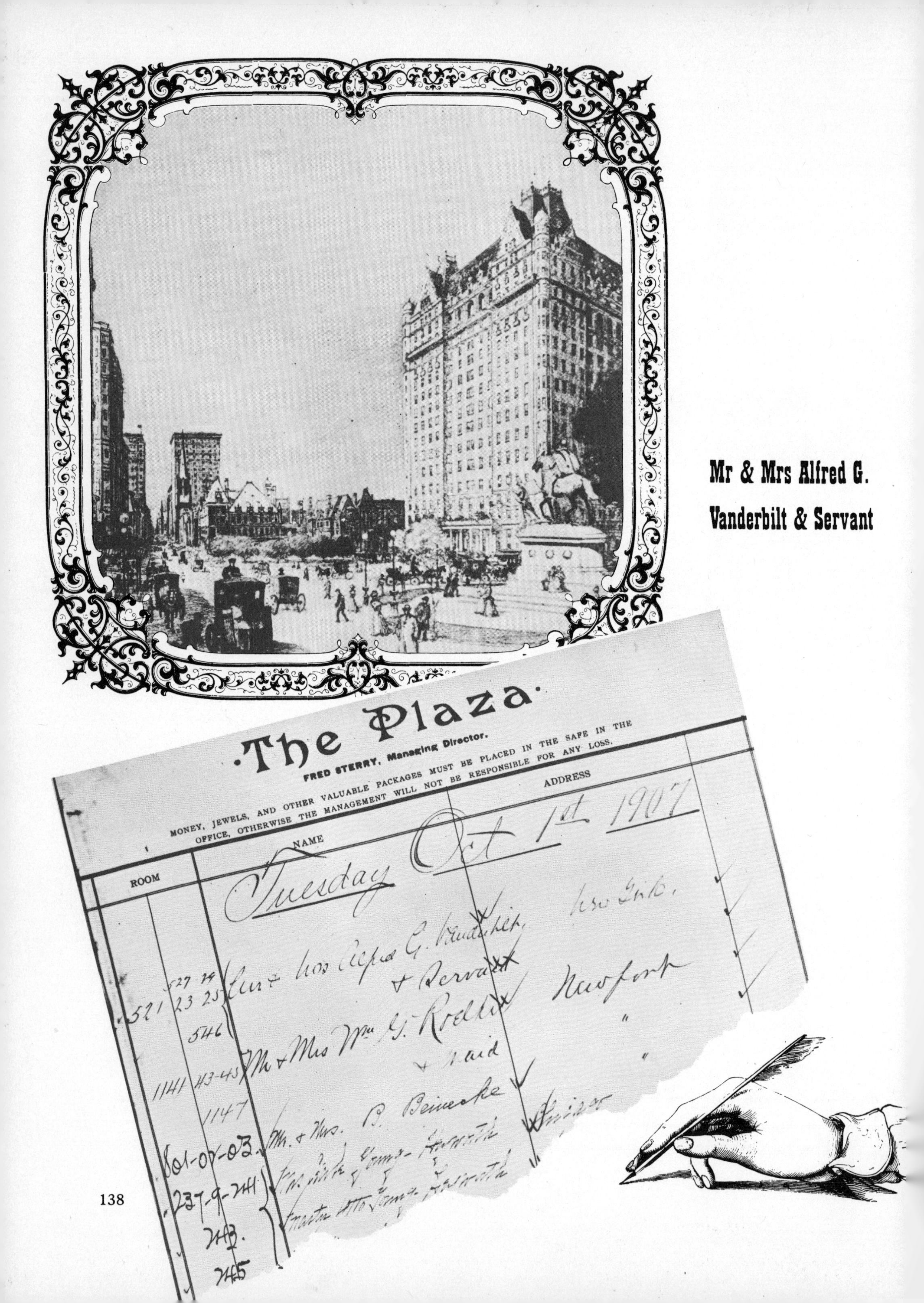

Mr & Mrs Alfred G. Vanderbilt & Servant

PLAZA HOTEL TO BE HOME OF N. Y. BLUE BLOOD AND RICHES

A. G. Vanderbilt, George J. Gould and Oliver Harriman Have Apartments.

WILL OPEN ON OCTOBER 1

Appointments of $12,500,000 Hostelry Costliest of Any in the World.

With the assured distinction of sheltering as permanent guests the largest millionaire colony in this city, or, as a matter of fact, in the entire world, the new $12,500,000 Plaza Hotel will be viewed by official invitation for the first time to-day. All is complete with the exception of a few finishing touches in arranging furniture

Photograph of the new Plaza Hotel, and diagram sketch showing location of choice corner apartments facing Central Park South and the Plaza leased by well-known millionaires.

"Essentially the Home of Millionaires"

Suites of the society tenants of the new Plaza; at upper left Mrs. Alfred G. Vanderbilt, Mrs. John W. Gates; in center Mrs. Oliver Harriman; lower right, Mrs. George J. Gould. This widely publicized newspaper article indicated a fine disregard for jewel thieves to whom this neatly diagramed information might be useful.

AN OPULENT PAST TO CHERISH

Tea time in the Plaza's elegant Palm Court is still a time for soft lights, muted music, and young romance. Now, as half a century ago, the mirrored panels reflect a sheen of silk and satin, the occasional flash of a jewel as comely debutantes and their beaus hold hands and make betrothal plans and even decide on the wedding date.

The tradition of "courting at the Palm Court" began during the first week of the Plaza in October, 1907, when society belle Gladys Vanderbilt walked across the street from the family's French Renaissance chateau to meet and become engaged to Count Laslo Szechenyi. There, too, Diantha Fitch had her first date and their romance flourished over tea and *petits fours.*

In the very heart of the Plaza, the Palm Court was once described by Clara Bell Walsh, who lived there for nearly fifty years, as "an oasis of calm, dignified elegance." Its sixty marble-topped tables stand decorously among the plumy ferns and palms in their vast Chinese *cachepots.* Tall candelabra of crystal and bronze bring out the glow of *Fleur de Peche* marble pillars and light the four famous caryatids, copies of those made in 1598 by Donato Donati, pupil of Michelangelo.

TAXIMETERS FREE TODAY!

Like fussy little upstarts, a line of motor cabs with "the new French taximeters" stood on opening day before the Central Park South entrance of the Plaza. The "taximeters" were symptomatic of the urge of Americans for the newest, the biggest, and the best. The Plaza itself was proof of that spirit. It all began around a table at the St. Regis in 1905, when John W. "Bet-a-Million" Gates remarked that the old Plaza ought to give way to a truly first-class luxury hotel, whereupon a man identified only as "a millionaire known on two continents" said he would back such a project if Fred Sterry could be persuaded to manage it. The suave Mr. Sterry had won a patrician following at Hot Spring's famous Homestead as well as at Palm Beach. So it was that the multimillion-dollar Plaza became a reality. Its design was entrusted to H. J. Hardenbaugh, of Waldorf-Astoria fame, who, according to the toastmaster on opening night, "threw up the chance of becoming a great Hamlet to become a great architect."

Many a visiting dignitary has crossed the Plaza's baronial lobby with its floor of exquisitely wrought mosaic, a detail of which is shown below.

The polished Edwardian manners of the Rose Room were enhanced by the presence of such society luminaries as Mrs. Stuyvesant Fish and Mrs. Herman Oelrichs, while at a nearby table might be seen Mr. John Drew with his young niece, Miss Ethel Barrymore.

At lunchtime the Rose Room's feminine clientele had begun to look to their wasp waistlines and temper the number of courses they ordered. A cup of bouillon and "a wafer-thin cracker spread with jelly and another with *pâté de foie gras*, laid together," sufficed for many of them. *The Steward's Handbook* also advised that women were fancying "a sandwich which is an ethereal vision of bread and meat—like two thin pieces of muslin."

On gala evenings the gilded grillwork elevators deposited guests in one of the most famous "marble rooms" in the world, the foyer off the gold and white ballroom. When some gala was taking place there, yellow candles were alight, glowing in golden candelabra beneath the twinkling chandeliers.

Chauncey Depew, his famous whiskers bristling, shared honors with Nicholas Murray Butler in welcoming the Lord Bishop of London (the Right Reverend Arthur Foley Winnington Ingram) to the first major public function on October 15, 1907. Four hundred guests sat down to a Buffet à la Russe, much fancied by gourmets of the day. They had hors d'oeuvres lobster, oysters, roast plover, salad, and ices plus such *amuse-gueules* as olives, almonds, fruits, and bonbons. The wines were vintage Moselle, Bordeaux, Burgundy, and of course champagne. Cocktails came before dinner and rare liqueurs were passed around with the coffee.

Eugene Laperreque, first head chef at the Plaza, posted French menus outside his office door, knowing that his eighty-two cooks could read them perfectly. Reading and speaking French were prerequisites for cooks and waiters. But to make certain that his own methods were followed precisely, M. Laperreque always added an explanation for each dish, such as:

JOINVILLE—Sauce vin blanc truffes champiognes en des crevettes
RICHELIEU—Roti poele tornate farcie et laitues braisees sauce tomate reduite par mottie a une demi glace courtons caneles

Over the Pastry Room stood Henri Pichenot of Paris, his ovens placed in niches and the fires controlled by thermometers. An early form of automation was employed in the gleaming marble kitchens of the Plaza, where electricity heated the broilers and peeled carrots and even served out "a pistache of ice cream."

No one ever succeeded in obtaining the secret of the Plaza's still famous Cream of Chicken Soup, but Chef Letard's trick of making Crab Meat Remick was disclosed a decade ago by Charles Campion, who came to the Plaza fresh off the boat from France and watched the old chef invent the dish, using:

1 lb. large crab flakes
6 slices bacon, fried crisp
1 tsp. dry mustard
½ tsp. paprika
½ tsp. celery salt
Few drops Tabasco sauce
½ cup chili sauce
1 tsp. tarragon vinegar
¼ cup mayonnaise

Pile crab flakes in six buttered ramekins. Heat through in hot oven; top with crisp bacon.

Blend mustard, paprika, celery salt, Tabasco. Add chili sauce and tarragon vinegar, mix well and stir in mayonnaise. Spread sauce over warmed crab meat and brown under broiler.

"Wine is the intellectual part of the meal and is to be served at the proper temperature," instructed a reigning authority on the subject. And the Plaza was nothing if not fastidious about its wine cellars and bottling rooms, into which came great vintages from all over the world.

"Bottle the wine on a clear cold day. Avoid stormy weather . . . and if possible select a day when the wind blows from the Northeast."

Equipment required in the bottling room included a special mallet to force in the corks, which were first dipped in warm water, then forced into the bottle and carefully cut an eighth of an inch above the top to allow the wine to ripen without disturbance. Two years was the generally accepted period for bringing a red wine to perfection, while a white wine required less time, usually eighteen months, to achieve the desired dryness. A mixture of yellow wax and mutton tallow, colored ocher or black, gave the cork extra protection, especially from insects. The bottles went into the specially constructed wine racks at exactly the correct angle, leaving the corks touching the liquid.

Decanting was often done by the wine waiter before dinner, so that the wine in its crystal decanter shone in limpid perfection when it arrived at table. Certain wines were reserved by chefs for their own special creations, such as those Plaza favorites of many years' standing, Côtelette Kiev and the Shashlik d'Agneau Caucasian with its heady wine marinade.

...HE SPENT MANY

The light shines softly down on a richly carved alcove in the Oak Room where George M. Cohan used to hold court at five o'clock every afternoon with fifteen or twenty men and women gathered round to listen to his gentle voice and marvelous stories. Today above the small table there is a bronze plaque:

"Here in this corner where he spent many happy hours the Lambs have placed this tablet in honor of the most brilliant and versatile gentleman in the theater of his day, George M. Cohan."

For all the years up to prohibition the Oak Room was a man's domain, and it still remains sacrosanct to the male during lunchtime. The adjoining Oak Bar takes its patrons backward in time to a snowy evening in Central Park in the early 1900's, when the mansard rooftop of the Plaza still dominated the skyline. These distinguished paintings, by Everett Shinn, also picture some of the great Fifth Avenue mansions of the era.

HAPPY HOURS...

The Oak Room and Bar as well as all the other cafes and restaurants have always been dependent on the meticulously kept wine vaults deep in the basement where the wines are not exposed to vibrations or shocks which might make the dregs rise or turn the wine sour. No green wood was permitted within the vaults, no vegetables within tainting radius where undesirable fermentation might occur. Thermometers kept count on the temperatures; fifty to fifty-five degrees, with the Bordeaux kept at the highest and the Burgundy coolest. The barrels stood well apart so that air might circulate (but never a through draft) and were always refilled to guard against spoilage.

Wine stewards saw to it that waiters knew the correct order of service, spelled out for them in a small leatherbound book titled *Menu Terms*: "Oysters, white wine; soup, sherry or Madeira; Releves, 2nd grade Burgundy, temperature, 42 to 45 deg. Far; Entrees, 2nd grade Bordeaux, temperature 52 to 56 deg. Far; Punch or Sherbet; Roasts, 1st grade Burgundy; Dessert, Champagne, cold or frappé; After dessert, Alicante, Tokay, etc.; Cordials, Cognac, Fine Champagne, Pousse Café, etc.; Divers Beers."

The Plaza . . . how define it? Clara Bell Walsh, "first lady of the Plaza," who lived there for nearly fifty years, once said it was "the sweet sadness of all the Christmases . . . the blazing beauty of Easter . . . the crush of the most exquisitely dressed people in the world . . . Diamond Jim Brady and Lillian Russell waltzing in the Grill as dusk washed down the city that was their oyster . . . the roaring of the lions in the Zoo only a few blocks away." Her life at the Plaza spanned it all.

The Breslin, on Broadway

The Astor, on Long Acre Square

The Seville, on Madison Avenue

Fifty Million Dollars' Worth of Hotels

Some of the Elaborate Structures that have been Opened in New York within the Past Five Years

The Marseille, 103d Street

THE *Plaza Hotel, recently opened in New York City, marks the top-notch in hotel size and cost in a city which has more expensive hotel buildings than any other city in the country. It represents an investment of $12,500,000 and has 800 living rooms. The Belmont has 800 rooms and cost $9,000,000. The Ansonia houses 1,500 guests and cost $4,000,000. The Gotham and the St. Regis cost, together, $9,000,000 and they accommodate 800 guests. The cost and capacity of the others* are: *the Knickerbocker, $7,000,000, 700 guests; the Astor, $6,000,000, 600 guests; the Breslin, $3,000,000, 600 guests, the Seville, $1,000,000, 350 guests; the Marseille, $1,000,000, 300 guests. A [illegible] investment to house 6,000 guests*

The new Plaza Hotel

The Belmont, Forty-second Street

The St. Regis and the Gotham

When the Plaza was new, the above newspaper feature heralded New York's grand splurge of hotel-building which took place within five years in the early 1900's. It was claimed that New York had "more expensive hotel buildings than any other city in the country," yet you will note that only three of them survived to 1963 complete with stature and prestige.

THIRD COURSE
BOUNTY FROM LAND & SEA

Choicest Viands Chosen By The
Steward For Demanding Appetites

...FROM WHENCE CAME THE

New York City, face to the sea and a continent stretching away at her back, has always had to reach into the far corners of the world for the food necessary to sustain her island-bound people.

Even in the 1750's when Manhattan was no bigger than a country town, the importing business was part of the city's lifeblood. Ships arrived loaded with raw sugar, tea, chocolate, coffee, tropical fruits. The markets then were small and innkeepers did their own buying . . . beef at sixpence or less per pound; pigeons a penny apiece; one-and-six for a roasting chicken.

More than a century later the game markets were still abounding in venison, bear, wild duck, quail, pheasant, pigeons and succulent little rice birds.

Fulton Market, pictured here during the holiday season of 1877, offered a festive variety of game to tempt the hotel steward in search of delicacies for his Christmas and New Year menus. In this scene a fussy steward in high silk hat takes out his glass to examine the bird offered him while a butcher in bowler hat looks over his haunches of venison and his racks of hanging game birds and hare.

By 1890, sophisticated New Yorkers were taking it for granted that, as *Harper's Weekly* put it, "the limitations of season have ceased to be any bars to the demands of the appetite." Thanks to improved transportation, to new and better refrigeration, and to the discerning eye of the men who saw to it that New York's famous hotels kept their reputations as the best in the country, the "epicure" could then "feast on pecan-fed turkey and canvas-back duck on the Fourth of July" as easily and with as much relish as he could at Christmas.

GAME...

...TO MARKET, TO MARKET...

Washington Market, which first opened in 1772 as the old Bear Market, had by the mid-1800's become a sprawling affair of sheds, stalls, piers and an occasional market house of brick. *Harper's Weekly* considered it a disgrace and called upon the city to build "a superb public edifice which should be one of the architectural glories of the city and a monument of civic enterprise." Nothing happened, however, and Washington Market grew in a noisy disorder of repatched and rebuilt structures, its cobbled streets crowded with wagons, drays, and basket-carrying people on foot.

First to arrive were the stewards from the big hotels, intent on outdoing their rivals in cornering the biggest and best, the rarest and most expensive, for as G. T. Ferris, a writer of the late 1800's noted, New York's hotel clientele now reveled in "the delicious sophistries of a French cuisine . . . truffled turkey and green turtle soup . . . tribute from the whole world to supply his table."

The hotel steward was up before dawn, lists in hand, and at market by four or five in the morning. He had to appreciate what *The Steward's Handbook* called "the delights of commissions and percents," and at the same time "be a sort of policeman, austere, unsympathetic" and sociable enough to keep the market men on friendly terms so that they would hide a rare item under the counter until his arrival or scheme with him for a purchase of the last shad of the season or the first spring peas. The steward was next in rank to the hotel proprietor and usually had the responsibility of hiring the head chef and headwaiter, as well as the pastry cook or confectioner. . . . He had to know all about dishes and the modes of preparing them and about literary composition."

This Washington Market scene shows one of the countless cul-de-sacs where produce was displayed outdoors and where weary buyers and market people could find a hasty meal (even if the proprietor spelled his Saloon with a backward "n"). An interesting device was a sort of awning rigged of sail canvas which the market dealers spread from the rooftops to keep the hot summer's sun from spoiling the fruits and other perishables.

If the buildings were patched and ramshackle, the contents surely left nothing to be desired. A hotel steward whose menu that day listed cold buffalo tongue or "filet of prairie chicken aux truffles" knew he could find them somewhere in the vast complex of the city markets. There was so much of everything and at such comparatively reasonable prices that *Harper's* somewhat sententiously noted: ". . . nowadays the man of the proletariat may easily have varieties of food which a well-to-do gentleman of the Elizabethan period could not have obtained. The grand development of productive industry and of transportation facilities have made this whole big world of ours, farm, fish-pond and game preserve, available for the owner of the horny hand as well as him of the kid glove."

South Street was a busy and romantic thoroughfare as shown here in the spring of 1876, when the bowsprits of ships lying at dock jutted over the street and heavy carts and drays rumbled over the cobblestones where a short time before the tides had flowed back and forth. For South Street was on "made land" at the foot of Manhattan Island. Wharves, shipping sheds, ferry houses and docks lined it on one side; sail lofts, chandlers, offices of maritime lawyers, brokers, and occasional restaurants on the other.

Produce poured into the city markets in the long night hours. *Harper's Weekly* described the waterfront scene at the turn of the century:

"There are dancing lights and the air is burdened with the rattle and rumble of wagons and the shouts of drivers and clerks and stevedores and checkers. An incessant and murmurous procession of hand-trucks moves in and out of the shadowy, spacious dock-houses, unloading from railroad barges the incredible number of boxes and crates and barrels in which fresh fruit and vegetables have come from the South . . . Everyone hurries, for these products of faraway gardens are perishable."

"What is to be done with these mountains of food which are melting away so fast?" asked *Harper's*. "Whither and to whom? This rushing, unresting world that they call a city renews itself from day to day . . . By and by there are only the leavings, the debris and the market-man, his smile undiminished, his pockets heavy with dollars."

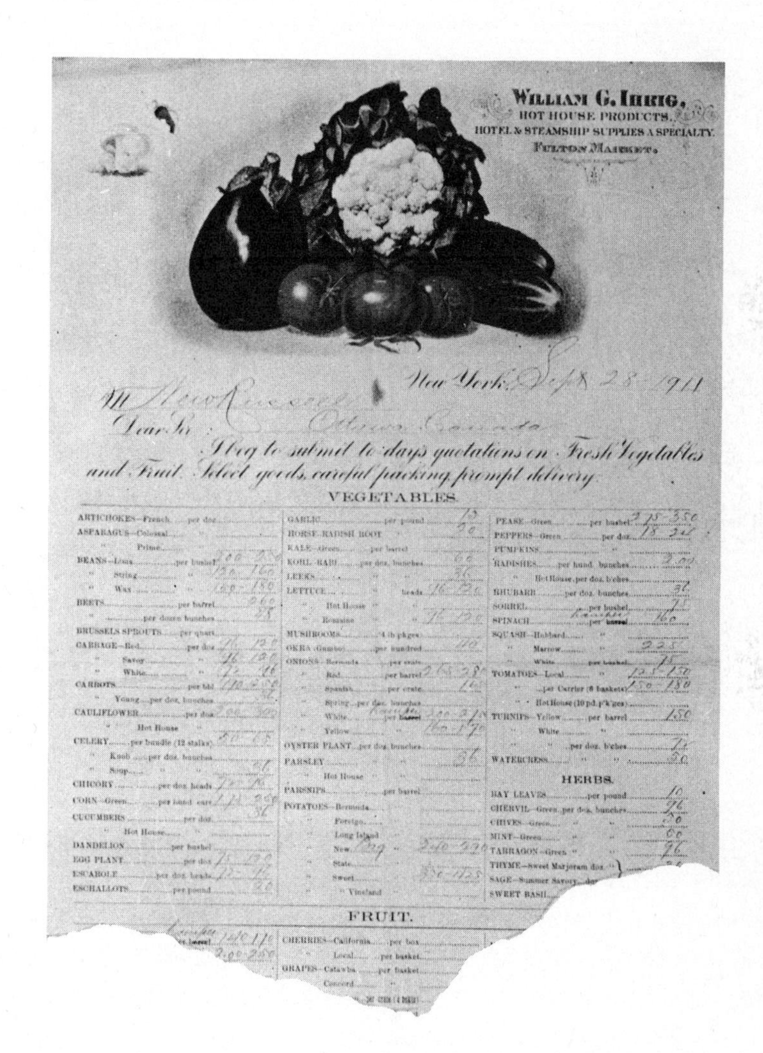

WILLIAM G. IHRIG,
HOT HOUSE PRODUCTS,
HOTEL & STEAMSHIP SUPPLIES A SPECIALTY.
FULTON MARKET.

New York, Sept 28 1911

Dear Sir:
I beg to submit to-days quotations on Fresh Vegetables and Fruit. Select goods, careful packing, prompt delivery.

VEGETABLES.

Item	Price
ARTICHOKES—French ... per doz.	
ASPARAGUS—Colossal ... "	
" Prime ... "	
BEANS—Lima ... per bushel	[illegible]
" String ... "	150 160
" Wax ... "	160 180
BEETS ... per barrel	[illegible]
" ... per dozen bunches	[illegible]
BRUSSELS SPROUTS ... per quart	
CABBAGE—Red ... per doz.	96 120
" Savoy ... "	96 120
" White ... "	72 96
CARROTS ... per bbl	[illegible]
" Young ... per doz. bunches	[illegible]
CAULIFLOWER ... per doz.	200 300
" Hot House "	
CELERY ... per bundle (12 stalks)	[illegible]
" Knob ... per doz. bunches	
" Soup ... " "	[illegible]
CHICORY ... per doz. heads	72 96
CORN—Green ... per hund. ears	[illegible]
CUCUMBERS ... per doz.	36
" Hot House ... "	
DANDELION ... per bushel	
EGG PLANT ... per doz.	75 100
ESCAROLE ... per doz. heads	72 96
ESCHALLOTS ... per pound	20

Item	Price
GARLIC ... per pound	15
HORSE-RADISH ROOT	10
KALE—Green ... per barrel	
KOHL-RABI ... per doz. bunches	60
LEEKS ... " "	36
LETTUCE ... " heads	[illegible]
" Hot House " "	
" Romaine " "	[illegible]
MUSHROOMS ... 4 lb pkges	
OKRA (Gumbo) ... per hundred	[illegible]
ONIONS—Bermuda ... per crate	
" Red ... per barrel	[illegible]
" Spanish ... per crate	[illegible]
" Spring ... per doz. bunches	
" White ... per barrel	[illegible]
" Yellow ... "	[illegible]
OYSTER PLANT ... per doz. bunches	
PARSLEY ... " "	36
" Hot House " "	
PARSNIPS ... per barrel	
POTATOES—Bermuda ...	
" Foreign ...	
" Long Island "	
" New ... "	[illegible]
" State ... "	
" Sweet ... "	[illegible]
" " Vineland	

Item	Price
PEASE—Green ... per bushel	275 350
PEPPERS—Green ... per doz.	18 24
PUMPKINS ... "	
RADISHES ... per hund. bunches	2 00
" Hot House, per doz. b'ches	
RHUBARB ... per doz. bunches	36
SORREL ... per bushel	75
SPINACH ... per	160
SQUASH—Hubbard ... "	
" Marrow ... "	225
" White ... per bushel	75
TOMATOES—Local ... "	125 150
" ... per Carrier (6 baskets)	150 180
" Hot House (10 pd. p'k'ges)	
TURNIPS—Yellow ... per barrel	150
" White ... "	
" " ... per doz. b'ches	75
WATERCRESS ... " "	30

HERBS.

Item	Price
BAY LEAVES ... per pound	10
CHERVIL—Green, per doz. bunches	96
CHIVES—Green ... " "	50
MINT—Green ... " "	60
TARRAGON—Green " "	96
THYME—Sweet Marjoram doz. "	
SAGE—Summer Savory ... doz.	
SWEET BASIL ...	

FRUIT.

Item	Price
CHERRIES—California ... per box	
" Local ... per basket	
GRAPES—Catawba ... per basket	
" Concord ... "	

"I beg to submit..."

The busy hotel steward was aided in his marketing by colorful lists submitted to him daily by purveyors of foodstuffs. The one shown here was a smartly got up affair with the eggplant, cauliflower, tomatoes, and cucumbers in full color and the day's price quotations written in after every item available. Few hothouse products were needed when this list was submitted, as September still saw fresh fruit and vegetables in good supply and reasonably priced. Later, Mr. Ihrig would be offering hothouse parsley, radishes, California melons, Jamaica oranges, Tokay and Malaga grapes.

The People of the State of New York, by

the Grace of God Free and Independent; To all to whom these Presents shall come, Greeting:

Know Ye, *That* **We,** *reposing especial trust and confidence in the ability and integrity of* Ichabod Postwick of our County of Columbia

Have *nominated, constituted and appointed, and by these presents,* **Do** *nominate, constitute and appoint* him *the said* Ichabod Postwick Inspector of Beef and Pork in and for our said County of Columbia

hereby giving and granting unto him *all and singular the powers and authorities to the said office by law belonging or appertaining.* **To have and to hold** *the said office of* Inspector of Beef and Pork *together with the fees, profits and advantages to the same belonging, for and during our good pleasure, to be signified by our Council of Appointment.*

In testimony whereof, *WE have caused these our letters to be made patent, and the Great Seal of our said State to be hereunto affixed:* **Witness** *our trusty and well beloved* De Witt Clinton Esqr *Governor of our said State, General and Commander in Chief of all the Militia, and Admiral of the Navy of the same, by and with the advice and consent of our said Council of Appointment at our City of Albany, the* Thirtieth *day of* August *in the year of our Lord one thousand eight hundred and* Seventeen *and in the forty* Second *year of our Independence.*

De Witt Clinton

Passed the Secretary's Office the 30th day of August 1817

Chas. D. Cooper **Secretary.**

"DeWitt Clinton, Esq. 30th day of August, 1817"

The serious business of inspecting New York City's markets was by no means a nineteenth-century innovation, but it did assume a more official status and greater proportions as the inbound stream of produce tried to keep pace with the mounting population and the daily influx of visitors.

The document on this page, dated 1817 and signed by Governor De Witt Clinton, also noted that this was "the forty-second year of our independence." Ichabod Postwick was enjoined to inspect all beef and pork coming into Columbia County, New York, for sale.

Meat was always big business in New York. The scenes on the opposite page show what was happening in July of 1877 when beef "on the hoof" was a commonplace, since refrigerated train transportation and storage had not yet been developed on a major scale. The big meat companies had their own docks and the cattle, as shown here, were driven through a tunnel to the slaughterhouse. Icehouses, fairly primitive but at least a moderate safeguard against spoilage, were part of the Manhattan abattoir. Hotel stewards were the best customers, since beef was practically a round-the-clock item on their menus; it was not at all unusual for a hotel's broiling ovens to be filled with steaks sizzling for breakfast.

THE MANHATTAN ABATTOIR.—FROM SKETCHES BY V. L. KINGSBURY.—[SEE PAGE 530.]

TRADING FOR STOCK.

A GLIMPSE AT THE B

WEIGHING SIDES EN ROUTE FROM REFRIGERATOR TO CAR.

FRESH BEEF

In 1827, Mr. Archibald Clybourne established a small slaughterhouse on the north branch of the Chicago River for supplying the garrison at Fort Dearborn and the little settlement nearby with fresh beef. Five years later the slaughter-house was moved "away out on the prai-rie," to the present intersection o Chicago's Madison Street and Michigan Avenue. Thus began the story of Chicago's colossal meat empire.

It took twenty-two days to get from New York to Chicago in 1846, the yea a Mr. H. R. Smith came out to gather the first herd of Illinois cattle for the New York market. The return trip took a hun

SHIPMENT EAST AND TO EUROPE.

THE

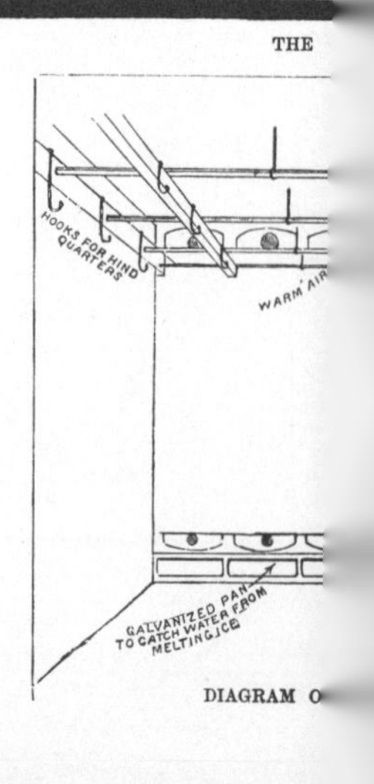

DIAGRAM O

E ENGLISH MARKET.

HOW CATTLE ARE SLAUGHTERED.

FROM CHICAGO

red days, but he cleared a profit of more
han $18,000.

Chicago's Union Stock Yards opened
n 1865, on Christmas Day, increasing
ach year until they became the nucleus
f thriving South Chicago. *Harper's
Weekly* sent a staff artist to Chicago
o record the entire procedure from
he initial on-the-hoof trading through the
aughtering, weighing, cooling, and the
nal shipment in the new refrigerator
ars to the East. Hungry Americans demanded more and more steaks and rib
oasts and the annual total by 1882, the
ear of *Harper's* article, had risen to
,125,000,000 pounds!

FRESH MEAT FROM ICE-HOUSE TO CAR.

NG-ROOM.

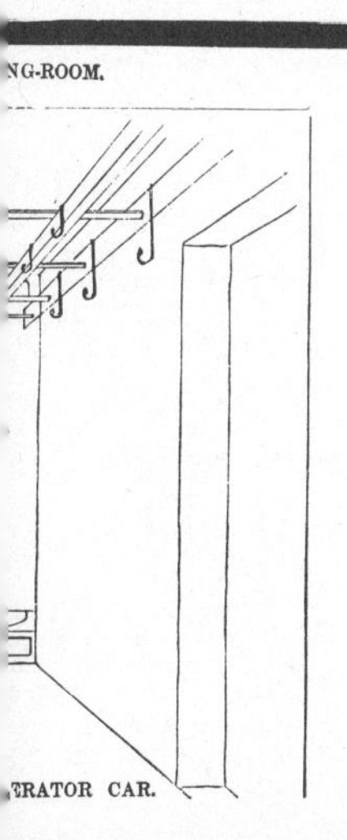

RATOR CAR.

INTERIOR OF REFRIGERATOR CAR.

New Yorkers were getting tired of having "that swindled feeling" every time they ordered beef, said an indignant news article deploring high prices and predicting that the year 1882 would usher in "at last" an era of beef at more reasonable prices, due to the active competition building up between purveyors of dressed beef in refrigerated cars and beef on the hoof.

Within a decade, beef was not only "depressed" in price by four and more dollars per hundredweight, but was available in the form of ready cut rib roasts, boned, "coiled up and bound around, skewered, ready for putting in the oven." Not only that, but summer hotels could have their roasts wrapped in paper and in a "frozen condition" while fillets could be bought from the packers as a separate cut by the hundred or thousand pounds.

To go with the prized beef, four or five canny mushroom fanciers in Philadelphia were growing those succulent dainties the year round, although as late as 1899 they were still a luxury item, and "a one dollar note will buy you about two mushrooms." But it was a cachet for any steward to be able to add fresh mushrooms to his bill of fare in midwinter, just as it was for him to obtain Grenoble snails which *The Handbook* informed him were "collected by vine dressers in the evening from stone heaps where they gather to enjoy the dew."

The fancier menus offered beef in various guises which must have proved as unpronounceable as they were surprising to a majority of the patrons. *Aloyau de Boeuf à la Provençale*, for instance, turned out to be larded sirloin spread with marrow, anchovies, garlic and other seasonings, roasted and served with *piquante* sauce; *Filet de Boeuf au Jus d'Orange* was tenderloin served like duck with an orange sauce. Stewards were advised not to call upon their cooks for a Baron of Beef, since, it was explained, this was served at the Queen's table in England at Christmas; it weighed about three hundred pounds and was flanked on either side by a boar's head and a woodcock pie. It had to be "roasted at Windsor Castle and thence despatched to Osborne . . . why the 'baron' of beef has so lordly a title is not quite clear. As the joint consists of the beef's two sirloins—or Sir Loins' as some people spell the word—not cut asunder, the name may possibly have been given on the principle that one baron is equal to two knights."

WHERE NEW YORK LANDS ITS FISH

In the small hours lights blink in Fulton Market as fishing smacks from New England and the Jersey shore tug at their moorings. By the 1880's, when *Harper's* published the scene opposite, picturing the fish landing-slip at Fulton Market, the daily food bill of New York City stood at $1,500,000 and seafood comprised no small part of it.

"Probably no city in the world has so varied and interesting a fish-market. A sea-coast of two thousand miles of ocean contributes to its resources, and the largest lake system known adds varieties of fresh-water fish. Salmon are set off against pompano and red snapper. . . . There are no less than three-score excellent kinds of food fish in their different seasons.

A well-organized "fish express" brought additional supplies to New York by rail, and a dealer could send an order by telegraph in the afternoon and have his fish from Gloucester the following morning.

Opening of the Oyster Season (*Harper's Weekly*, 1872)

1. Dredging through the ice. 2. Oyster shell covered with young. 3. Dredging from a boat. 4. Drumfish. 5. Opening oysters for export. 6. Oyster knives. 7. Starfish. 8. Dredge. 9. Young oysters. 10. Oyster sloops at foot of West Tenth Street.

OYSTERS R IN SEASON

"An oyster, sir, is one of the elements of social existence, a delicacy of no age, sex or condition, but patent to the universal family of man."

In that all-inclusive quotation, *The Steward's Handbook* reflected the extravagant devotion Americans expended upon the oyster. What historian William E. Woodward called "the great oyster craze" spanned more than half a century in all, and an evening on the town was considered a failure if it did not take in a visit to an oyster bar, oyster saloon, oyster cellar, or oyster parlor.

Thus New York City's oyster season found hotel and restaurant stewards conspiring for the choicest hauls and often cornering the entire catch as a heavily loaded sloop put in at the foot of West Tenth Street. By the time *Harper's Weekly* recorded the animated scenes on the opposite page (March, 1872), the oyster season was rigorously observed.

Such was the demand for the sweet and luscious American oyster that a curious system known as the "oyster express" used to convey the mollusks hundreds of miles inland. The "express" was in the early years a wagon and team of horses which headed west from such points as Baltimore or Long Island. Horses were changed, à la Pony Express, and the oysters were kept alive in straw moistened with seawater. For points beyond Pittsburgh, Pennsylvania, the "oyster express" changed to boats and the prized cargo was kept alive in tanks of salt water.

Because of the gargantuan appetite for oysters, the more ingenious of the oyster "farmers" began planting them in beds adjoining Long Island and even imitating the English fashion of forcing them in "ambulances," or boxes covered with galvanized wire in which the oysters grew rapidly.

By the 1890's a delicacy of a century before, pickled oysters, had again "come into gastronomic fashion," according to *The Steward's Handbook*, but the waiter was also advised that oysters on the half-shell were the American classic. "Always insist on one point," the instructions continued, "that the dainty morsel is opened on the *deep* shell, so as to preserve every drop of liquor. This done, the American asks only crackers, butter, a slice of lemon and the pepper cruet."

Clams were another nineteenth-century delicacy and it was said that Sam Ward, known as widely for his gourmet tastes as for his skill as a lobbyist, knew "more than a dozen ways of cooking the delicious bivalve."

Harper's Weekly sent a staff artist to Great South Bay, Long Island, in 1877, to find out how New Yorkers acquired the juicy tonnage that arrived daily via the clam fleet. The most esteemed clam was the Little Neck, "a small round clam of a charming flesh color." Hotel stewards bought it in quantity, for it was an important first course in "dinners of the highest order."

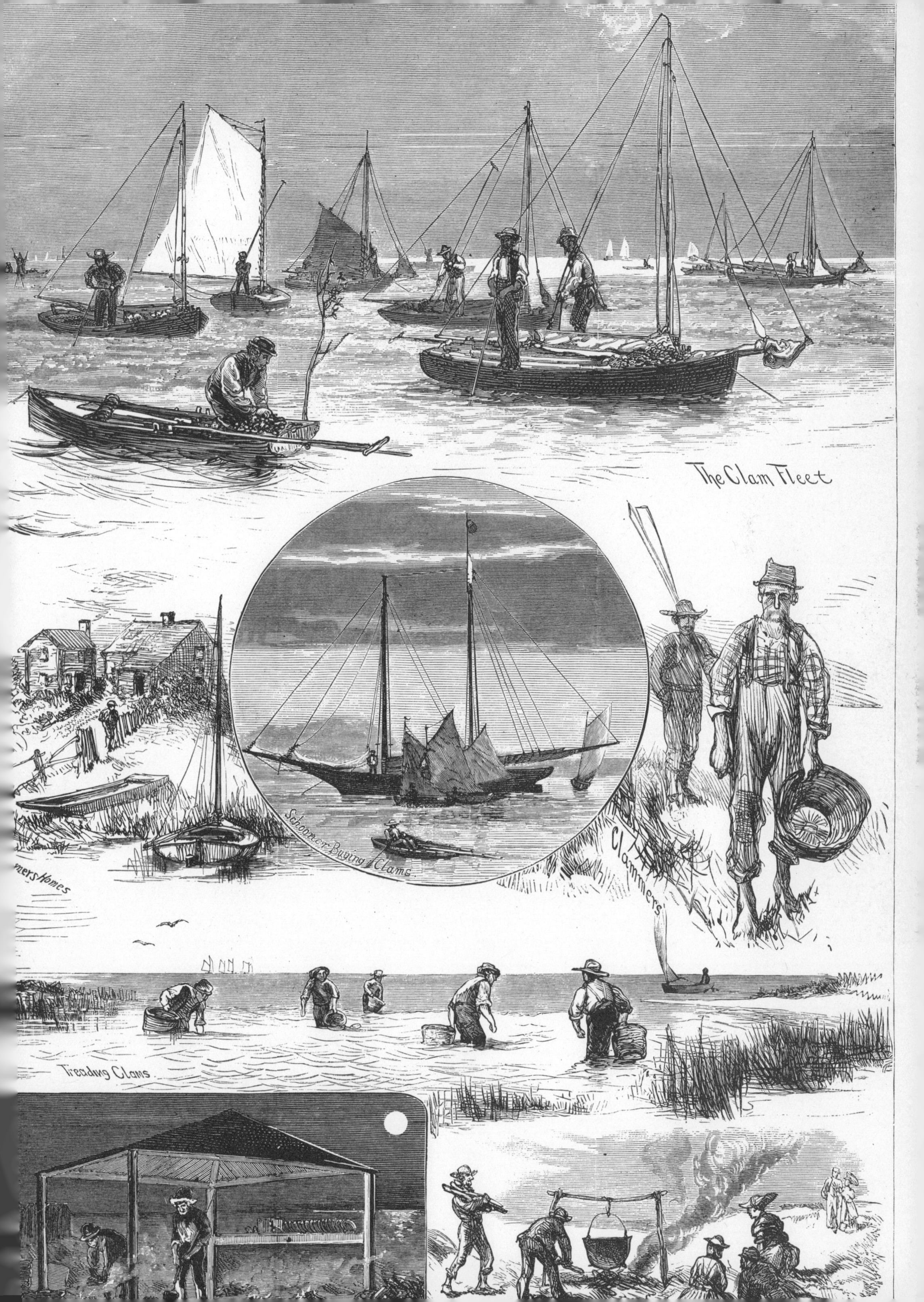
The Clam Fleet
Schooner Buying Clams
Clammers
Treading Clams

A MILLION EGGS A DAY

By 1873 New York's appetite for eggs brought in a million per day, and of these the hotels and restaurants bought a major portion, for eggs were on the menu from breakfast through after-theater suppers. It was the pride of chefs in the fashionable hotels that they knew five hundred to a thousand ways of preparing eggs and that it would be no trick at all to emulate the respected Marin of Paris who in the early 1700's served a dinner for twelve and a supper for seven, "all wholly and solely of eggs." There were skewered eggs, meringues of eggs, eggs as sole and eggs as whiting, a hot pie of fresh eggs; the dinner contained twenty and the supper nineteen dishes of eggs!

Before eggs could come to the New York market they had to be candled, as is being done in the *Harper's Weekly* drawing on this page. Candling determined their freshness and, of course, their acceptability to the knowing buyer. The "million eggs a day" arrived by basket and barrel and were sorted in the predawn hours before market opened. Some farmers kept them fresh by packing them in bran. Others, resorting to a strong brine to preserve the eggs, commanded a somewhat lower price on the regular market quotations. Cold-storage chambers were just beginning to be used, and by the turn of the century were widely accepted.

Up from the Tropics and the Deep South

The hotel steward who went marketing in the 1870's and 80's was advised by *The Steward's Handbook* that "cash in hand will draw the last and best thing from the darkest back corner." The cash the steward carried was in mills and three-dollar pieces, eagles and double eagles, and with it he shopped cautiously and knowingly for the tropical fruits at the sprawling open-air markets around the waterfront. He knew his importers and his marketmen by name and was on hand when ships arrived with cargoes of prized pineapples, oranges, lemons, bananas. Imagine the agonies and machinations of the nameless steward who had to see to it that the fantasia dreamed up by a rich New Yorker was complete on the evening of the "tropical dinner" he had ordered for his guests. *Steward's,* which reports the dinner in its 1899 edition, does not identify the hotel, but does say that the dinner cost $ 175 per cover. "The wine and music were extra."

The twenty-course menu included all the foibles of the era: a punch called Balaklava Cup served before the game, which was choice partridge (punch before game and salad after was said to be copied from the French); diamond-back terrapin, filets of beef, endless vegetables and side dishes. But, in addition to shopping for such items, which the average experienced steward always knew where to find, this poor fellow also had to arrange for the importation of "bouquets" of ten strawberries each (the season was just before Lent; the steward billed the strawberries at ten dollars per guest). The truffles

he had brought from France. The hotel's damask and linen went into the supply closets that evening, since the host had requested the steward to have the tables polished and bare, with a perfect palm leaf at each place serving as a table mat. There was a Roman punch, too . . . but, since mandarin trees had been brought in from Florida and other tropical spots, this punch could only be served from the oranges hanging on the natural trees, "the pulp of the fruit having been deftly removed so that the favored guests could pick their own fruit."

By 1890, sophisticated New Yorkers were taking it for granted that, as *Harper's Weekly* put it, "the limitations of season have ceased to be any bars to the demands of the appetite." Thanks to improved transportation, to new and better refrigeration, and to the discerning eye of the men who saw to it that New York's famous hotels kept their reputations as the best in the country, the "epicure" could then "feast on pecan-fed turkey and canvas-back duck on the Fourth of July" as easily and with as much relish as he could at Christmas. When the Deep South began to ship its wares to the big city, hotel stewards were down in the markets in the chilly pre-dawns to see that their guests would have "green peas and strawberries before the winter blasts have done howling."

The practiced steward, added the *Handbook,* has to avoid the pitfalls of small potatoes, stale eggs, produce that will not keep, and overpriced gourmet items, else the proprietor of the hotel will deprive the steward of "the delights of commissions and percents" and will himself march down to the markets at five o'clock in the morning to make sure that his hostelry's cuisine is not only up to scratch but returns him a profit as well.

The 1890's were an era of elaborate eating, and the purchasers of hotel provender had to take into account the demand for what a critical Englishman, Dr. Ian Maclaren Watson, called "a huge amount of curious and superfluous food." Dr. Watson asked one hotel proprietor why this over-abundance was necessary, and Mine Host replied:

". . . one of the charms of going to a hotel, for people who live poorly at home, lies in this power to order expensive dishes they rarely or never see on their own tables. To be served with a quantity of food that he has no intention of eating is one of an American citizen's dearest privileges."

LOOK OUT

FOR

Hotel Jumper AND Dead Beat.

The undersigned wishes to warn Hotel and Livery-men to look out for

ROBERT GALISPIE of Rochester, Vt.,

who, on the night of Sept. 23rd, 1885, got away from an officer at Hancock, Vt., ... dy to start for Middlebury

FOURTH COURSE

Small Town Talk

A Nostalgic Look at the World of the Commercial traveller

pass him ... ong.

He is a young man about 24 years old, weighs about 160 pounds; very dark complexion, with dark eyes; about $5\frac{9}{12}$ feet in height, a State-prision countenance; was dressed in a dark suit, with black soft hat, when last seen.

For further particulars address

M. L. FAULKNER,

Proprietor Rochester House, ROCHESTER, VT.

Rochester, Vt., Sept. 24, 1885.

GOOD PLAIN FOOD & PLENTY OF IT

The commercial traveler, in his heyday during the last half of the nineteenth century, had developed a keen nose for the small town hotel which spread an ample board. The dining room was apt to be large, airy and unadorned as is the one shown below, in the town of Reading, heart of the Pennsylvania "Dutch" country, where everything came to table at once. One bemused traveling salesman reported that his waitress told him when he asked for more potatoes that "ter bodatiss iss all." "And thus I learned," he went on, "that the Pennsylvania Dutch never say anything is 'gone.' If the bar runs out of beer, the beer is 'all' . . . when the sauerkraut barrel is empty, the kraut is 'all.' But there is one thing that is never 'all.' That is pie. Not only pie, but a whole pie, and not only one whole pie, but sometimes three or four whole pies, all of different kinds. The black-eyed girl . . . placed four uncut pies on the table . . . a cheese custard, a cranberry tart, a sweet potato custard and a snitz pie. The only thing that is short about Pennsylvania Dutch pies is the crust."

TERRITORIAL ENTERPRISE...

Travel was still rugged for the "bagmen" who ventured as far as Minnesota, a riproaring frontier territory until it achieved statehood in 1858. The bagman, so called because he invariably carried a carpetbag on his travels, had to put up with primitive sleeping cars which had rows of bunks on one side and day seats on the other. The cars boasted potbellied stoves and large spittoons; no such frills as sheets or blankets graced the bunks, and passengers slept in unwashed, unpressed discomfort. The same year that Minnesota became a state, two remodeled day coaches were put into service as Pullmans and a new era of traveling comfort and luxury began.

The 1850's saw a zigzag ribbon of rails across the country and an army of strangers disembarking from "the cars" and seeking bed and board as hotels sprang up near every railroad depot. As early as the mid-1840's, the young town of Buffalo, New York reported that more than five thousand people passed through on their way to the West in a period of only seven months, putting up at railroad hotels and depot houses. The commercial traveler kept pace with the westward march of population and soon became a pet object for jokes and cartoons, in his flashy waistcoats, diamond stickpins, checkered coats, and with his ready flow of beguiling talk.

HUFF'S HOTEL

HUFF'S HOTEL.

R.N.WHITE. Greenwood. M.T.

WINONA,

MINNESOTA TERRITORY,

F. M. COCKRELL & Co., - Proprietors.

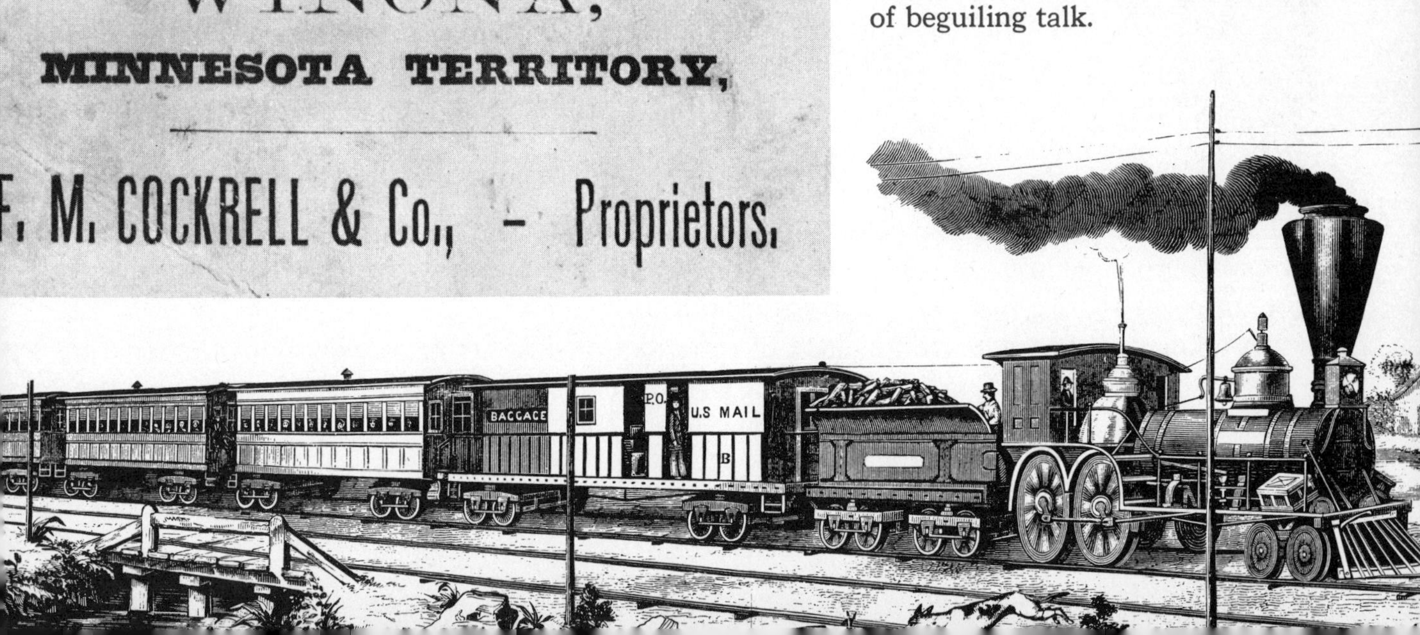

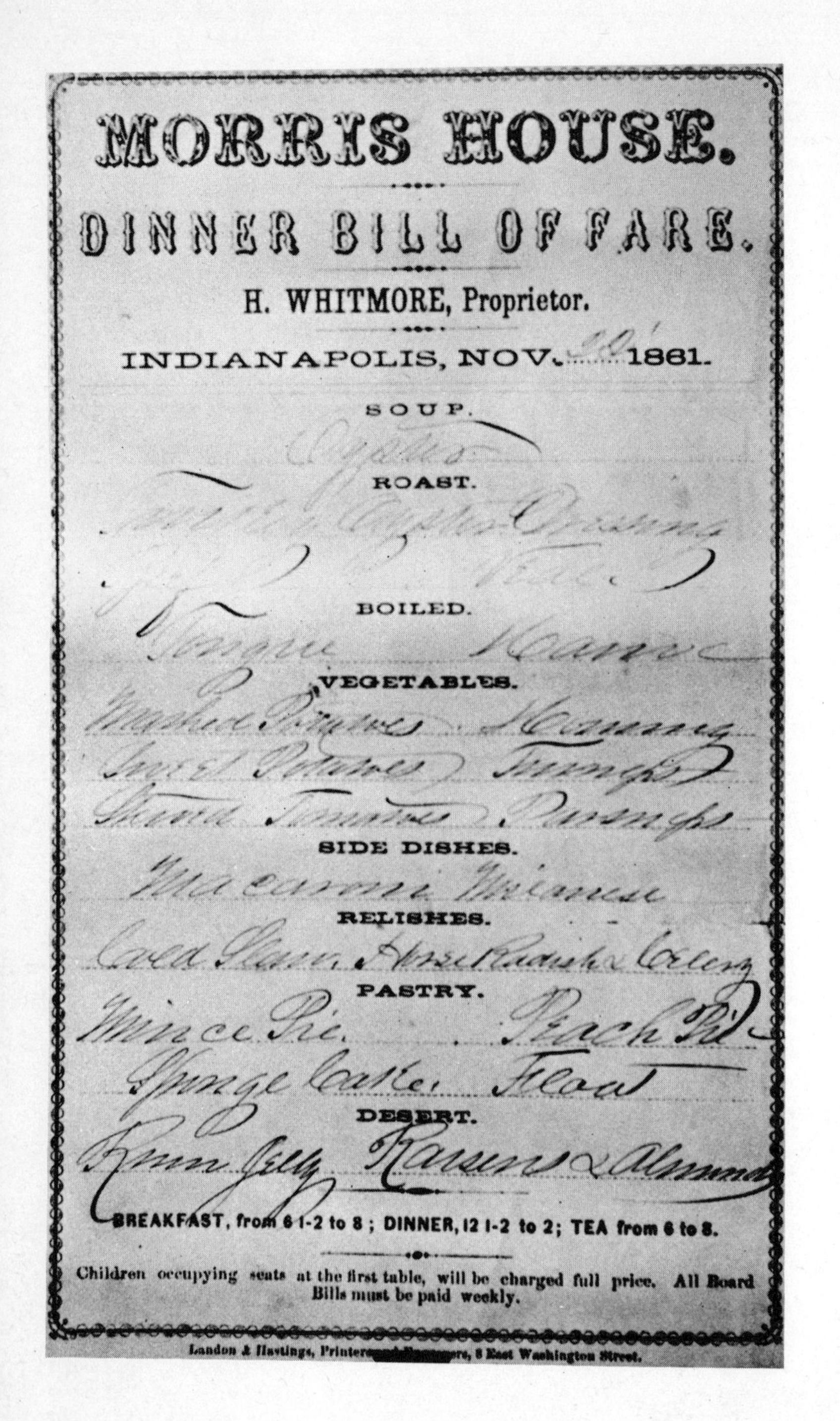

MORRIS HOUSE.

DINNER BILL OF FARE.

H. WHITMORE, Proprietor.

INDIANAPOLIS, NOV. 20' 1861.

SOUP.

Oysters

ROAST.

Turkey, Oyster Dressing

[illegible] Veal

BOILED.

Tongue Ham

VEGETABLES.

Mashed Potatoes Hominy

Sweet Potatoes Turnips

Stewed Tomatoes Parsnips

SIDE DISHES.

Macaroni [illegible]

RELISHES.

Cold Slaw, Horse Radish & Celery

PASTRY.

Mince Pie. Peach Pie

Sponge Cake. Float

DESERT.

Rum Jelly Raisins & Almonds

BREAKFAST, from 6 1-2 to 8 ; DINNER, 12 1-2 to 2; TEA from 6 to 8.

Children occupying seats at the first table, will be charged full price. All Board Bills must be paid weekly.

Landon & Hastings, Printers and Engravers, 8 East Washington Street.

In stout hands, jangling as it fell
Near a white apron, rang a bell.
Its tones are sounds that all may know
It gives the languid pulse a glow,
It tinkles, jingles, rings and rings,
And talks of sweet and savory things,
"The roast, the broil, and on the shell,"
It's the dinner bell, "sweet bell."

Breakfast was *over* at 8 A.M. and the big meal was served at midday, with a light supper, often called tea, in the evening. Most hotels in the Midwest offered a plain bill of fare on which the proprietor wrote out by hand the day's offering, often, as in the case of the Morris House in Indianapolis, allowing the guest little or no choice. If he did not like oyster soup, he could proceed to the next course, where indeed oysters popped up again in the sauce for the roast veal. The vegetables were a rather uninspired array of parsnips, turnips, hominy, stewed tomatoes, and potatoes. The Morris House apparently discouraged the presence of children at its first seating, by charging them full price unless they waited for a later table.

The old-time Yankee peddler had graduated into the bagman and the bagman now metamorphosed into commercial traveler and drummer. Everywhere he went he was met by omnibuses offering free rides to hotels or by runners with a sales talk as fast as his own. The traveling salesman was the lifeblood of the small town hostelry as well as the larger commercial hotels. By the early 1880's there were a quarter of a million salesmen hawking their wares across the country.

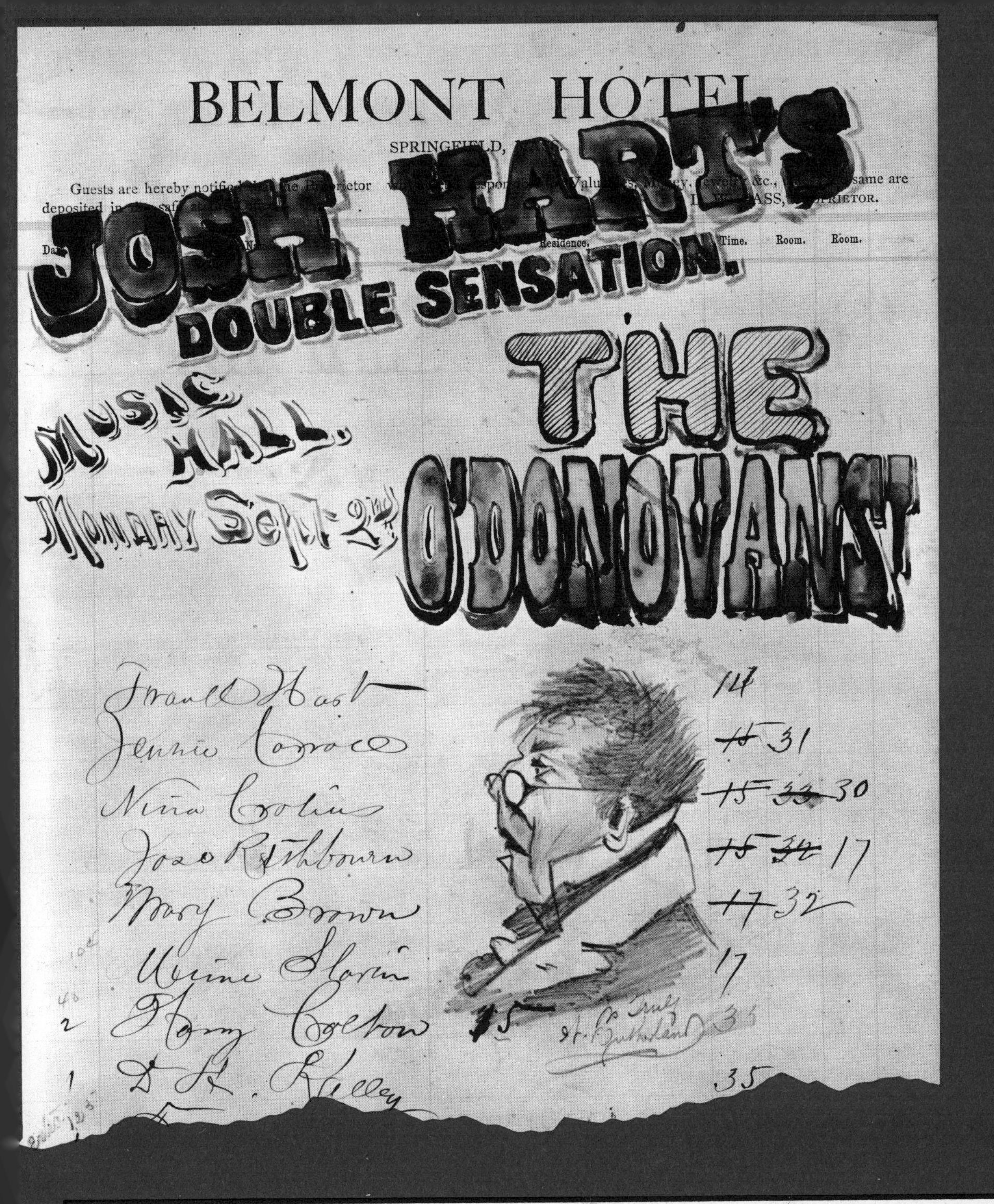

It was not until after the Civil War that whole troupes of actors began to travel. Prior to that only the star and principals went around the country, and local actors were hired to fill out the cast. It was important, but not easy, for a barnstormer to claim at least one "New York performance." A James E. Murdoch, said to be the "most genteel comedian in the country," in the 1870's could not obtain an engagement in New York because he was "deemed a Western actor."

Hotel keepers frequently looked askance at the road company, which as often as not brought along a menagerie of pets, slept late in the day, burned the lights until late at night, and cooked in their rooms. Not to mention the too frequent occurrence of an entire company stranded and unable to pay the hotel bill.

Toward the end of the 1800's hotels in the rapidly growing towns and cities were discovering that more of their patrons wanted dinner in the evening instead of the noon-to-two hours. Trainloads of passengers arriving in the late afternoon and finding only "tea" or "supper" available were apt to complain. *The Steward's Handbook* reported that by the late 1890's "people of fashion were contending in favor of the late dinner."

To effect a compromise, most hotels still served a big midday meal, but added dinner dishes to the bill of fare at supper. This resulted in some odd combinations, such as a first course of oatmeal porridge, followed by broiled pig's feet, stewed kidneys, cold mutton and venison, salmon salad, potatoes, and an assortment of French, graham and cream breads, currant buns, toast and flannel griddle cakes served with maple syrup or New Orleans molasses, with fruit and assorted cakes for dessert. On another supper menu, the rolled oats were followed by fried oysters!

Vienna coffee was in demand at suppertime, and so were Mandarin, Japanese, and Gunpowder teas. *Demorest's Monthly Magazine* received a letter from a grateful proprietor of a family hotel, saying that the Demorest formula for Mandarin tea had made her famous . . . "there is nothing that so cheers an exhausted body, or spirit as a cup of good tea, and nothing more hurtful or disappointing than adulterated or sham tea."

Demorest's also was in receipt of a lengthy communication from "a frontier boarding house," advising that breakfast held on as a stalwart meal well into the first two decades of the twentieth century, especially in the smaller towns and cities where life became real and earnest at six in the morning and a good deal of physical exercise took place before a substantial feed at noonday.

A ROCKY MOUNTAIN *Pensione*

The houses behind their picket fences stand quietly along the tree-shaded streets of Georgetown in the heart of the Rocky Mountains. A carload of tourists empties at the doorway of a small solid building whose sign proclaims it to be the Hotel de Paris. The tourists look curiously at the gilded statue of Justice, scales swinging in the breeze, and the couchant metal lion above the side entrance. Once more the strange story of Louis du Puy is told, a story that dates back to 1875, when Georgetown had as many as ten thousand people roaring through its streets of a Saturday night.

The hotel was a legend in its own time. Who would expect to find truffles, pâté de foie gras, vintage wines, imported *champignon* served by candlelight in a frontier mining town nine thousand feet above the plains! The look of the Hotel de Paris was entirely continental, inside and out, which was exactly as M. du Puy intended when he set out to create a corner of his native Alencon in faraway Colorado.

Louis du Puy presided over all the public rooms in his Hotel de Paris. He was the factotum who met guests in the lobby pictured here, as well as being chef in his kitchen and *maître d'* in the delightful dining room shown on the right-hand page.

"French Louie" as he was nicknamed, had a reputation as a woman-hater. Some believed his misanthropy was the result of an unhappy love affair. At any rate, a lone woman arriving at the hotel was nearly certain to be told politely that all the rooms were booked.

People in Georgetown knew very little about Louis du Puy during his lifetime. He simply arrived with a burro named Fleurette, a tent, and camping equipment. He had come as a sort of free-lance reporter, but the quick money lure of the silver mines dimmed his enthusiasm for journalism. Shortly afterward, in March of 1873, he was nearly killed in a freak explosion and warned by doctors not to return to mining. He himself said in later years that he thought of opening a restaurant simply because a good cup of coffee was not to be had in Georgetown. He launched his dream by working in a bakery, saving his money, and finally, in 1874, beginning to build the Hotel de Paris. The thick masonry walls and windowed facade were copied after inns and taverns he remembered in France.

HOTEL DE PARIS

AND

Restaurant Dining Rooms.

ORDER BILL OF FARE.

OYSTERS.

Half Doz. Raw. -	35c.	One Doz. Raw, -	65c.
Half Doz. Stew, -	40c.	One Doz. Stew, -	75c.
Half Doz. Fried, -	50c.	One Doz. Fried, -	80c.
Coffee, - -	10c.	Milk, per Glass, -	10c.
Tea, - - -	10c	French Chocolate, -	25c.

2,000 MILES FROM AN OYSTER BED

Oysters were an absolute passion with Americans in the late nineteenth century . . . especially Americans who happened to be two thousand miles from the nearest oyster bed.

So it is not surprising to find that the gourmet proprietor of the Hotel de Paris hauled them by the barrel across the mountain passes to adorn the magnificent table he set. Nearly everything in the hotel had to be brought across oceans and continents. The tall breakfront cabinet in the dining room (above) was filled with Limoges and Haviland china and Belgian glass. The floor was of inlaid strips of maple and walnut and the wainscoting was striped to match. In the center stood a delightful little fountain copied from one in Florence, Italy; the ceiling was gaily painted and the walls hung with Western paintings.

The fame of the Hotel de Paris was out of all proportion to its size and location. By the time the narrow gauge railroad reached Georgetown it was not unusual for people to take the afternoon train from Denver on Friday, in the hope that "French Louie" would regard them kindly and allow them to stay for the weekend. Actors, writers, opera stars, lecturers, and the higher class traveling salesmen made for Georgetown and De Paris as soon as they were within a day's travel. But Louis du Puy, he of the mercurial moods and whims, could be icily indifferent to those he did not fancy.

HARPERS WEEKLY 1874

"ON THE WAY TO NEW DIGGINGS"

The scene here is typical of the frontier days of Louis du Puy, when the three largest towns in Colorado were nearby Central City in the heart of the gold mining region; Denver, the distribution point for supplies; and Georgetown, "The Silver Queen" lying almost at the foot of the Continental Divide. The lure of silver brought an army of prospectors and for nearly a quarter of a century the flash of new money . . . and lots of it . . . turned Georgetown into a boisterous metropolis, complete with two opera houses, churches, saloons, lodge halls, livery stables and a scenic narrow gauge railroad called "The Loop," which for a time was as popular as Niagara Falls or the Grand Canyon.

The vast silver mining region around Georgetown was known as "The Argentine" and among its famous mines were the Bethany, the Terrible, the Cashier, the Phoenix, and the Mendota. The silver ore found at such mines as the Anglo-Saxon was assayed at twenty-three thousands dollars a ton. It seemed that the boom would never end.

One day the train pulled into Georgetown with a group of passengers whose total wealth was estimated at more than two hundred million dollars. These gentlemen, including

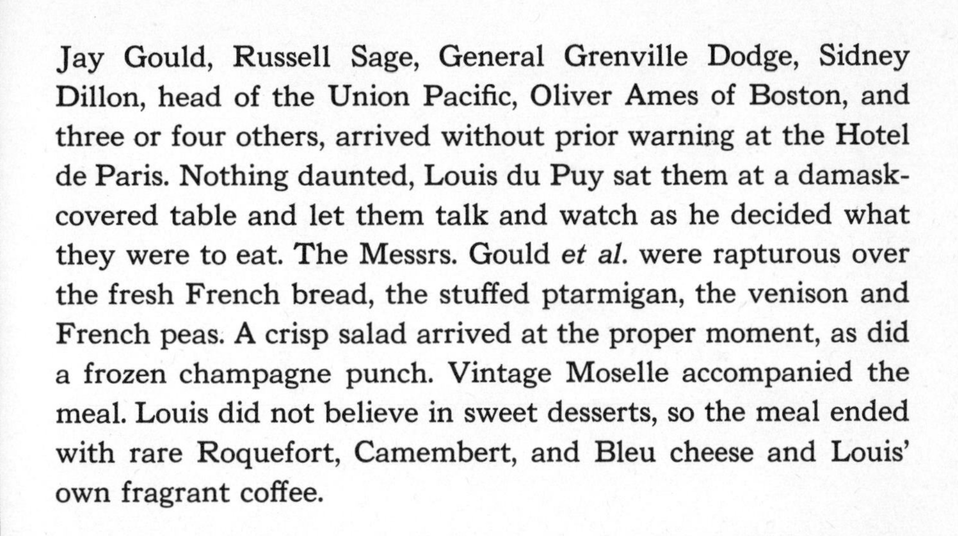

Jay Gould, Russell Sage, General Grenville Dodge, Sidney Dillon, head of the Union Pacific, Oliver Ames of Boston, and three or four others, arrived without prior warning at the Hotel de Paris. Nothing daunted, Louis du Puy sat them at a damask-covered table and let them talk and watch as he decided what they were to eat. The Messrs. Gould *et al.* were rapturous over the fresh French bread, the stuffed ptarmigan, the venison and French peas. A crisp salad arrived at the proper moment, as did a frozen champagne punch. Vintage Moselle accompanied the meal. Louis did not believe in sweet desserts, so the meal ended with rare Roquefort, Camembert, and Bleu cheese and Louis' own fragrant coffee.

When Louis du Puy arrived in Georgetown, it looked much like the scene above, with a population of 3,000 in the year 1874. There was a bristly frontier newspaper, one of whose reporters, Jesse S. Randall, later started the *Georgetown Courier*, which carried trenchant editorials that made the paper known throughout the West. Once, Editor Randall, bemoaning the fall weather, wrote:

"The melancholy days are here,
The saddest of the year!
It's most too warm for whiskey straight
And most too cold for beer."

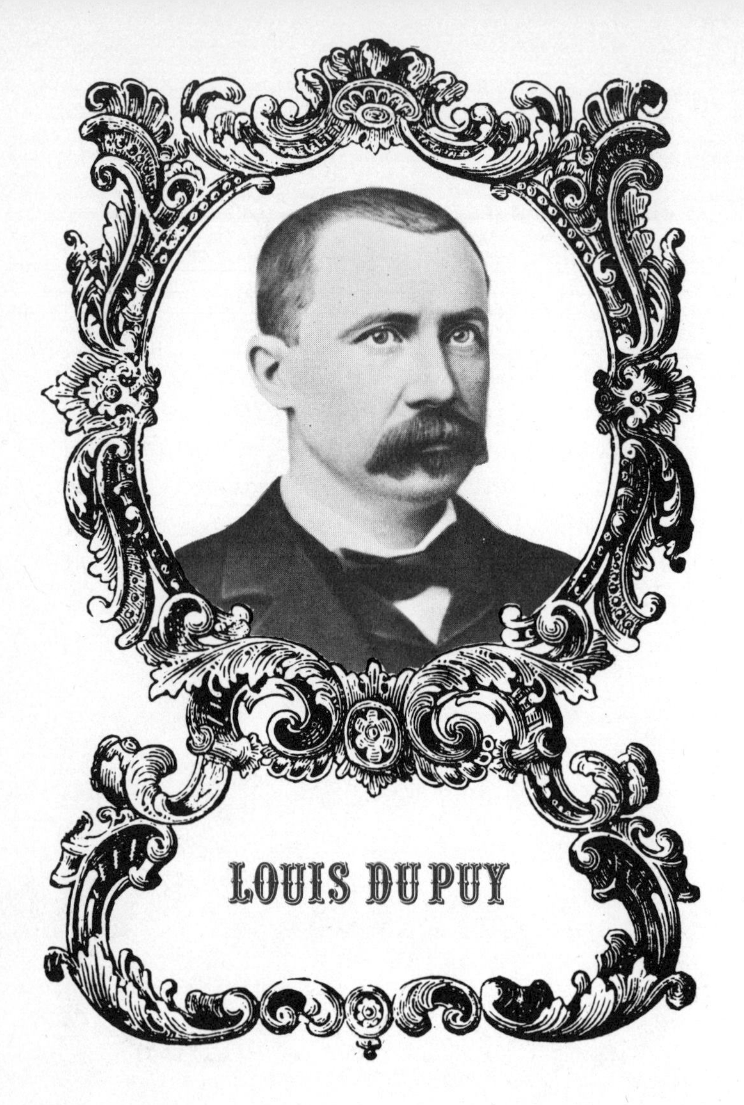

Louis du Puy was never in doubt about the rightness of his taste or his ability to "provide oysters, game and all the delicacies of the season" and to have "one of the best cooks in the Territory to provide the viands" (none other than Louis himself!). His wine cellar was a distinguished one, and he imported his own machine to do the bottling from the great casks.

Louis confided in very few people, but among them they managed to piece together a sort of chronology which traced him back to Alençon and a birth date of October 14, 1844. His erudition —he was often spoken of as "the best educated man in the country"—was attributed to schooling at a seminary in France. He picked up some of his knowledge of food and cooking when he worked in restaurants in Paris and London. After a brief try at soldiering in the United States Army, Louis deserted, changed his name from Adolphus Gerard to Louis du Puy. Men with assumed names and shadowy reputations were a commonplace in the Old West. But Louis with his courtly manners, his aloofness from the rowdy night life, his pursuit of philosophy . . . he was different. Those who saw him in cap and apron presiding over his stoves . . . found it difficult to reconcile that figure with the ascetic gentleman who liked to retire to his book-lined library, to read and meditate long past midnight.

Whatever the truth about a frustrated romance, the fact is that Louis du Puy is known to have associated with only one woman during his Georgetown years. She was Sophie Gallet (or Gally), known as Aunt Sophie. She came to the Hotel de Paris after her husband's death and stayed there for twenty-two years, looking after the table linens, silver, and glass, and tending the flower garden.

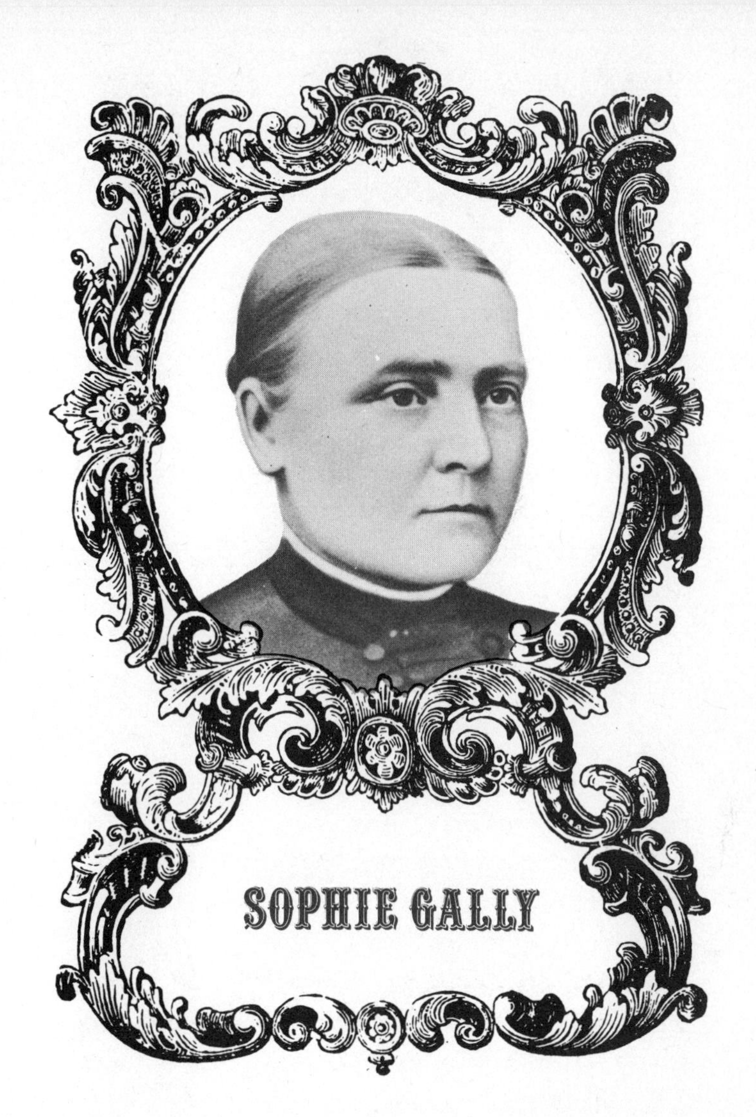

Wilton carpets muffled the footsteps of those fortunate guests who were deemed acceptable by Louis and allowed to register for one of his dozen or so suites. The bedchamber pictured here does not look lavish, but it had luxuries nearly unobtainable in the mining towns of the Rockies. The black walnut furniture was carved and polished; there was hot and cold running water in the marble washbowls, beautiful corner mirrors and, best of all, central steam heat. Louis' kitchen was every bit as much a beloved domain as his library. There copper pots gleamed along the walls and a big brick oven, four by six feet, turned out the crusty French bread for which the De Paris was famous. Trout were popped into the pool below the dining room fountain to be picked out and cooked to a guest's order.

The glory days of Georgetown were brief. When Congress repealed the Sherman Act which had required the U.S. Treasury to buy four and a half million ounces of silver per month, the result was sheer disaster. In the panic of 1897 people in Georgetown simply walked out of their homes, leaving furniture, china, and other possessions behind and heading for somewhere, anywhere, where a living might be made.

But people talked for a long time about the picturesque Frenchman, Louis du Puy. A Georgetown woman who was a little girl in 1882, when Louis decided to build an addition to his Hotel de Paris, remembers how he used to play host to the small girls of the town on summer afternoons. Louis had been engaged to supervise a crew of Chinese laborers who were building the grade for the Colorado Central Railroad. Louis worked as diligently as his crewmen. But at midafternoon the little girls would come to the courtyard of the Hotel de Paris and sit around on stones or lumber until Louis emerged, balancing a tray containing a curious lead box, a decanter of French wine, and glasses. This he would hand to one of the Chinese workers. Then the girl who had been chosen "queen" for that day came forward and was given the lead box to pass around. It was filled with tiny sugar-iced petits fours from Paris. When everyone was served, Louis would lift his glass and give the toast *"Avec santé, messieurs, mademoiselles."*

In a letter describing the events of October, 1900, when Louis fell sick, a contemporary comments that "he was an atheist . . . a man of determined viewpoints on all religious matters. Sophie was a devout Catholic and when the end was near Sophie cried and cried and begged Louis to become a Catholic, and so to quiet and please his very old friend, he was baptized as a Catholic about three days before his death. Realizing that the end was near, he called for two bottles of France's most celebrated champagne . . . and defying the doctor's orders, he drank the contents . . . and died soon after."

Sophie followed him in death within the year. On the tombstone in Georgetown cemetery is the inscription, "Deux Bons Amis" . . . Two Good Friends.

Isaiah Rogers, a native of Marshfield, Massachusetts, never compromised with his ideal of architectural beauty, based on the chaste symmetry of the Greek Revival. He translated the Tremont look to New York's Astor House and went on to design the million-dollar Merchants Exchange in New York, with its magnificent Ionic columns; the famous St. Charles Hotel in New Orleans, and a series of other distinguished hotels including the Bangor House in Maine, Richmond's Exchange Hotel, Battle House in Mobile, the Galt House in Louisville, the Maxwell in Nashville, and the Burnett in Cincinnati.

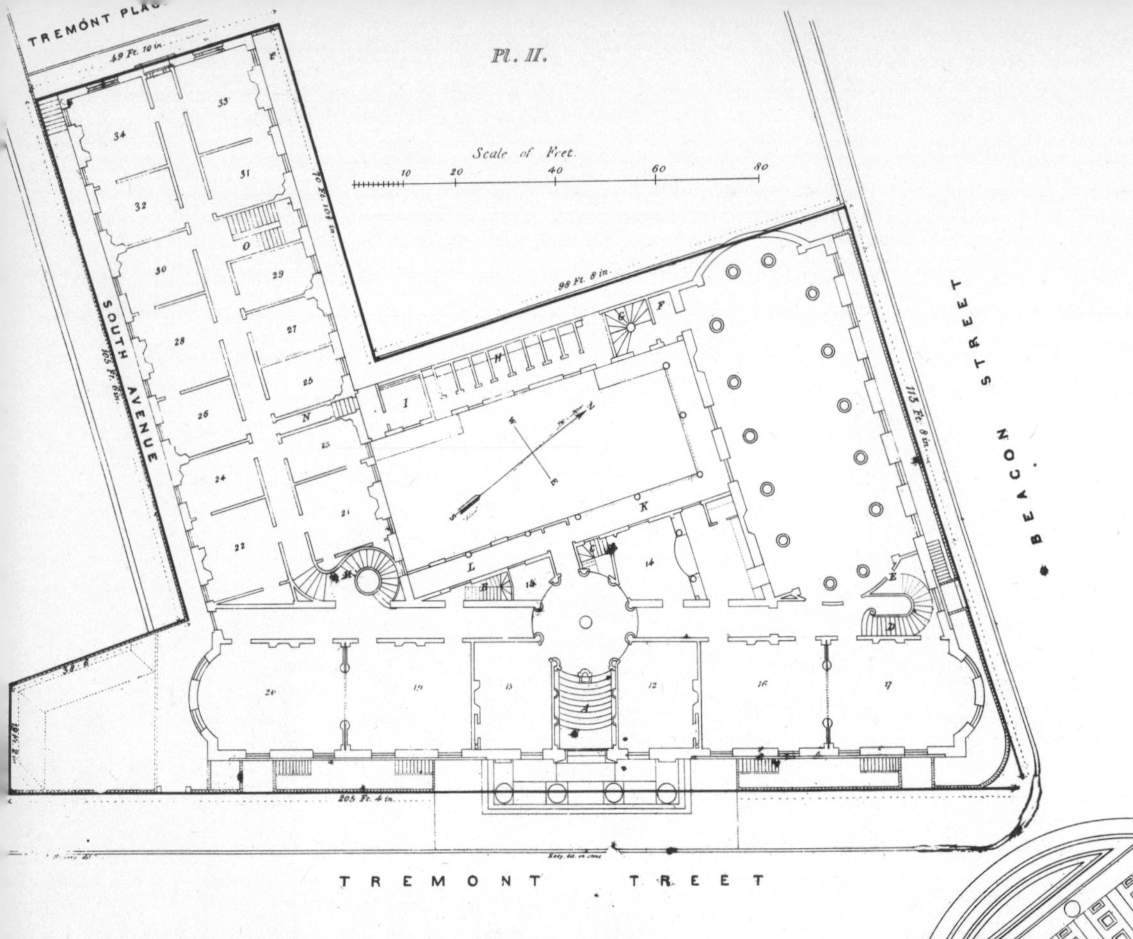

PLANNING THE FIRST HOTEL

The remarkable floor plans shown here are from a book published in 1830 by Gray & Bowen of Boston, titled *A Description of Tremont House with Architectural Illustrations.* It was to become the standard reference work for hotel construction. The Rogers blueprints marked the end of the casual era of innkeeping and the start of a period of intensive competition in which hotel builders outdid each other in providing lavish accommodations.

The plan of the first floor indicates the spaciousness of the Tremont House. Facing Tremont Street, it occupied an entire square block. Standing three and a half stories high, its Doric entrance was adorned with four Grecian columns and its roof was topped by a graceful cupola . . . which, as is evident from later pictures of the actual hotel, was never built, possibly for reasons of economy.

The dining room, seventy-three feet long and thirty-one feet wide, had a fifteen-foot-high ceiling and was warmed by two great open fireplaces. Back of these was an air furnace which conveyed heat from the kitchen into the vast dining room . . . another Isaiah Rogers innovation. It was the talk of the town that two hundred guests could be served here at a single sitting.

The Tremont had an awesome list of "hotel firsts" . . . not the least of which was a lobby presided over by a clerk. Earlier hostelries had a sort of man-of-all-work who signed in the guests, carved the roast, served at the bar, and carried guests' luggage. The Tremont not only had a lobby, but a separate baggage room as well. And it offered the unheard-of luxury of single and double bedrooms, each equipped with its own key . . . quite a contrast to the old inns where guests slept in lots of five, six, or more and the door was always open. The immediate popularity of the Tremont's private rooms would seem to contradict Madame Fanny Kemble's acidulous comment in 1830 that Americans . . . "have an aversion for solitude whether eating, sleeping or under any circumstances."

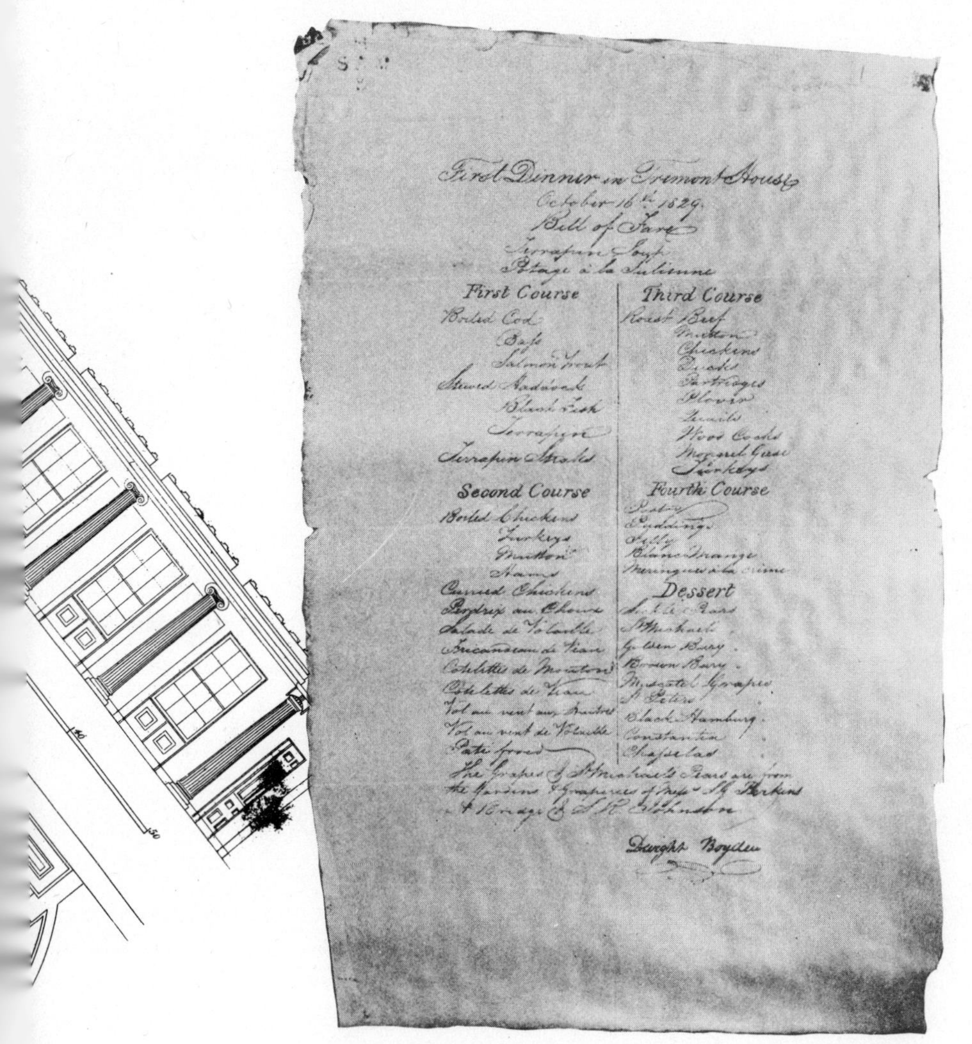

First Dinner in Tremont House
October 16th 1829.
Bill of Fare
Terrapin Soup
Potage à la Julienne

First Course
Boiled Cod
Bass
Salmon Trout
Stewed Haddock
Black Fish
Terrapin
Terrapin Steaks

Second Course
Boiled Chickens
Turkeys
Mutton
Hams
Curried Chickens
Perdrix au Choux
Salade de Volaille
Fricandeau de Veau
Cotelettes de Mouton
Cotelettes de Veau
Vol au vent aux Huitres
Vol au vent de Volaille
Paté [illegible]

Third Course
Roast Beef
Mutton
Chickens
Ducks
Partridges
Plover
[illegible]
Woodcocks
[illegible] Geese
Turkeys

Fourth Course
Pastry
Puddings
Jelly
Blanc Mange
Meringues à la Crème

Dessert
[illegible] Pears
St Michael
Golden Bury
Brown Bury
Muscatel Grapes
St Peters
Black Hamburg
Constantia
Chasselas

The Grapes & St Michael's Pears are from the Gardens & Graperies of Messrs S G Perkins & Bridge & S R Johnson

Dwight Boyden

Here is the opening night dinner menu of Tremont House, October 16, 1829. More than a hundred eminent Bostonians attended, including Daniel Webster and Edward Everett. Dwight Boyden, proprietor who signed the menu, was the son of Simeon Boyden, head of a justly famous family of New England hotel keepers.

The Tremont opening night dinner menu shows the inroads being made by the French cuisine, as note the *potage à la julienne, perdrix aux chou, côtelette de mouton,* and the like. But American classics were there too: Terrapin soup, boiled cod, roast beef, and plenty of game. For a dessert a fascinating assortment of fruits: S. S. Michael's grapes and pears from the "gardens and graperies" of Messrs. Perkins, Bridge and Johnson.

Banquet to Colonel N. A. Thompson, Captain of the Boston City Guards.
Gleason's Pictorial, 1852.

During its prideful sixty-five years, the Tremont House was visited by a regular Who's Who of politics, literature, business, and society. Charles Dickens, whose comings and goings in America were usually tempestuous, arrived at the Tremont in 1842 to meet a young man, James T. Fields, who was later to be his publisher in this country. Fields recalls the bleak winter evening "when I first saw the handsome, glowing face of the young writer who was even then famous over half the globe. He came bounding in . . . fresh from the steamer . . . 'Here we are!' he shouted as the lights burst upon the merry party just entering the house, and several gentlemen came forward to greet him."

When the waiter asked whether he would like his dinner "right away," Dickens stared for a moment and then said no, he'd like it where he was. The confusion was finally cleared up by a perceptive Bostonian who whispered to the waiter that Dickens wanted his food "directly." Dickens says in his journal: "I saw now that 'right away' and 'directly' were one and the same thing. So I reserved my answer and sat down to dinner in ten minutes afterwards, and a capital dinner it was."

Good talk was a concomitant to eating when the Saturday Club began meeting in Boston hotels during the 1850's. Its membership included Emerson and Longfellow, Dr. Oliver Wendell Holmes, Asa Gray, the botanist and taxonomist; Charles Eliot Norton, editor of the *North American Review* and founder of *The Nation*; Benjamin Peirce, mathematician

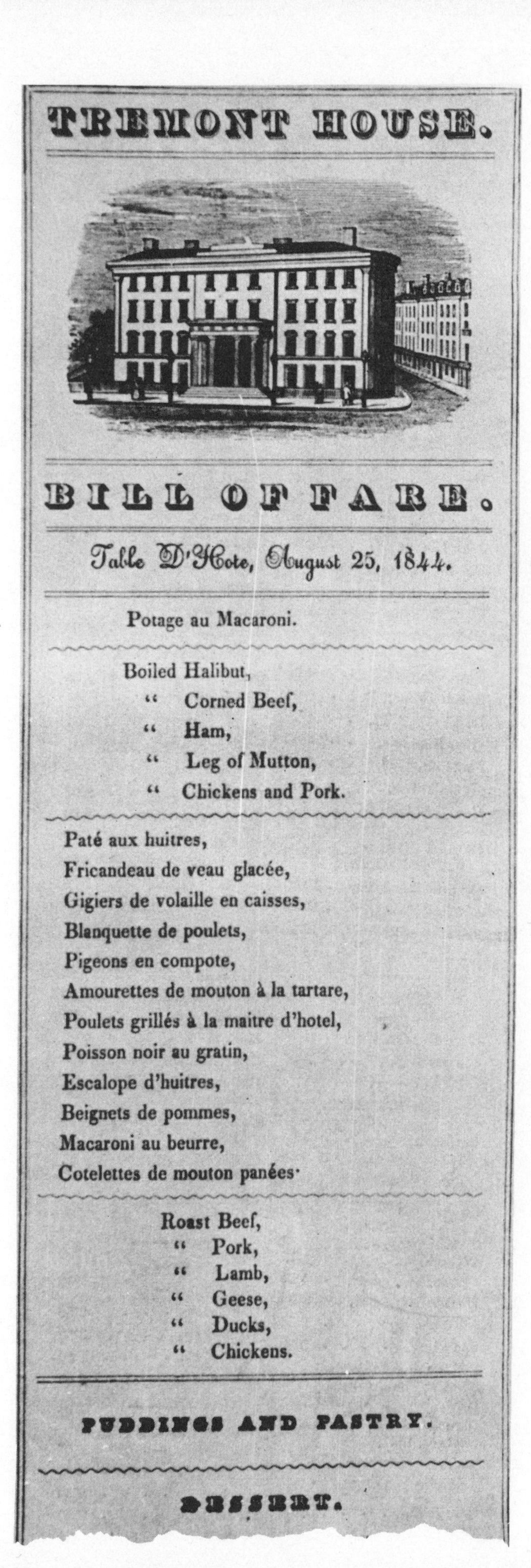

TREMONT HOUSE.

BILL OF FARE.

Table D'Hote, August 25, 1844.

Potage au Macaroni.

Boiled Halibut,
" Corned Beef,
" Ham,
" Leg of Mutton,
" Chickens and Pork.

Paté aux huitres,
Fricandeau de veau glacée,
Gigiers de volaille en caisses,
Blanquette de poulets,
Pigeons en compote,
Amourettes de mouton à la tartare,
Poulets grillés à la maitre d'hotel,
Poisson noir au gratin,
Escalope d'huitres,
Beignets de pommes,
Macaroni au beurre,
Cotelettes de mouton panées.

Roast Beef,
" Pork,
" Lamb,
" Geese,
" Ducks,
" Chickens.

PUDDINGS AND PASTRY.

DESSERT.

and physicist. They dined on venison and guinea fowl at the Tremont, and selected their wine with knowing taste, for as Holmes observed, wine was "the grand specific against dull dinners."

By the time this Tremont House menu appeared in 1844, the cuisine had taken a turn toward fancy French terminology, although corned beef, pork, lamb, goose and other native fare was in still plain English.

The Tremont's dining room was brilliant at night under the gaslight, which was as much a conversation piece as the annunciator system. Baltimore had a commercial gas plant in 1817, but the Tremont claimed to be the first hotel to employ it. As for the annunciator, it was the first push-button device to appear in a hotel, replacing the raucous hand-bells with which guests formerly had to send out alarms for water or other supplies.

...THEY SAW THE FLAMES ON THE EASTERN STAR 65 MILES AWAY

On a late winter afternoon in 1856 one of the Tremont's guests, Thomas Thompson, happened to glance from his window just as a yellow spurt of flame shot from the roof of the Tremont Temple across the street. Since Mr. Thompson had his art collection, worth some $50,000 stored in the Temple, he quite naturally dashed toward the fire and tried to enter the big granite building. Firemen held him back, warning that roof and walls might cave in at any moment. Back at the hotel, he joined other guests at the windows to watch the spectacular blaze and, in his case, to see with especial agony bits of canvas and statuary among the ruins.

From the cupola of *Ballou's Pictorial* building a staff artist sketched this lurid night-time scene. The Temple, opened two years before the Tremont House, was a city landmark. It had been a famous theater for some sixteen years, at which time it was purchased by a Baptist group which used it for public worship and also rented some of the rooms as studios, offices, and storerooms.

When the great roof fell, showers of sparks and cinders turned the atmosphere into a fiery rain. At least one man was killed and a number rushed to the Tremont House for assistance. According to *Ballou's* the immense volume of flames illuminated the whole of the city . . . and . . . "we understand that the light was clearly visible on board the steamer *Eastern Star* which was off Boon Island sixty-five miles in a direct line from Boston."

Along Tremont Street in the same year of the Temple fire, 1856, tracks were laid for the Metropolitan Horse Railroad. *Ballou's Pictorial* commissioned an artist to make the drawing on this page, showing the terminus of the line at the Tremont House and the gateway to the Granary Burying Ground. The proximity of the hotel to the graveyard prompted the poet Fitz-Greene Halleck to say that the proprietors wanted to give their guests "prospects beyond the grave." He also noted that when John Jacob Astor hired Isaiah Rogers to build New York's Astor House in imitation of the Tremont, he even chose a site next to a cemetery . . . St. Paul's Churchyard.

A year after the Metropolitan Horse Railroad was opened, six more lines were running in Boston, and *Ballou's* stated that "the comfort, convenience and economy of horse railroads, benefitting all classes of the community, are now almost universally recognized." The cars were painted in circus colors, straw yellow with green lights, blue edged with gold and red with red lights at either end. The terminal offices were "fitted up very liberally" and had "a complete suite of apartments for the ladies, provided with all modern conveniences."

CENTENNIAL CITY

1876

"Wherever one is traveling this year, whether on cars or steamboats, the universal topic of conversation is 'The Centennial.' "

And the universal destination was Philadelphia, where the great Exhibition opened on May 10, 1876, to the unfurling of flags, a band playing a march written for the occasion by Richard Wagner and a procession headed by President Grant. The ceremonies closed with a hymn by the poet Whittier and a chorus of six hundred voices singing Handel's "Hallelujah Chorus."

There were two thousand hotels and boarding-houses awaiting the rush of visitors, but they were inadequate on opening day and scenes such as the above occurred often during the Centennial summer. Among the hostelries were the two pictured here: the Continental, and the Girard.

The flags of all nations whipped in the breeze and pennants fluttered from everything including the manes of smartly curried carriage horses. Hanson cabs vied with gaily decorated coaches and every other conceivable conveyance on the Centennial's gala opening day. In this picture can be seen one of the gigantic hotels built especially for the Centennial, the Transcontinental of Philadelphia, with accommodations for a thousand guests at five dollars a day. At right is a corner of the sprawling Hotel Globe with a similar five-dollar rate but with room for two thousand. The crowded intersection here is at Elm and Belmont, close by the Centennial and route of official parades.

The fair was a challenge to the hardy visitor who wished to see it all on foot. Guidebooks estimated that he would have to trudge twenty-five miles outdoors to cover the entire two hundred and thirty-six acres. The main building alone encompassed more than two acres and eleven miles of indoor walking. The great Corliss engine, started on opening day by President Grant, was the star showpiece; its fourteen hundred horsepower engine could, if necessary, drive the entire shafting machinery required to operate the exhibits.

Visitors could eat in a number of languages at the nine major Centennial restaurants. *Harper's* warned that at the Trois Frères Restaurant "you shall find the mere fragments from a breast of veal or the segments of a calf's head so bedecked and so dressed with piquant sauces, and so flanked with savory vegetables that you shall come to a new knowledge of the triumphs of cookery."

1857 ENDEMIC OF THE NATIONAL HOTEL

WASHINGTON, D. C.

MAY 7, 1857.

The undersigned have been appointed a committee by the Board of Health of Washington to communicate with residents of this city and persons elsewhere, in order to procure, if possible, further authenticated information in regard to the malady which recently prevailed at and was known as the "Endemic of the National Hotel." No fatal cases have occurred in this community; but, as vague and unauthenticated statements have reached us that persons have died elsewhere from this cause, we take this as the only sure mode of calling upon physicians and persons abroad to favor us with statements of the names and residences of the persons who thus have died. We desire to obtain a description of the course and symptons of their disease; the opinion formed as to its origin and the reasons therefor; the treatment adopted in the cases and the results of the *post mortem* examinations or chemical analyses of the dejections from the sick, if any such were made. As the guests of that hotel are wide cast over the land, it is impossible for us to obtain the names and residences of their physicians, and must therefore appeal to them through the public press for the information desired. Their prompt attention (by letter to the committee) will confer a great favor upon the Board of Health and this community, and perhaps be of great service in promoting the cause of public health and medical science.

Papers friendly to the above objects will confer a favor on the Board of Health by publishing this card.

ROBERT KING STONE, M. D.
JAMES E. MORGAN, M. D.
Committee of the Board of Health.

WASHINGTON, MAY 7, 1857.

"You exchange nods with governors of foreign states; you elbow illustrious men and tread on the toes of generals; you hear orators and statesmen speaking in their familiar tones . . . You adopt the universal habit of the place, and call for a mint-julep, a whiskey-skin, a gin-cocktail . . ." So wrote Nathaniel Hawthorne on a visit to Willard's Hotel during an assignment to cover Civil War battlefields. He might have been describing the scene in the gaslit marble-floored oyster bar pictured opposite.

Various WILLARDS

The Willards, a remarkable quartet of brothers who began their careers as bartenders on Hudson River steamboats, emerged on the Washington scene in pre-Civil War days and made hotel history. First came the Ebbitt House, opened by Henry A. and Edwin D. Willard. Joseph D., most eccentric of the lot, engaged in a feud with brother Caleb and the two communicated only through newspaper letter columns.

Both the Ebbitt House and the various Willard hotels became headquarters for lobbyists and that lobbyist par excellence, Sam Ward, had a favorite cocktail: chipped ice, four drops of Angostura and a liqueur glass of green Vermouth.

First venture of the Willards was Ebbitt House (at top). Then came the earliest of the three hotels bearing the family name, Willard's (at center), and finally the present Willard's Hotel.

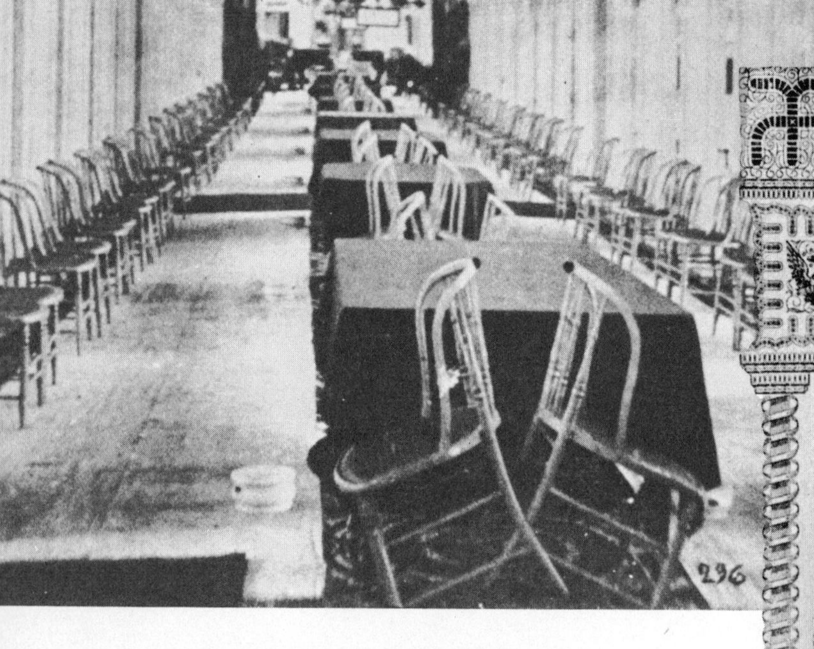

FLOATING PALACES

Mississippi steamboats were truly "floating palaces" in the mid-nineteenth century. Dining saloons in such as the *S.S. Red Wing* pictured above offered "a table as good as money and skill could make it." En route to gay New Orleans passengers found that "every succeeding day's dinner was better than the last."

New Orleans was a culinary oasis in a desert of corn pone, fried ham, yams, and chitlins and the passengers who disembarked there went on a spree at the fine hotels and restaurants. In the 1730's the French girls who arrived on "brides' ships" rebelled against the daily fare, and officials, explaining that "For corn the newcomers have a dogged aversion," sent an SOS for provisions, and New Orleans famed Creole cuisine was born.

GENTLEMEN'S ORDINARY.

BILL OF FARE,
ST. CHARLES HOTEL,
SUNDAY, 16th March, 1845.

SOUPS & FISH—Turtle Soup.
Italian Soup.

Boiled Redfish, Anchovy sauce.
Redfish, stewed in white wine.

BOILED.

Corned Beef and Cabbage.
Ham.
Chicken and Pork.
Leg of Mutton.
Beef Tongues.
Fulton Market Beef.
Leg of Corned Pork.

Cold Pressed Corned Beef.
Cold Roast Beef.
Round of Beef, à la mode.
Pork and Beans.
Mutton Chops, with green peas.
Fried Oysters.

ENTRÉES.

Vol au vent garni de fricassée de poulet.
Tête de veau en marinade.
Côtelettes de mouton aux petits pois.
Noix de veau braizé à la Bourgeoise.
Cervelle de veau en matelot.
Haricots au Porc.
Rognons sautés au champagne.
Macaroni au gratin.
Becassines sauce Madere.
Huitres frites.

VEGETABLES.

Mashed Potatoes.
Onions.
Beets.
Cabbage.
Baked Potatoes.
Marrow Fat Squash.
Rice.
Turnips.
Spinnage.
Sweet Potatoes.
Horse Raddish.
Boiled Potatoes.
Carrots.
Lettuce.
Parsnips.

ROAST.

Beef.
Chicken.
Turkey.
Mutton.
Capons.
Veal.
Lamb, mint sauce.
Pig.

PASTRY & DESSERT

Mince Pies.
Cranberry Pies.
Blackberry Tarts.
Papillons D'ores.
Almond Puddings.
Ice Cream.
Almonds.
Pecans.
Apples.
Filberts.
English Walnuts.
Raisins.
Oranges.
Figs.
Prunes.

N. B. Oyster Supper, will be given every Monday Evening, until further notice

Pickled Onions,
Pickled Red Cabbage.
Jelley,
Pickled Cucumbers.
Apple Sauce,
Cranberry Sauce,
Pickled Peppers,
Pickled Olives,
Tomatoe Ketchup,
Pickled Tomatoes,
Walnut Ketchup,
Mushroom Ketchup.

ORLEANS CULINARY OASIS OF THE SOUTH

The shining, gilded dome of the first St. Charles Hotel, opened in February of 1837, made it a landmark on the New Orleans skyline. It was as well a center of fine food and gracious Southern living. Many a chapter of ante-bellum Louisiana history was written in the St. Charles where gathered Creole social leaders, dashing young officers, bankers, and politicians. This menu is from the Gentlemen's Ordinary in 1845; here and in the adjoining barroom slave auctions were held regularly.

The St. Charles reserved a sixteen-thousand-dollar gold service for its gala dinners and banquets when "delightsome music" filled the air, everyone danced, and the evening ended with a midnight supper of "cold meats, salads, salamis, gallantines quaking in jellied seclusion, an infinite variety of a-las . . ."

When the gold-domed St. Charles burned in 1850, that ubiquitous architect, Isaiah Rogers, was called upon. Although the dome was omitted, the second St. Charles, pictured below, was a lavish house of three hundred rooms with a rotunda, grand ballroom, and private parlors. Fire, the demon of the nineteenth-century hotel, accounted for this structure too on April 28, 1894, when four people lost their lives. The third and last St. Charles was built on its site, to be the scene of many celebrant Mardi gras parties.

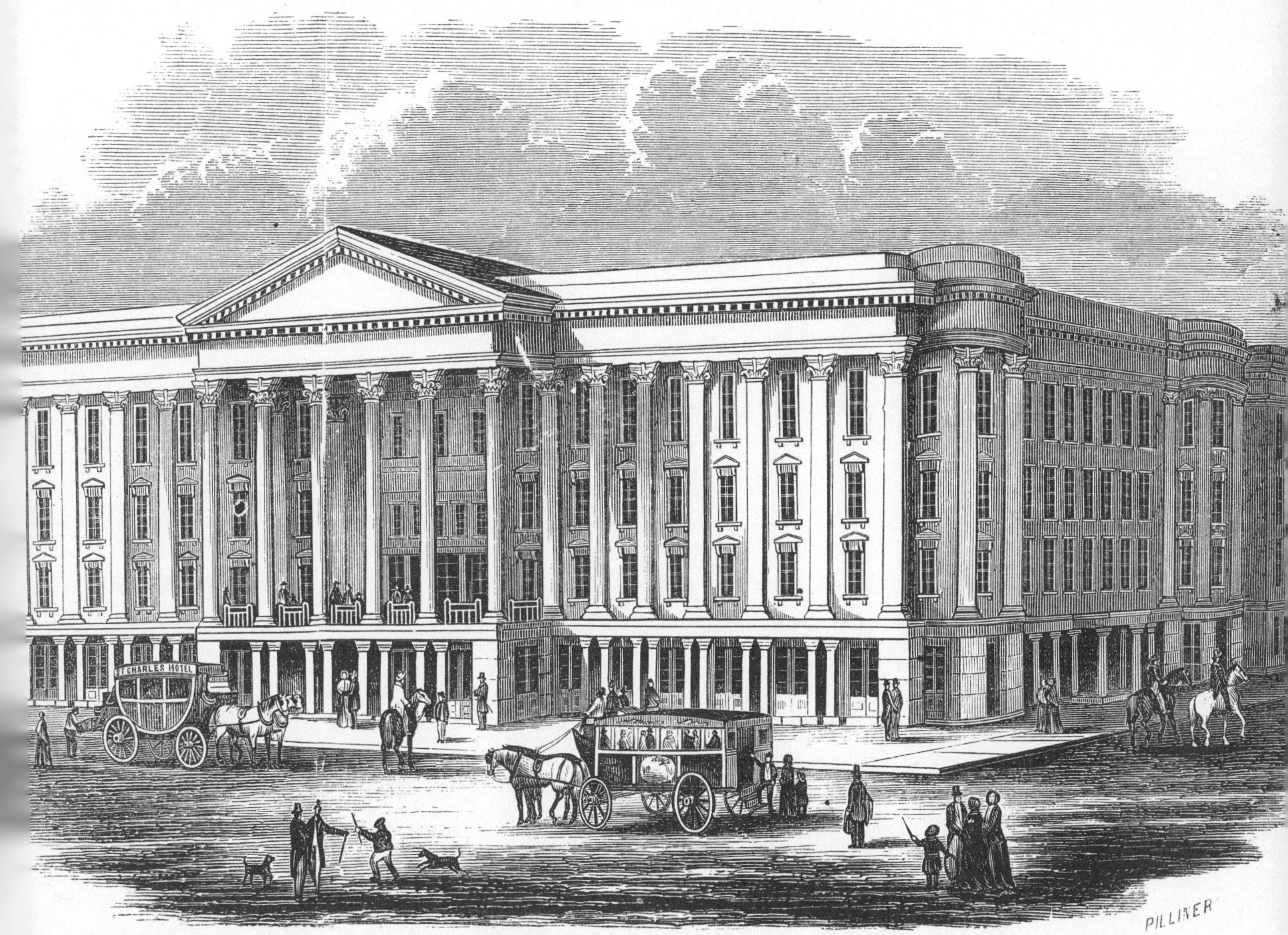

ST. LOUIS

Four brief but glamorous years were all that fate allowed the Lindell House in St. Louis. St. Louis was burgeoning in the 1860's with a population nearing 170,000, and it was thought only fitting that it should have the "most aristocratic hotel" and the "grandest opening night ball" in the entire West. This it achieved when the Lindell House, a massive stone structure six stories high, opened in November of 1863. On July 4, 1865, high society and political bigwigs thronged the Lindell House for a triple-barreled celebration . . . national independence, the fall of Vicksburg, and the opening of the Mississippi River. They were served St. Lawrence salmon, ham with champagne sauce, and "cold ornamental dishes," followed by Supreme of Chicken à la Pré de Pois, and Timbale de Servilles à la Milanaise . . . and for those still in the running, Roman punch and ice cream!

Actually the Lindell had not quite reached its fourth birthday when tragedy overtook it. It had five hundred and thirty rooms and claimed at the time, 1867, to be "the largest building for purposes of accommodation ever erected in America." It was valued at more than a million dollars.

There were four hundred guests in the Lindell on March 30, 1867, when a small, insidious fire broke out in an attic chamber. For some unexplained reason, the hotel's elaborate system of "hose connections" was not put into use and within two hours the flames had shot through the roof in a twisted column of fire and smoke. In the story accompanying this picture in *Harper's Weekly* for April 20, 1867, it was noted that "from the sixth story downward the hotel presented its ordinary aspect, the lights still burning in the rooms and there was neither flame nor smoke to be seen. But from the broad plane of the roof rose a pyramid of fire, roaring and cracking with irresistible fury." By morning "the once imposing hotel was a mass of crumbly blackened ruins." No loss of life was recorded. And as so often in the disaster-riddled chronology of the American hotel, the proprietors looked at the wreckage and immediately began planning another hotel on the site.

GATEWAY TO THE WESTERN TERRITORIES

In 1877 *Harper's* noted that "hotels are beginning to post notices in conspicuous places announcing that 'guests will find ropes at the ends of the halls in case of fire.' "

"GOD'S WILL BE

Thirteen proved a disastrous number for the original Palmer House shown above. Opening September 26, 1871, it was a smoldering ruin thirteen days later, one of ninety-five buildings lost by Potter Palmer in the Great Fire.

A few pious persons may have believed that "wicked Chicago" had sealed her own doom, but the world in general admired the lusty young city and along with *Harper's Weekly* mourned the "dire calamity . . . the flames blown by the winds of heaven from house to house . . . the terror-stricken men, women and children flying from burning homes and spreading out, a helpless, half-starving multitude on the open prairie." Fire-fighting equipment was rushed from as far off as Cincinnati; trainloads of food, tents, medicine, blankets, and clothing poured out of the East. There was pandemonium as crowds sacked deserted saloons and went barreling down the streets drunk and hysterical. Millionaire members of the Chicago Club, meeting at a champagne breakfast to assess the disaster and plan the future, had to leave when the flames took over their building. They moved some crimson velvet chairs and sofas to the lake shore, finished their champagne, and revised their plans.

The fire, which began on Sunday evening, October 8, did not catch up with the Palmer House until nine o'clock the next morning, just about the time the *Tribune* staff, its Fire Extra editions on press, had to flee the building.

DONE, OH WICKED CHICAGO"

Potter Palmer, who was in the East when the fire occurred, rushed home, borrowed more than a million and a half dollars with his signature as the only collateral, and began to rebuild. He ordered round-the-clock construction for the new Palmer House. In the picture below crews are working by calcium flares.

The story of Mrs. O'Leary's cow upsetting a lantern and starting the fire has been discredited many times, but it is interesting to note that *Harper's Weekly*, reporting the calamity, stated that on the night of October 8 "a woman went into a stable on Dekoven Street, near the river on the west side, to milk a cow, carrying with her a kerosene lamp. This was kicked over by the cow and the burning fluid scattered among the hay and straw." Thus the legend, if so it be, began right along with the fire and spread just as rapidly!

NOTHING SHORT OF THE BEST!

The urbane Potter Palmer was not accustomed to doing things on a small scale. When he bought real estate, he bought it by the mile. When he jaunted off to Saratoga, he wagered on the thoroughbreds, played for high stakes at the Casino, gave late and lavish champagne suppers. When he married in the summer of 1871 at the age of forty-four, he married the belle of Chicago, beautiful Kentucky-born Bertha Honore. There was sterling silver at the reception and the guests numbered over seven hundred. And the bridegroom's wedding present to his bride was a half-million dollar hotel!

It followed that when Mr. Palmer set out to build another Palmer House after the great fire, this Palmer House would not only be bigger and more lavish . . . it would also be the "most fireproof" in the world. To demonstrate this last claim he made a standing offer to permit any hotel keeper to set fire to any room in the Palmer House. If the fire failed to spread within an hour the wager was lost and the other hotelman must pay the damage. If the fire did spread, Mr. Palmer would pay. No one took up this highly publicized challenge.

In keeping with the spectacular night-and-day construction was the Palmer announcement that as soon as a room or suite was completed it was ready for occupancy! As a result Chicagoans were treated to the odd spectacle of guests going in and out of a hotel which was finished only as far as the third floor! By New Year's Day of 1874 the Palmer House was completed, and looked as it does here with its unique rounded corners, gleaming plate glass curved to fit the wide windows, heroic statuary topping the ornate entrance on State Street.

The lavish Palmer House was a prideful proof of the prediction made by *Harper's Weekly* at the time of the fire that "Chicago will soon recover from this great calamity, more magnificent and beautiful than she was before." Indeed, the little mud town of 4,000 population had come a long way since 1837. In less than half a century the plank sidewalks and frame buildings (there were 40,000 of them in 1871) had been superseded by the magnificent buildings along Lake Shore Drive, the fashionable shops of the Loop, the luxury hotels, expensive restaurants, and the domed and turreted mansions of the rich.

Many rich Chicagoans chose to take up residence at the Palmer House, including General "Little Phil" Sheridan and his family, and practically every visiting dignitary signed the Palmer House register or at least attended a celebratory function there. Its domed rotunda echoed to speeches by such as James A. Garfield, Generals Sherman and Grant, Mark Twain and Roscoe Conkling.

The dignified sweep of the grand stairway of the Palmer House was a proper setting for Grover Cleveland when he descended it to receive the news that he had won the Democratic nomination for President. Down this same staircase over the years came such varied notables as Mme. Helena Modjeska, Oscar Wilde, Rudyard Kipling, and most of Chicago's society leaders and tycoons.

The dining room of the old Palmer House opened into a series of other rooms to afford more dining space than any "refectory west of the Alleghenies." There the wining and dining of the exclusive Commercial Club took place as did the dinner meetings of the Sunset Club and St. Andrew's Society.

The scene must have been far more resplendent than the evening pictured here, on the occasion of General Grant's welcome home from his journey around the world on November 14, 1879. That afternoon the general stood on the Palmer House balcony to review a procession of his old Federal Army leaders. At dinner the bill of fare was long, the speeches short, with General William T. Sherman as toastmaster. The *pièce de résistance* was a speech by Mark Twain which reduced the usually stolid Grant to laughing "until the tears came and every bone of his body ached."

MENU.

OYSTERS.
Blue Points on Half Shell.
SOUP.
Cream of Chicken, a la Juisenne.
FISH.
Boiled Sheep's Head, Sauce Hollandaise.
(Croquettes of Potatoes.)
RELIEVES.
Fillet of Beef, Larded, a la Financier.
Sweet-breads, Brazed, with Green Peas.
JOINTS.
Turkey, Christmas Beef, Veal,
Saddle of Mutton,
Capon Egg Sauce, Tame Duck,
Leg Mutton, Caper Sauce,
Ham, Champagne Sauce,
Ox Tongue.
ENTREES.
Omelette Suffle au Rum,
Escolloped Oysters on Half Shell,
Potted Pigeon, with Mushrooms,
Broiled Quail on Toast, Maitre d'Hotel.
COLD.
Boned Turkey, with Allspice Jelly,
Gallinteen of Quail, with Truffles,
Game Patty, a la Glase,
Spiced Round of Beef, with Jelly,
Pickled Lobsters,
Spiced Oysters.
SALADS.
Lobster, Potatoe, Chicken,
Shrimp.

GAME.

Young Bear,
Maryland Coon, Mephis-
to Sauce,
Mallard Ducks, Partridges,
Leg of Elk, Prairie Chicken,
Reed Birds, in Paper Cases,
Loin of Buffalo.
RELISHES.
Celery, Sweet Pickled Tomatoes,
Mixed Pickles, Lettuce and Egg.
VEGETABLES.
Asparagus on Toast, Mashed Potatoes,
Spinach, Baked Tomatoes,
String Beans,
French Green Peas, Sugar Corn.
PASTRY.
Sliced Apple Pie, Mince Pie,
Lemon Merangue Pie,
English Plum Pudding, Brandy Sauce,
Marble Cake,
Golden Cake, Citron Cake,
Lady Fingers, Rosa Diamonds, Fancy Cake.
DESSERT.
Neapolitan Ice Cream,
Edam Cheese,
Champagne Jelly,
Bon Bons, California Pears,
Malaga Grapes,
Oranges, Apples,
New Figs,
Mocha Coffee.

The menu above with its elaborate silk fringe and colorful birds and butterflies gives very much the sort of feast tendered on that brisk November evening to General Grant, except that this one happens to be for a gala Christmas dinner. But the same specialties of the house prevailed: young bear, Maryland coon with Mephisto sauce, mallard ducks, partridges, leg of elk, prairie chicken, reedbirds in paper cases, and loin of buffalo, giving an authentic American flavor to the hot game course.

Even at Christmas oyster were *de rigueur,* the filet of beef was served *à la Financier,* the cold quail came in a "gallinteen" with truffles, and there was a festive English plum pudding flaming with brandy.

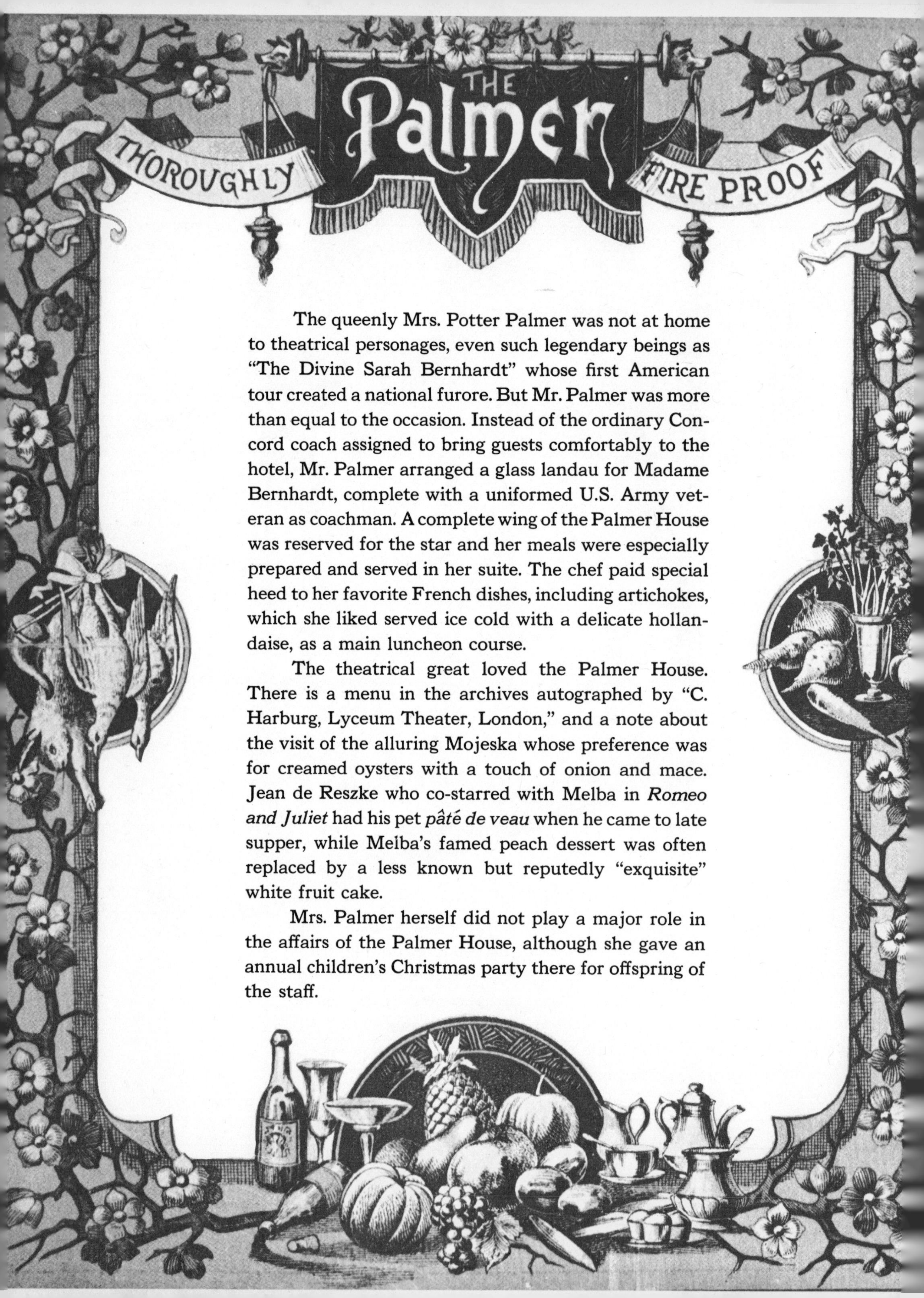

The queenly Mrs. Potter Palmer was not at home to theatrical personages, even such legendary beings as "The Divine Sarah Bernhardt" whose first American tour created a national furore. But Mr. Palmer was more than equal to the occasion. Instead of the ordinary Concord coach assigned to bring guests comfortably to the hotel, Mr. Palmer arranged a glass landau for Madame Bernhardt, complete with a uniformed U.S. Army veteran as coachman. A complete wing of the Palmer House was reserved for the star and her meals were especially prepared and served in her suite. The chef paid special heed to her favorite French dishes, including artichokes, which she liked served ice cold with a delicate hollandaise, as a main luncheon course.

The theatrical great loved the Palmer House. There is a menu in the archives autographed by "C. Harburg, Lyceum Theater, London," and a note about the visit of the alluring Mojeska whose preference was for creamed oysters with a touch of onion and mace. Jean de Reszke who co-starred with Melba in *Romeo and Juliet* had his pet *pâté de veau* when he came to late supper, while Melba's famed peach dessert was often replaced by a less known but reputedly "exquisite" white fruit cake.

Mrs. Palmer herself did not play a major role in the affairs of the Palmer House, although she gave an annual children's Christmas party there for offspring of the staff.

But Mrs. Palmer was far from the genteel female whose stiff proprieties and self-proclaimed purity characterized so many ladies of the period. She was gay and sophisticated. A talented linguist, she traveled widely and assembled a magnificent collection of French impressionist paintings as well as a collection of jade which she impatiently whisked from Chicago to her Paris home when she decided that her Middle Western friends were not quite up to appreciating the subtleties of Oriental craftsmanship.

She was sharply aware of the need for women to play a more active part in world affairs. As president of the Board of Lady Managers for the Columbian Exposition of 1893 she exhibited a rare talent for leadership, yet with such grace and finesse that a fellow manager said, "All the good fairies must have hovered over her christening."

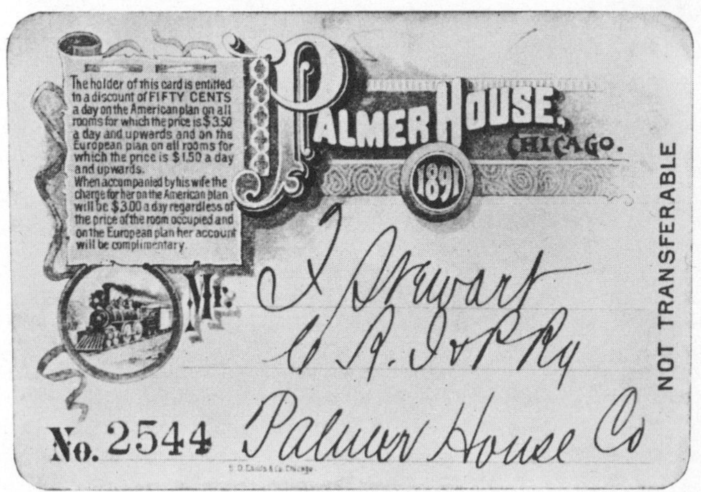

The holder of this card is entitled to a discount of FIFTY CENTS a day on the American plan on all rooms for which the price is $3.50 a day and upwards and on the European plan on all rooms for which the price is $1.50 a day and upwards.
When accompanied by his wife the charge for her on the American plan will be $3.00 a day regardless of the price of the room occupied and on the European plan her account will be complimentary.

PALMER HOUSE, CHICAGO.

1891

Mr.

No. 2544 Palmer House Co

NOT TRANSFERABLE

Certainly the glamorous Mrs. Palmer (shown above) must have approved when her husband's hostelry decided to encourage traveling husbands to bring along their wives, by the use of devices like this 1891 ancestor of the ubiquitous modern credit card. In addition to offering a fifty cent per day discount on American plan rooms costing $3.50 and up and European plan rooms above $1.50, the card offered a flat rate of $3.00 a day American plan, "regardless of the price of the room" to gentlemen accompanied by their wives. If the gentleman preferred the European plan, his wife's account "will be complimentary."

The bedrooms to which a gentleman and his wife were ushered were always comfortable, luxuriously carpeted, outfitted with the best of beds, bureaus, chairs, and tables. But they were not all as elegant as the state chamber pictured here, its floor to ceiling windows hung with cut velvet and lace, the massive carved bedstead, the frescoed ceiling with elaborate chandelier to augment the soft light from wall brackets. In the state chamber a fire blazed merrily in season and the glow

was reflected in the great pier glass over the mantel as well as in the full-length mirrors arranged for a lady's vanity and pleasure. Ballroom-size carpeting was needed for such a room, and the center table with its carved gilt legs and marble top was large enough for the elaborate breakfasts of the time . . . which might and frequently did see a cold game pie side by side with a broiled partridge, hot waffles, and delicate chops in curl papers as well as a choice of fifteen varieties of toast, rolls and sundry hot breads!

The Palmer House breakfast menu also had an elegant list of breakfast wines: Sauterne, Haute Sauterne, Medoc, St. Julien claret, and a white Chablis. These could be had for seventy-five cents per pint of Sauterne to three dollars and a half for the Chablis.

A jewel box of marble and glass, the Roof Garden of the Palmer House was an enchanting place for a promenade among the royal palms, the trailing vines, the hanging baskets and tubs of flowers and greenery. It is pictured here during the late 1870's, era of silk toppers, Prince Albert coats, canes and gloves for the gentlemen, bustles and bows and trailing skirts over gauzy petticoats for the ladies.

The old Palmer House sailed into the twentieth century with all the aplomb of Mrs. Potter Palmer herself. The silver dollars gleamed bright in the floor of the famous Palmer House barbershop run by W. T. Eden. The literary talk shone, too, when the hotel was host to the annual summer Book Fair Dinner was still moved forward to high noon on days when society attended the trotting meets. The procession of visiting royalty, statesmen, stars of opera and theater, and the rich and famous from everywhere continued during the half century of the old hotel's existence, and when it finally moved offstage, there was a fine Palmer House heritage to hand along to its successor.

Fred Harvey

"GOOD FOOD & SERVICE

"When you leave home, carry a good substantial lunch in your satchel, say, nice rusks, fruit, dried beef, cold chicken and a glass of jelly, all of which will last several days and be good as long as they do last."

So advised *Demorest's Monthly Magazine* in a how-to-travel-by-railway article. The year was 1878 and *Demorest's* had found restaurant meals "meagre" at most of the depots across the continent. The "ten-minute stop" for meals which was standard practice on trains meant a pell-mell dash for the lunch counter and a usually indigestible combination of cold food and bad coffee.

Yet two years before the article in *Demorest's* an event had taken place which in some ways was to have a more far-reaching effect than even the spectacular Centennial Exhibition in Philadelphia.

The event took place a thousand miles from the Centennial City, at one end of a wooden railway depot in Topeka, Kansas. It was the opening of the first Fred Harvey restaurant, in 1876. With it began a new concept in good food, good service, and comfort for the traveling public. People traveling weary miles in elegant Palace cars like the one pictured above were delighted to find Mr. Harvey's well-scrubbed little havens like the one in Topeka, pictured here in the 1880's.

Fred Harvey had good reason to know about the greasy steaks, bad coffee, and dingy lunchrooms available to railway travelers. For a time he rode the rails as a mail clerk and his digestion was none the better for the experience. The English-born Harvey, who had arrived in New York at the age of fifteen with something like ten dollars in his pocket, worked briefly as a dishwasher and once owned a small restaurant in St. Louis. The Civil War and typhoid fever switched his career to the post of mail clerk, but the business of serving bad food he still considered inexcusable.

TO THE TRAVELLING PUBLIC"

It took considerable persuasion to convince officials of the Sante Fe Railroad that his was a sound and profitable idea, but from the small lunch counter in Topeka, the Harvey standards of food and service sped right along from station to station. Now the trains stopped regularly at mealtimes and there was a Harvey House with a piping hot dinner for seventy-five cents. Typical was this Harvey Hotel (below) at Wallace, Kansas, in the 1880's.

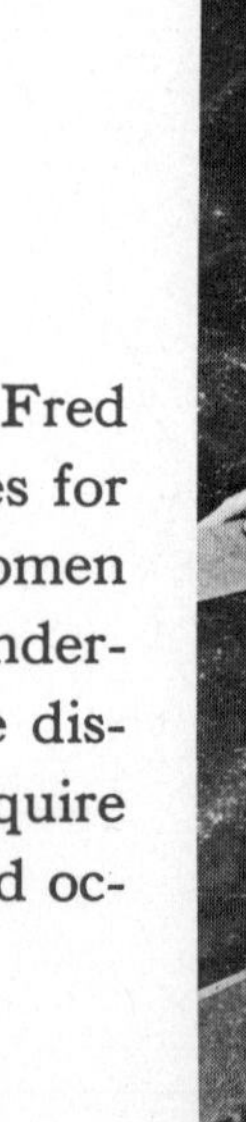

"The Great Civilizer" was a title the press often attached to Fred Harvey's name because he had not only civilized the eating facilities for the great train-traveling public, but also he had imported "young women of good character, attractive and intelligent" as waitresses. They underwent the knowing scrutiny of Mr. Harvey himself before they were dispatched to points west . . . there in a happy majority of cases to acquire husbands from the lonely ranks of rangers, ranchers, prospectors, and occasional young scions wandering afield in search of adventure.

"YOUNG WOMEN of GOOD CHARACTER, ATTRACTIVE & INTELLIGENT, 18 to 30"

Harvey Girls were domiciled in clean, properly chaperoned quarters where their gentleman callers were asked to leave their guns outside on the porch and not to "walk out" except to church on Sunday. At top, the girls wait in smiling readiness at the Syracuse, Kansas, lunchroom in the 1800's. Center, another neatly uniformed group at Chanute, Kansas, in the early 1900's, and last a winsome trio at Rosenberg, Texas, 1908.

PURE IS THE FOOD, PURER ARE THE GIRLS

Electric fans whir and the marble counter gleams in the noon sunlight as this Fred Harvey lunchroom in the Sante Fe Station at Houston, Texas, awaits its lunchtime customers (1880's).

If Fred Harvey demanded high standards of beauty, manners, and morality from his girls, he was no less sparing when it came to his food, his chefs . . . even his customers. No man was served in his dining room unless he wore a jacket. The shirt-sleeved customer had to be content with the lunchroom unless he would accept one of the jackets kept on hand for such emergencies.

The cuisine was justifiably praised for the first-rate meat which Fred Harvey chose himself; the local supplies of fresh eggs, milk, cream, butter, and poultry, the regional game and fish. Where the state or local laws did not forbid, Harvey restaurants offered an excellent wine list. The same applied to dining cars when the Harvey cuisine went aboard the rolling stock. In those dear dead days of fifty years ago and more the seventy-five cent special â la Harvey began with a purée of tomato soup, stuffed whitefish with potatoes, a choice of mutton, beef, pork, or turkey, small turnovers of chicken, shrimp salad, a choice of rice pudding, apple or cranberry pie, assorted fruits, fancy cakes, ice cream, and finally Edam and Roquefort cheese with crackers and French coffee!

Here is a Fred Harvey eating house at Guthrie, Oklahoma, in the 1890's. Note the contour swivel chairs, the immaculate counter. The indomitable Mr. Harvey had, indeed, revolutionized the business of eating en route, and when he was finally able to induce the Santa Fe to add dining cars with Fred Harvey food and Fred Harvey service, his menu did not exaggerate when it pictured the pioneer in his covered wagon on one side and on the other the traveler of less than half a century later ordering a complete dinner as his train sped him westward.

1892

The BROWN PALACE

When Denver's Brown Palace Hotel opened in 1892 a writer who remains happily anonymous described it as "unique . . . superb . . . a miniature world in itself," adding it had been only a few years since "the snowy gleam of tents was exchanged for the polished whiteness of marble; the flimsy canvas, swayed by every breeze, replaced by glistening granite, whose solid foundations fear not the fiercest gale."

In spite of this gentleman's verbal pyrotechnics, it is true that the Brown Palace was the most imposing building in the Rocky Mountains.

Denver, the "mile high city," decided to go even higher for the hotel's opening night banquet. Here the enormous horseshoe table of the Brown Palace is agleam with glass, damask, silver, and spun-sugar symbols of the Knights Templar for the "gallant men and beautiful women from every State in the Union" who journeyed to Colorado for their annual conclave and the debut of the Brown Palace. The banquet hall was atop the ten-story hostelry, which was christened Brown in honor of the man on whose farmland it stood and also lived up to its name in the warm color of Arizona sandstone and Colorado red granite. The banquet hall pictured at the top was sturdily bulwarked as may be seen in the center illustration showing the construction technique. Perhaps it was not, as our nameless press agent states it, "as enduring as the Pyramids of Egypt," but it was satisfactorily sturdy for its day. From the top-floor dining halls the hotel descended through parlors, suites, and more modest single rooms to the ground-floor rotunda. In this picture the lone patron reading his newspaper in the lobby is obviously unimpressed by the fireplace which "our man in Denver" explains was "an Arabian Nights fantasy of rare and beautiful gems." The gems were actually onyx from a Colorado mine, and the fireplace had two solid onyx columns weighing three thousand pounds.

A MILE HIGH

PARLOR BEDROOM

"Matrimony has been cynically compared to a gilded cage. Every one outside wants to get in —everyone inside wants to get out." Once again we are indebted to the inspired fellow who wrote the 1890's pamphlet intended to lure the public to the new Brown Palace. He was working up to a description, needless to say, of the hotel's Bridal Suite. He was anything but speechless when he walked into the parlor of the suite and found "Colorado's life-giving sunlight" pouring through the velvet-hung windows onto the flowered pale green carpet. The bed canopy, he decided, "might have been copied from a maiden's blush" . . . "the path of the bride is literally strewn with roses. . . . Hopeless old maids and bachelors would be legally justified in hanging themselves or each other, after a view of these lovely apartments."

& BATH

The Victorians were enamored of American plumbing and hotels of the period made a great thing out of the number of water closets, tubs, bathing chambers, and marble sinks available. But it is a rare thing to find such a detailed illustration of an 1892 bathroom as this one in the Brown Palace. Once again our pamphleteer explains that electric exhaust fans were installed to draw the air from bedrooms and baths . . . "so even if the stealthy microbe gains admission, instead of lurking in some dark corner until he can pounce upon his prey, he finds himself in a sort of maelstrom of fresh air and rapidly whirls onward and upwards till he presumably congeals in the frigid upper regions." Notable in the picture is the sitz bath, the pink marble washbasin, the shower, and the vase of peacock feathers.

A PEEK AT THE PEAK

The 1890's Brown Palace booklet from which we have been quoting featured this idyllic view from the top-floor dining room, with the shady streets of Denver stretching away toward a view of Pike's Peak in the distance and "a range of the Rocky Mountains over three hundred miles in extent . . . in all their glory of changing color." The dining room was two stories high with onyx wainscoting, stained glass panels above the windows, and pilasters and columns of stucco made to look like Oriental carvings.

"Fresh milk, rich cream and clover-scented butter" were guaranteed by the hotel's own herd of pedigreed Holstein-Fresians. On the same farm were immense vegetable gardens as well as hedges of blackberry, raspberry, and currant bushes and large strawberry beds.

The Irish linen, Haviland, Limoges, Royal Doulton and Dresden china, the cut glass, candelabra, and imported statuary all contributed to the cost of the Brown Palace, estimated at more than two million dollars. Banquets given in the sky-high dining halls matched the luxury of the hotel itself. Champagne, *pâté de fois gras,* caviar, quail, venison, Rocky Mountain trout all adorned the menus for seventeen-course "collations" which went on for hours to the music of two orchestras.

Buffalo Bill and the "Unsinkable Molly Brown" were among the headline making personalities who signed the Brown Palace register and enjoyed its views, its comfort, and its cuisine. Sir Harry Lauder's suite was filled with adoring visitors at all hours, but Mary Garden demanded privacy after her concerts. Evalyn Walsh McLean glittered as brightly in the lobby and public rooms as did her famed Hope diamond. And presidents, too, were partial to the Brown Palace. Starting with Theodore Roosevelt, who hunted and fished the Rockies with tireless Rooseveltian vigor, the Brown Palace was a favorite vacation spot for chief executives and their staffs, and during the Eisenhower administration became known as the Summer White House.

The PALACE...

San Francisco has always been a city of tall dreams. It began when the forty-niners headed west singing the theme song of the Gold Rush:

I came from Salem City
With my wash bowl on my knee.

I'm going to California
The gold dust for to see.

The San Francisco they found was only three years away from the sleepy little town of Yerba Buena with its population of three hundred living in adobe houses and shingle shacks. Gold shook the little village from its long nap in the sun and changed its destiny as quickly as its name was changed to San Francisco. By the time the brig *Eliza* set sail in 1849 from Salem, Massachusetts, with a gold-hungry crew of adventurers aboard, San Francisco was awash with tent saloons, makeshift frame sheds, mattresses for rent at three dollars a night (in the open air). Oranges from Tahiti sold for a dollar each; a plot of land with four apple trees for eight hundred dollars; potatoes were a dollar each, cooked, and you could get, if you were lucky, a slice of freshly baked bread for a dollar . . . plus another dollar if a blob of butter was added. One man milked his cow twice a day and sold the milk in whisky bottles, a dollar each.

The Palace Hotel was part and parcel of the dream . . . a perfect expression of the exalted state of mind that was San Francisco. Even the free-wheeling forty-niners wouldn't have taken a wager that in a quarter of a century their town would be adorned with such a crown jewel as the white and gold Palace, built at a cost of nearly five million dollars!

The Palace was always front-page news and the hectic scene below was a commonplace during the 1870's when the iron skeleton of the hotel was rising above the crazy-quilt pattern of the young city. The newsboys on horseback must have had a wilder race than usual on the August day in 1875 when William Chapman Ralston, entrepreneur of the Palace, learned that his Bank of California had failed . . . and so walked out to his death in San Francisco Bay. It was the end of a skyrocket career that began on Mississippi river boats and climaxed in a mansion down the Peninsula where he often entertained a hundred guests, seating them in small gold chairs for a musicale at the conclusion of which the wall at one end rose to reveal an enormous gaslit dining room with a pigtailed Chinese servant for each guest.

The Ralston tragedy tuned to a minor key the opening on October 2, 1875, of his dream hotel, and the main event of the evening was a tribute to his vision and courage by his partner, Senator William Sharon. There was quiet music from a string orchestra and everyone went home early to await the fanfare of the banquet on October 14 in honor of General Sheridan. "Little Phil" Sheridan had to climb on one of the banqueting tables "amid pyramids and castles of tuberoses, camellias and lillies" in order to be seen by the celebrant guests who were feasting on *Pâté de Canard à la Perigeaux, Artichauts à la Barigole, Becassines Anglaises, Poulet Rosolio* and *Pouding à la Diplomate.* The affair lasted nearly four hours. The Palace had indeed been opened.

PEARL OF THE PACIFIC 1875

Fit for a King...

AND KINGS THERE WERE

Less than six months after its opening, the Palace entertained its first visiting royalty in the person of Dom Pedro II, emperor of Brazil, who browsed through museums, went to the opera, and amiably handed out autographs. Perhaps the most lordly of the lot was the last king of Hawaii, David Kalakaua, welcomed with a salute of Navy guns and an artillery band in December of 1890 but fated to leave in less than a month, in a flag-draped casket with a funeral cortege of some fifteen hundred persons.

The Grand Court became the most famous hotel entrance in the world. Crowds filled the tiered galleries to look down into the brightly lighted court, brave with palms and echoing to music as a chariot with six white horses brought in General Ulysses S. Grant, whose arrival in the Golden Gate from the Orient had been watched by thousands atop Telegraph and Russian Hills and who was hero-worshipped by an adoring and nearly hysterical city.

The Palace was nearing its fourth birthday when Grant arrived in September of 1879. Songs were composed in his honor; parades, balls, dinners, and parties filled every waking moment; and, following his visit, came a regular *Who's Who* of Civil War generals, including Sherman, McClellan, West, Parker, Garrison, and Greeley.

In the 1890's, the Palace was at a pinnacle of prestige. Gentlemen in cutaways and four-in-hands met for lunch in the bar, an imposing room with a vaulted stained-glass ceiling with sunlight softly filtering through during the day and the glow of electric light suffusing it at night. The bar was mahogany and red marble, the fixtures bronze.

Shops occupied part of the lower floors, a chemist selling "English milkweed face powder, used exclusively in the courts of Europe" and another offering "silk veils . . . a genuine satisfaction in the high winds and dust." There was G. T. Marsh & Co.'s Japanese Emporium. In the summer of 1888, the *News Letter* reported that Mr. Marsh had been "arrested for exposing a nude figure in his window," and commented: "We are growing fearfully modest. At this rate even the luscious oyster will be compelled to appear on the half shell in bathing drawers."

"The fine residences on Nob Hill surpass anything we have in the East," wrote a visiting New Yorker in 1880, adding that "we are stopping at the Palace Hotel . . . by far the largest caravansary in the world and to my mind the best kept." She was waiting eagerly to "view their highnesses" from Nob Hill when they drove into the Grand Court in their polished carriages, traps, and phaetons for a dinner party or after-theater supper in the lovely colonnaded dining room pictured here. The Palace was *the* place to be seen for the budding Four Hundred of San Francisco whose social mores were being dictated by Edward M. Greenaway, brash "West Coast Ward McAllister."

WHEN NOB HILL DINED OUT

The sheer splendor of the Palace made it a prime target for satirists of the day. Said *Harper's Weekly* just before the opening:

"An exchange informs us that the head waiter at the new Palace Hotel, San Francisco, will wear a purple velvet suit, powdered wig, silk hose and pumps. He will receive guests at the dining-room door to the sound of opera music and gently assign them seats by a slight inclination of the head and a graceful wave of his hand. On Sundays he will walk on rosewood stilts . . ."

Even the *San Francisco News Letter* imagined a dinner with "all the entrees sprinkled with gold dust" and at the conclusion "Mr. Leland and Mr. Smith will enter . . . on solid bonanza silver velocipedes."

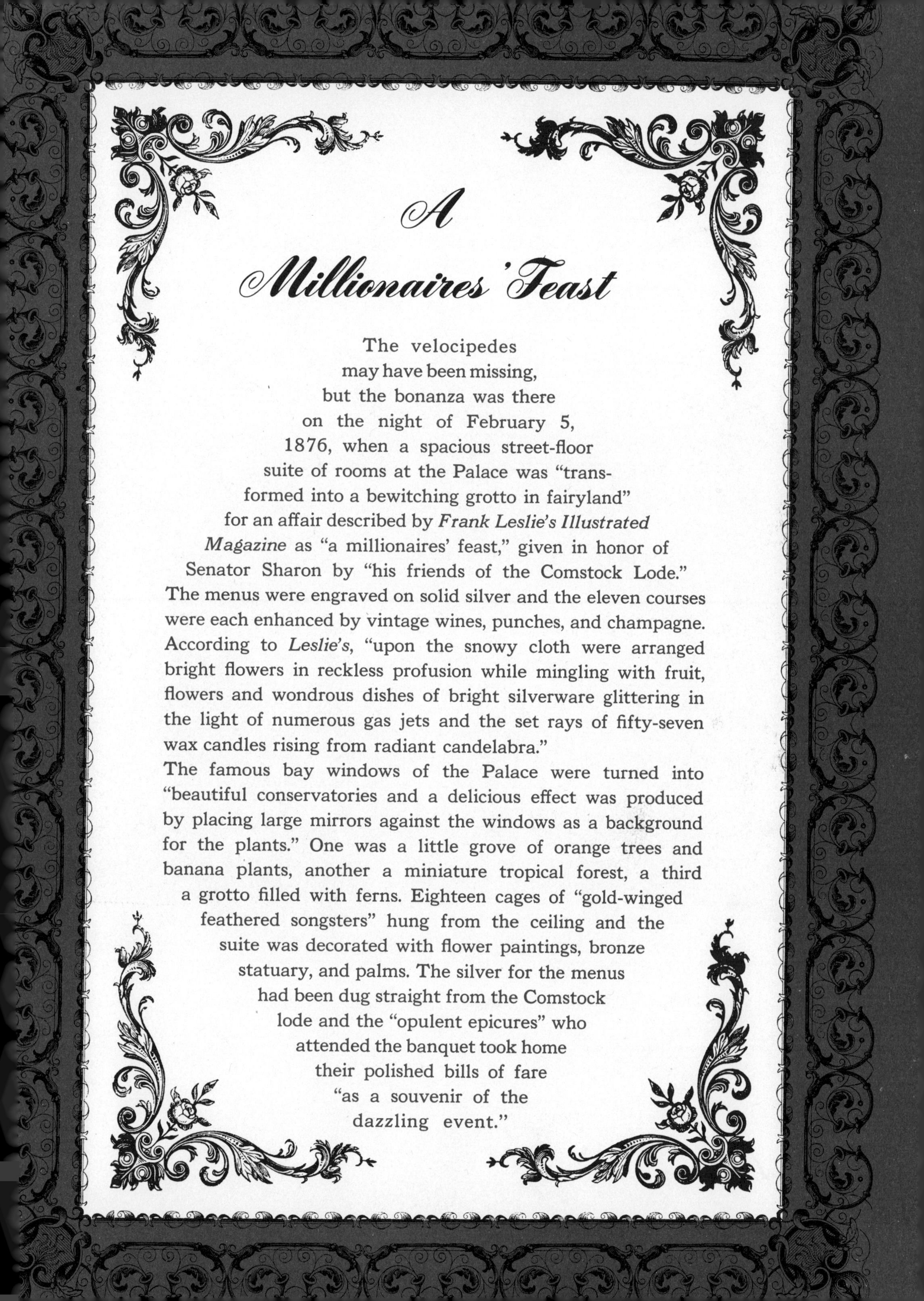

A Millionaires' Feast

The velocipedes may have been missing, but the bonanza was there on the night of February 5, 1876, when a spacious street-floor suite of rooms at the Palace was "transformed into a bewitching grotto in fairyland" for an affair described by *Frank Leslie's Illustrated Magazine* as "a millionaires' feast," given in honor of Senator Sharon by "his friends of the Comstock Lode." The menus were engraved on solid silver and the eleven courses were each enhanced by vintage wines, punches, and champagne. According to *Leslie's*, "upon the snowy cloth were arranged bright flowers in reckless profusion while mingling with fruit, flowers and wondrous dishes of bright silverware glittering in the light of numerous gas jets and the set rays of fifty-seven wax candles rising from radiant candelabra."

The famous bay windows of the Palace were turned into "beautiful conservatories and a delicious effect was produced by placing large mirrors against the windows as a background for the plants." One was a little grove of orange trees and banana plants, another a miniature tropical forest, a third a grotto filled with ferns. Eighteen cages of "gold-winged feathered songsters" hung from the ceiling and the suite was decorated with flower paintings, bronze statuary, and palms. The silver for the menus had been dug straight from the Comstock lode and the "opulent epicures" who attended the banquet took home their polished bills of fare "as a souvenir of the dazzling event."

"A COSEY CORNER"

The Grand Court had many "cosey corners" like this one where ladies might keep a rendezvous for luncheon or tea. Their comforts were well attended to by owner Sharon, proprietor Leland, and chef Jules Harder, whose culinary laurels had been won at Delmonico's in New York and the Grand Union in Saratoga. An especial delight of his female clientele was an omelet made with the delicate little West Coast oysters. They dressed to the nines, many in gowns like the carriage costume of the 1870's shown here.

Beneath the two-acre roof of the Grand Court passed a glittering procession of celebrities: Patti celebrating her forty-seventh birthday at a gala Palace dinner, where the menus were white satin and Patti's gown pink satin decked with diamonds; beauteous Lily Langtry arriving with thirty-two trunks; Sarah Bernhardt checking in with her pet baby tiger; Anna Held, Ellen Terry. . . .

And to the "ooohs" and "aaahs" of every female within miles, Sandow the Strong Man, in pink silk tights, held court in the Maple Room of the Palace.

DID CARUSO SLEEP HERE?

It's certain that the great tenor *did* sleep in the Palace on the fateful April night in 1906 which saw a brilliant performance of the touring Metropolitan Opera Company, Alfred Hertz conducting *Carmen.* The Opera House had been "a garden of roses and orchids and blossoming boughs," not to mention "the bloom on the cheeks of the fair patronesses and the sparkle of their jewels."

Just such a suite as the one above provided an abundance of comfort and perhaps an overabundance of decoration for the visiting opera stars. Ormolu, velvet, tasseled cushions, pier glasses in carved walnut, brocade, marble fireplaces, gilded harps, stuffed birds, and portraits made even the spacious, high-ceilinged parlors and salons look overcrowded. The stuffy Victorian and the elegant Edwardian were just beginning to sort themselves out when the events of April, 1906 did it for them, at least in the case of the Palace and most of the rest of the gay, unlucky city.

SAN FRANCISCO'S CALAMITY

The Palace survived the shattering earthquake of early morning, April 18, in regal fashion but the guests were mostly assembled in panicky disarray, Caruso said to be wearing pants and a Turkish towel and carrying his treasured autographed picture of Theodore Roosevelt. Outside was a chaos of twisted streetcar tracks, houses sliding downhill, buildings collapsing, bricks crashing into the streets, and everywhere bewildered people wondering where to go for refuge.

The ominous spirals of flame and smoke which rose to the morning sky from half a hundred spots in the city found the embattled defenders of the Palace ready for action, their system of pumps and private reservoir unimpaired by the quake. For a time it was a hopeful and inspiring sight to watch great jets of water spouting from the Palace roof as a wall of fire engulfed the entire business district.

But San Francisco's calamity was to be complete. By noon the Palace was deserted except for a gallant handful of men who stayed at the pumps until even the 675,000-gallon reservoir ran dry. Then the facade of bay windows glowed crimson as fire swept the Grand Court and raced through the cafes, corridors, and luxury suites.

The grim proclamation of Mayor Schmitz was tragically necessary.

PROCLAMATION

BY THE MAYOR

The Federal Troops, the members of the Regular Police Force and all Special Police Officers have been authorized by me to KILL any and all persons found engaged in Looting or in the Commission of Any Other Crime.

I have directed all the Gas and Electric Lighting Co.'s not to turn on Gas or Electricity until I order them to do so. You may therefore expect the city to remain in darkness for an indefinite time.

I request all citizens to remain at home from darkness until daylight every night until order is restored.

I WARN all Citizens of the danger of fire from Damaged or Destroyed Chimneys, Broken or Leaking Gas Pipes or Fixtures, or any like cause.

E. E. SCHMITZ, Mayor

Dated, April 18, 1906.

"Vale et Ave, Frisco," wrote William Marion Reedy in his pioneering little magazine, "the beautiful, the glad, the strong, the stricken, the invincible."

It might have been a requiem for the Palace.

But San Francisco, which Mr. Reedy delighted in as "a town of temperament in which lightness blent with a native beauty sense," began to rebuild almost before its smoking ruins had cooled. Down on Leavenworth Street at Post the Little Palace Hotel opened with twenty-three guest rooms on November 17, 1906, with as many more rooms in an annex across the street. The "Baby Palace . . . a neat little gem in a setting of dirty, jagged ruins," carried on while the old Palace was razed and a brave new structure rose on the same site.

The new Palace, all eight million dollars' worth of it, opened on December 15, 1909. As the San Francisco *Chronicle* noted, "Three years ago there was a tent restaurant on the old Palace lot serving coffee and sinkers to dusty laborers . . . Where in the stories of enchantment has imagination equaled this transformation?"

With a nice sense of drama, William Ralston's son opened the Palace with a golden key, and the key was then floated from the roof at the end of a cluster of balloons. Shining in the sun, it headed out through the Golden Gate.

"VALE et AVE..."

SIXTH COURSE

SWEET SUMMER OF RESORTS

"Suitable fishing tackle for those who may be fond of that amusement."

That was one of the inducements offered at the bucolic little retreat above, pictured in the late 1700's, only a few years after the Revolution. Even then summer-weary city dwellers were trying to get away from it all, traveling by horseback, carriage, or stage to bosky dells and breezy islands where inns provided them with food, outdoor fun, and ease of spirit. Macomb's Dam has long since vanished, along with the anglers, the innkeeper, and the inn itself; the site is now the crowded intersection of New York's Amsterdam Avenue and 155th Street.

A companion piece to Deagle's was Gray's Ferry, which opened in May of 1789. "A handsome Stage Waggon mounted on steel springs with two good horses" ran twice a day along the Schuylkill from the Indian Queen in Philadelphia to Gray's. There was "an elegant new House," surrounded with groves, arbors, "summer houses, alcoves and seats" and a greenhouse filled with "exotic plants in high perfection."

Over in Hoboken, New Jersey, Sybil's Cave was "the quickest resort of the New Yorkers" in the early 1800's. The Jersey shore was wild and rocky then with "walks, promenades and parks" surrounding the Grotto, and "overshadowed by the richest foliage."

Within a few decades these same New Yorkers were traveling far afield for their holidays. Sachem's Head Hotel at Guilford, Connecticut, which bragged that "mosquitoes are never seen at the Head," also announced proudly in May of 1860 that it was linked with the Tontine Hotel in New Haven by "a Telegraph line . . . which connects with all the lines in the United States."

Harper's Weekly continued full of advice to the vacationing public, along with handsome drawings of new resort hotels, pages of fashion illustrations showing what to wear on holiday, and articles on when and how much to tip.

New hotels were often front-page news. *Ballou's Pictorial* on July 21, 1855, gave its entire cover page to the Nahant Hotel in the city of that name in Massachusetts, then the most widely known watering place in the United States.

When the vacation fever had reached a national pitch, *Harper's* brilliant cartoonist, Thomas Nast, devoted his talents to the following interpretation of summer joys.

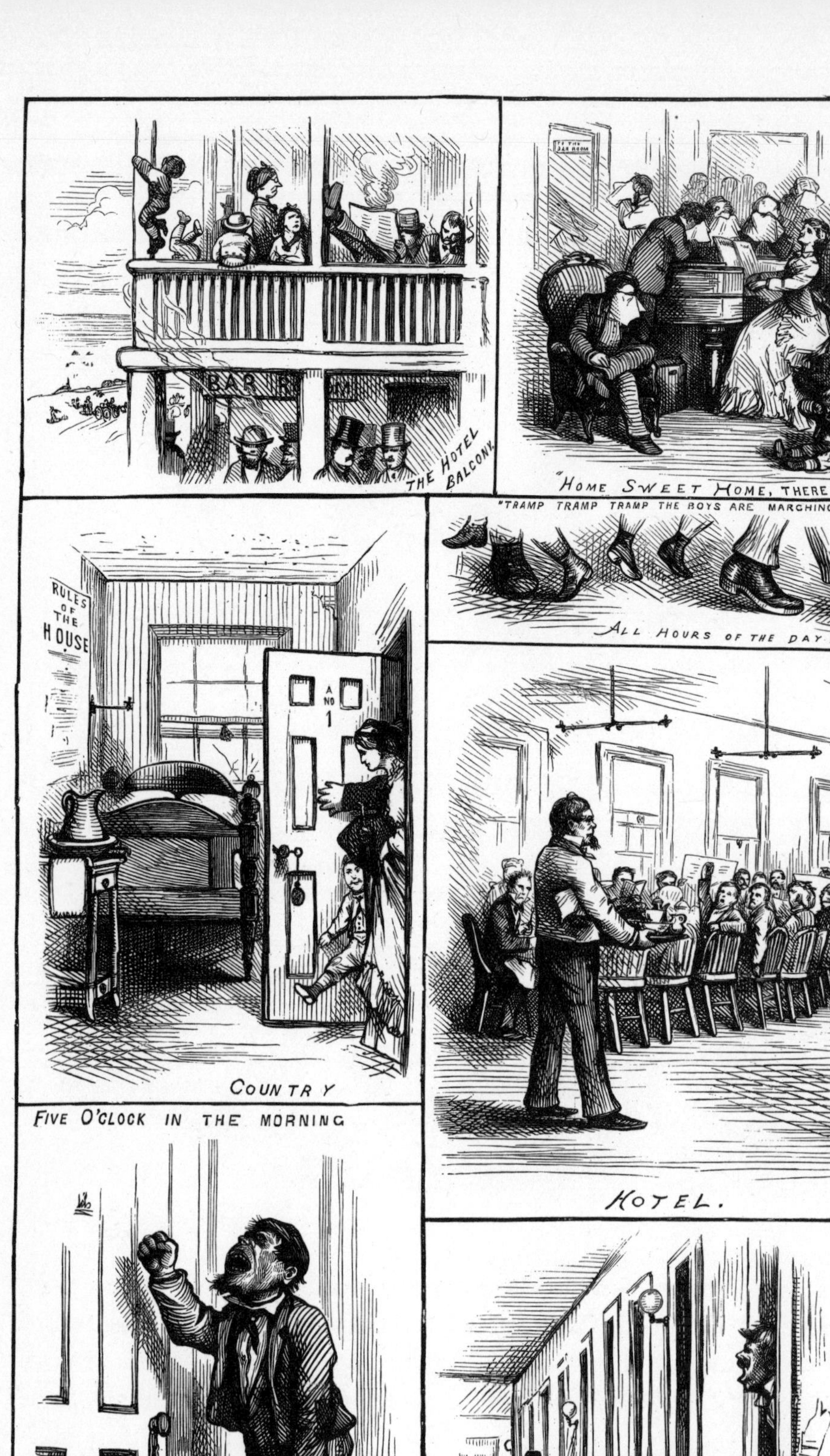
BAR R
THE HOTEL BALCONY.
"HOME SWEET HOME, THERE IS NO PLACE LIKE HOME."
"TRAMP TRAMP TRAMP THE BOYS ARE MARCHING."
ALL HOURS OF THE DAY AND NIGHT.
RULES OF THE HOUSE
A No 1
COUNTRY
HOTEL.

PUTTING UP

FIVE O'CLOCK IN THE MORNING
DEPARTURES FOR EARLY TRAINS

MAKING NIGHT HIDEOUS

GOING IN THE COUNTRY FOR
THE CHILDREN. — HEALTH. AND FASHION.
THE BALCONY AT HOME
EXPRESS
HOTEL
HOTEL.
"HOT AND COLD WATER"
BATH ACCOMODATIONS
TOWN.
"HOW GENTLY BREAKS THE MORNING"
HOME
Th. Nast.
AGAIN.
"WE WON'T GO HOME TILL MORNING."
"FIRST GONG" FOR BREAKFAST

The United States was just over a century old when these summer fashions appeared in *Demorest's Monthly Magazine*, indicating the sizable trunks required by milady if she planned to keep pace with the elaborate social ritual of the more elegant resorts . . . the morning promenade, the change of dress for luncheon and again for tea, for the formal dinners, musicales in the drawing rooms, *soirées dansantes*, and sundry other occasions such as picnics, clambakes, coaching balls, and receptions.

By this time, the summer of 1878, racing attracted a fast crowd at Saratoga, there was surf bathing at Long Branch, Coney Island, and other shore resorts. Newport glowed with social life and the Catskills were more popular than ever . . . all, according to *Harper's Weekly*, "never more serenely beautiful," Lake George, the White Mountains, Niagara, the Adirondacks, Lake Mahopac, Watkins Glen, Delaware Water Gap, Cape May, Old Orchard Beach, and "scores of other delightful localities." No wonder the editors concluded that at this time of year "proprietors of summer hotels begin to feel happy."

WHITE SULPHUR SPRINGS

THE PRIDE OF MR CALDWELL

13 DIFFERENT SALTS

The benefits of White Sulphur Springs were widely known even in Colonial times. In 1770, a Mrs. Anderson, tortured with rheumatism, was taken there and bathed in a hollow log filled with the water. People began coming in wagons from beyond the mountains, most of them camping out around the spring.

By the 1820's, White Sulphur—or, as it was affectionately called, the "White"—had launched its famous career as a resort. Men arrived on horseback, "carrying their entire 'springs' wardrobe in saddlebags, with a bottle or two of prime French brandy, a pack of cards, and a convenient pistol and rifle for venison or footpads."

Harper's New Monthly Magazine reported that, by the 1830's, "it had come to be known throughout the South that a true El Dorado or fountain of health and youth bubbled up in the Virginia mountains." . . . And to White Sulphur came "the wealthy old nabobs of James River and the shores of the Chesapeake, the elegant pleasure-loving country gentlemen of Maryland, and citizens of Baltimore" in their private carriages "drawn by six horses and driven by their portly black Jehus."

The spring, *Harper's* noted, had thirteen different, beneficial salts. It "bursts boldly from rock-bound apertures and is inclosed by marble casements." The resort was described as "a gem of natural loveliness—a tract of emerald meadows and foliage, encircled and embraced, as it were, by the loving arms of blue mountains . . . Nothing is more noticeable than the effect of a sojourn at the 'White' on the animal spirits."

The tall oaks shading the winding gravel walks and drives were "the pride and delight of Mr. Caldwell, the ancient proprietor." At his death in 1851 the leather-covered register of the "Old White" was a veritable *Who's Who* of Southern society and national politics. There was Henry Clay, who paid $4.50 in 1818 for three days' lodging and meals plus twelve cents a meal and the same for grog for his servant; there were Daniel Webster, Messrs. Calhoun, Van Buren, Fillmore, Tyler.

"But the war came at last, and the crowds no longer. The trim walks grew up in grass, the cottages went to decay, the hotel became a hospital . . ."

Recording this melancholy interlude, *Harper's* in its pictorial article on the resort in the year 1877 found it a greater success than ever before in its history, although the writer bemoaned "the fatal railway" which doomed the old stages and "shot you through in a Pullman Palace car" to the little valley in Greenbrier County, West Virginia which for so many years had been a peaceful "oasis in a desert of green and blue."

Now the "White" encompassed forty acres and the main hotel, pictured here, stretched four hundred feet at the heart of a complex of terraced cottages. Its plain, high-ceilinged dining room seated twelve hundred guests. Its cuisine was never fancy, but the kitchens were far-famed for hot breads and feathery biscuits. The bar (some claim it was here the Governor of North Carolina made that classic remark to the Governor of South Carolina), specialized in a mint julep made with brandy, loaf sugar, native mountain mint, and crushed ice plus whatever magic ingredient makes each mint julep the only genuine julep in the South.

PARADISE ROW...

The cottages, "their roofs brushed by the pendent boughs of laurels, maples, and the mountain ash," stood in long rows, each with its own name, such as Paradise Row, pictured here in the late 1870's. The style of architecture, known as "The Baltimore Cottage," was designed by John H. B. Latrobe, son of the Latrobe who rebuilt the Capitol at Washington and fathered a Gothic revival in this country.

The "Old White" continued to be a summer rendezvous for Southern belles and beaux and the scene of many gay parties, the most brilliant being the Lee Memorial Ball of 1877 given to raise funds for an equestrian statue to General Robert E. Lee. *Harper's* grew lyrical about this event:

"The little beauties, full of life and joy, with their sweeping trains, round arms, smiles, blushes and curls . . . natural or borrowed . . . are picturesque objects as they throng toward the ballroom, over the gravel-walks, or move in the waltz with the male-bipeds in dress-coats and snowy waistcoats, or promenade under the moon. Under the dazzling lights the sight is dazzling. The hours pass like dreams. And then toward dawn the white satin slippers pass again along the walks, lace handkerchiefs are waved in jeweled hands, tinkling laughter is heard under the oaks, gradually receding, and the ball is a thing of the past."

Harper's hastened to assure its readers that "frivolous amusement" did not always reign at White Sulphur and that "devout respect" was paid to the Sabbath when "profound quiet pervades the grounds . . . and the various places of worship are filled with attentive auditors."

In this charming scene at White Sulphur are two members of the "Billing, Wooing and Cooing Society" for which a group of young men wrote out a constitution on pale pink paper and posted it in the ballroom.

Symbolic of the summertime siestas on the verandas at the "Old White" are the mandolin and that "useful and pleasurable article," the hammock, both decorative accessories for the young lady, while the gentleman in the case seems to be depending upon his julep for courage. The activities of the couple may have been under surveillance by one Augustus Jenkins, Esq., who was a special correspondent for *The Glass of Fashion* and, according to *Harper's*, during his sojourn at the resort often stayed up very late at night so that next day there was "about his person a suspicion of morning cocktails." But he went about his duties, namely, "to interview every young lady he can scrape acquaintance with" and obtain descriptions of their smart summer wardrobes.

"Jenkins knows every belle, and what she is going to wear before she puts it on," added *Harper's*. "Her eyes and lips and figure are described with rapturous enthusiasm, and, spite of all the outcry made, it is doubtful whether this publicity is so distasteful to the subjects of it after all."

...AND PARADISE!

"...AND LOVERS PROPERLY PAIRED"

That was part of the recipe for a successful picnic luncheon, detailed by *Demorests's Monthly Magazine*, and this scene seems to indicate that the recipe has been followed enthusiastically by the six young guests of the "Old White."

Here, in "the little valley lost like a bird's nest in the foliage of the Alleghenies," were many delightful picnic spots, "with a spring bubbling up among the oaks and maples, blue mountains around and a fresh stream nearby."

Many romantically named walks led to picnic grounds near the hotel, and picnickers, choosing from Lovers' Walk, Courtship Maze, Acceptance Way to Paradise or Lovers' Rest, were usually accompanied at a discreet distance by one of the hotel staff bearing linens, hampers filled with food and wine, cushions, china, and silver.

For years the "Old White" succeeded in "preserving herself from the presence both of the *nouveau riche* and of Messrs. Tag, Rag and Bobtail," but finally, *Harper's* concluded, the Springs "lost their distinctive Southern character by the infusion of new elements . . . Change has begun."

And "change" made inroads deeper and deeper until in 1922 the hotel was torn down and famous "Old White" was just another, but gay and romantic, chapter in history.

SARATOGA

ueen

OF THE SPAS

"...THE CARS HAVE ROUNDED the last curve and speed on a homestretch for three miles, past the Geyser, whose crystal spray, thrown up forty or fifty feet, glistens in the sunlight as though Undine and her troupe of fairies were showering out a welcome to the coming guests . . . and now come the streets and houses of Saratoga and from the car windows we read in succession CLARENDON, GRAND HOTEL, GRAND UNION, CONGRESS HALL . . . There is an universal bustle—the whistle shrieks, the bell rings and the train slows up to the beautiful depot."

Thus was the expectant traveler by train ushered into "the most noted watering-place on the continent of America." The year was 1873 and Saratoga Springs was ringing with the carefree laughter of pretty women, the shouts of the racetrack crowds, the discreet murmur of male voices over the roulette and faro tables at the Club House.

The new United States Hotel "opened its great gates" in 1874 on the same site where fire had destroyed its fashionable predecessor. Its piazza stretched two hundred and thirty-three feet along Broadway. Its marble-floored lobby, pictured here, was a meeting place for bustling—and bustled—socialites arriving for the season and adorning the register with such names as Vanderbilt, Lorillard, Gould, Wanamaker, Flagler, and Plant. Regrettably the spa, in addition to attracting "the most wealthy, educated and refined Americans and foreigners," also "attracts those chevaliers who prey upon society wherever it is accessible, lavish in its expenditures, and free in its amusements."

Somewhat awed by the splendors of the great hotels such as the United States and Grand Union, *Frank Leslie's Illustrated Magazine* reported in 1875 that "not the Prater of Vienna nor the Unter der Linden of Berlin—not even the Champs Élysées of Paris—offer a more dazzling display of fashion, beauty and wealth than can be witnessed during the afternoon promenade on Saratoga's Broadway," which a staff artist portrayed elegantly in the drawing below.

August saw a garden party "in the beautiful grounds of the Grand Union . . . with simple outdoor sports, dancing on the lawn, music, refreshments and the ladies in walking dresses of light and gay colors."

The resort first flowered as a favorite vacation spot for aristocratic Southerners. In the antebellum years their great coaches rumbled north to the spa, carrying whole families and retinues of servants, with prized thoroughbreds in tow. The horses were raced in gentlemanly fashion on the old Oklahoma tract, with a gentlemanly wager or two made between friends. They drank the waters, danced at champagne balls in the old Congress Hall and the little three-story United States. Both hotels were important stops on the campaign trail of politicians during the 1830's and 40's. Henry Clay's barouche was hand-drawn down Broadway to the cheers of a holiday crowd, while his rival, Van Buren, escorted a bevy of lovely belles around town, . . . all helping to make August in Saratoga a joyous mixture of fun, intrigue, partying, and politicking.

"..."There's no place like Saratoga"...

And no place like the elm-shaded garden of the United States Hotel shown here in its opening year, 1874. There parasoled ladies and top-hatted gentlemen strolled beside the fountain, very probably discussing the latest arrivals in the hotel's luxurious cottage wing, an innovation of proprietors John Ford and James Marvin. The wing, stretching more than five hundred feet westward from Broadway, was divided into richly appointed suites of seven or eight bedrooms with bath and private parlor, offering "the pleasures and accommodations of an unexcelled Summer Resort and the seclusion and domestic comfort of a private dwelling." That the "pleasures" and "domestic comfort" sometimes included a mysterious "friend" or "cousin" . . . always female, always young, always beautiful... was a matter for raised eyebrows and whispered comment, but no open condemnation. The gentlemen concerned were too rich, powerful, and famous for ordinary censure.

The north porch of the United States became known as Millionaires' Piazza. There such moguls as Gould and on one occasion even John D. Rockefeller looked over the passing parade of Broadway, discussed vast financial deals, and conducted business via the hotel's telegraph line which connected with the Atlantic and Pacific Telegraph Company to reach "across the continent and around the world."

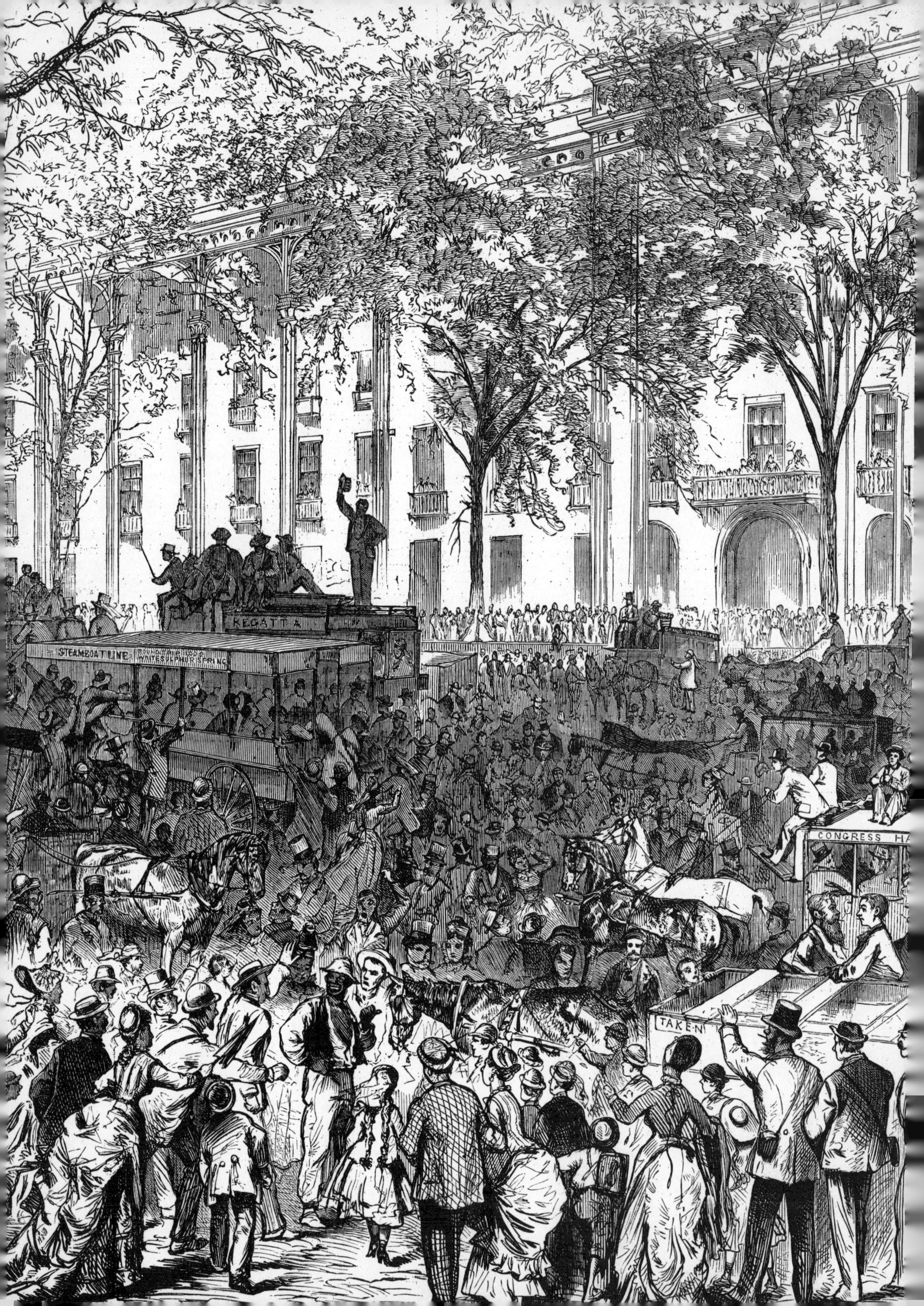
REGATTA
STEAMBOAT LINE
WHITE SULPHUR SPRING
CONGRESS HA
TAKEN

...AND LISTEN TO THE MUSIC OF THE BAND...

The morning concert on the Piazza of the United States Hotel was a time for casual listening and less casual discussion of the merits of the day's entries at the racetrack. It was also a time for making assignations as young ladies fluttered their fans and twirled their parasols, eyeing the young men considered to be the best "catches."

The early morning sun always found Saratoga astir for a draught of the medicinal spring water and a walk in the "tonic air" before breakfast. It was a ritual for the men to stop for a shine at one of the dozens of portable bootblack stands along Broadway, then to pick up a paper from one of the raucous little newsboys and perhaps buy a bag of famous Saratoga popcorn. The women and girls gravitated toward the glittering show windows of Tiffany or the jewelry shop of the enterprising and illiterate Dreicer. Legend has it that Dreicer walked out of his shop in the Grand Union Hotel one afternoon carrying a tray of expensive baubles which he proceeded to offer with his compliments to the ladies on the piazza. If true, it was a gesture quite in keeping with the exuberant, extravagant Saratoga of the late nineteenth century. The gentlemen did not yield to the ladies in glitter; rubies and sapphires sparkled on their fingers, tie pins, cuff links, and vest buttons were diamond-studded, walking sticks and canes were topped with gold and silver.

...UNPACKED SARATOGA TRUNKS...

The bulky Saratoga trunk with its curved top was the only possible answer to the elaborate wardrobes brought to Saratoga Springs. There had to be room for ruffles and flounces and bustles, acres of petticoats, bonnets and parasols for every occasion, dinner dresses and ball gowns, many bearing the unmistakable chic of the great Paris couturiers. *Demorest's* fashion columns reported that "white dresses are more than ever fashionable for morning and day as well as evening wear. Out of eight dresses made for one lady to take to Saratoga, seven were white and some were masses of lace and muslin or muslin and embroidery . . . All were made entirely by hand, that being the *ne plus ultra* of elegance."

Little wonder that ladies of the 1870's and 80's had no worry about being lost in the Saratoga crowds. They were pretty as nosegays, delicate as porcelain figurines.

But their escorts were just as visible in the Broadway promenade. A far cry from the modern male in his monotone worsteds and flannels were the Saratoga dandies in striped pants, vests of bright velvet or silk, boutonnieres, gloves, and sticks. In the late years of the

century their female companions adopted a gait known as "the Saratoga walk" . . . shoulders back, chest forward, chins up, stomachs in . . . "and then walk, wiggling head, limbs, body and especially the bustle."

Much speculation attended who would wear what and when. One time the noted Beau Brummel, Berry Wall, caused as much excitement as a stakes race by bringing a wardrobe of forty suits to Saratoga and claiming that he could wear them all in one day. He couldn't have done much more from early morning to late evening than change clothes, make a brief appearance, and retire to change again. But it is part of Saratoga's annals of high jinks that he did bring it off, entering the ballroom in correct evening attire to the applause of a crowd which had been wagering one way or the other all day long. On another occasion the world-renowned jockey Tod Sloane is said to have arrived at Saratoga complete with valets and a dozen trunks. Diamond Jim Brady brought twenty-odd Japanese houseboys to keep his wardrobe, his capacious self, and his suite in proper order.

Visiting writers and editors were forever criticizing Saratoga modes and manners—as though Saratoga cared a whit. One commentator decided in the late 1870's that the women at Saratoga "are educated to show off . . . They are veneered with the silver and gilt of a superficial education, perhaps to bait some luckless man on to matrimony."

A. E. BLITZ. GRA: DES. RUE DES ECOLES. 1 PARIS

"SARATOGA SPREADS ITSELF BRAVELY"

The food was passable, the quantities enormous, the table manners deplorable in Saratoga's early days. Guests at Union Hall in the 1860's staged a helter-skelter scramble into this barracks-like dining room the minute the gong rang. As can be seen here, dishes were often stacked on the floor as waiters rushed to keep up with hearty appetites and a rapid succession of "sittings."

All that began to change in the later years of the century as skilled chefs took over the cuisine in the spa's luxury hotels and fine restaurants. Then came terrapin and partridge, turtle soup, wild duck seared over open coals, broiled lake fish, lobster and salmon, champagne and more champagne.

The colored waiters were jewels of courtesy and swift, knowing service. They knew their clientele and their clientele rewarded them amply. One headwaiter, John Lucas, who made his reputation at the Grand Union, left an estate of sixty thousand dollars when he died.

Saratoga chips were perhaps the most famous food innovation, and many are the tales attendant upon their origin. Most widely accepted is the one attributing them to a chef and restaurateur named George Crum of Moon's Lake House, who, when a diner requested that his French fried potatoes be a bit thinner, cut a batch tissue-thin, dropped them in the hot fat . . . and lo, the first Saratoga chip!

After mass eating and "mile-long tables" gave way to damask, silver, crystal, fine china, and gourmet bills of fare, Saratoga waiters vied with each other to fold the serviettes in fanciful shapes, a favorite being the flower basket with its points turned up, then renamed the Saratoga Fold.

In the 90's, the "Philadelphia Cooler," invented by A. D. Kippe, bartender at the United States Hotel, was all the rage in Saratoga. *The Steward's Handbook* noted that "as it is made of champagne and costs something like a dollar a drink, it fitly represents the two main characteristics of the season—champagne drinking and extravagant pleasures."

The *Handbook* also advised that a favorite Saratoga breakfast dish among the ladies was "strawberries served on a hot morning from a block of clear ice, the berries dropped into a well in its center, surrounded by a cluster of yellow roses or ferns . . . Also muscatel grapes powdered with crushed ice and anointed with sparkling wine." A perfect send-off for a day of promenades, carriage parades, racing, dining, and attending the nightly concerts or hops.

"The Alpha and Omega of the daily Saratoga programme, is to drink and dance . . . the one in the earliest possible morning, and the other at the latest conceivable night," a traveler of 1857 observed. Things had not changed much when an artist from *Frank Leslie's Illustrated* sketched this gala night in the ballroom of the Grand Union in 1876, just after the death of Manhattan merchant prince A. T. Stewart who had owned the hotel for four years. The mammoth allegorical painting on the ballroom wall, "The Genius of America," executed by the artist Adolph Yvon for Mr. Stewart's New York mansion, proved too large and consequently was sent, all three thousand pounds of it, to the Grand Union. Between dances, guests might stroll through the mirrored parlor (left), marveling at the novelty of a hotel illuminated by electricity.

BOSTON DIPS & SARATOGA BENDS

After the ball it was Morrissey's gilded Club-House for the gentlemen, where to the whir of the roulette wheel and the click of chips they gambled away the rest of the night and sometimes a good deal of the morning. John Morrissey had a stunningly beautiful wife and a past which included a gaudy career as prize fighter, politician, and gambler. By 1871, the time of this scene in his brightly lighted, velvet-draped gaming room, the racetrack he was instrumental in founding had brought added éclat to Saratoga in the persons of eminent breeders of the thoroughbred . . . August Belmont whose flashy four-in-hand was an everyday August sight along Broadway; Pierre Lorillard, Travers, Jerome, various Whitneys and Vanderbilts. They were all familiar figures at the Club-House, where no woman was ever permitted beyond the drawing rooms and dining salons.

...THEN TO MORRISSEY'S

The flamboyant Jim Fisk once brought the entire band of New York's Ninth Regiment, National Guards, to Saratoga and of course to Morrissey's where they played martial music, ate, drank, and gambled until Fisk decided that the social atmosphere was slightly chilly and moved, band and all, to his pet New Jersey resort, Long Branch.

Morrissey (whose nickname "Old Smoke" dated from an unfortunate scuffle over a ladylove, ending in John being held on a hot stove lid by his opponent) lived right up to the pace of his casino and his racecourse. He fancied striped trousers, tail coats, white kid gloves and diamond solitaires. He hated it when ill health took away his zest for early breakfast of steaks, chops, and omelets. He would have hated it even more had he known that his death in 1878, at the age of forty-seven, occurred on the eve of Saratoga's greatest years of splendid extravagance.

Jockeys exercising their horses prior to the race (*Frank Leslie's Illustrated Newspaper,* 1875)

TURF SOCIETY

It was enchanting on an August noonday when the velvety lawns around the Saratoga racetrack bloomed with garden parties, when thoroughbreds tossed their heads under the ancient elms as they were saddled for the next race, when champagne bubbled inside gay striped tents, and when the road to the track was a dust-whirl of four-in-hands, tallyhos, barouches, drags, and other shiny equipages carrying the celebrities of society, the theater, and politics. Women spent hours over their racing costumes for the day. One, described by a reporter from *Demorest's* in 1879,was "of cream-colored linen, very coarse, embroidered with birds in red wool . . . The necktie was of red foulard, and the straw hat was trimmed with a batiste handkerchief with red stripes." The wearer carried a red parasol. Another was a short costume of white flannel, "trimmed with loops of black velvet, and the hat was that known as the 'Beef Eater,' of ivory chip, the brim lined with black velvet."

A start for the mile and three-quarter dash

Saratoga's old track, Horse Haven, opened in 1863, and the new track, still in use today, was inaugurated in that fateful Civil War year, 1864, with the running of the venerable Travers Stakes which was appropriately won by the great racehorse Kentucky, then owned by William R. Travers and a few months later by Leonard W. Jerome.

Both Mr. Travers and Mr. Jerome were leaders of the "turf society" which brought American racing and thoroughbred breeding to high prestige. Flat racing, steeplechasing and trotting were all fashionable pursuits, and at Saratoga the "sport of kings" was safeguarded by "the irreproachable character of its officials."

The pump in the betting ring at Saratoga was popular on hot August afternoons. Frank Sullivan, the famous columnist, was "pump boy" there when he was very young, and remembered one day when Lillian Russell came to his pump, reached for the cup, drank, and said,"My, it's good! Thank you, little boy." Miss Russell was, he remembered, "regal, but never haughty, generously allowing one and all to bask in the refulgence of her opulent, peaches-and-cream perfection . . . you felt sure that never in her life had this placid Aphrodite denied herself a broiled lobster with butter sauce or a second helping of creamd potatoes . . ."

Leonard W. Jerome

"A new era in American racing" was ushered in, according to *Harper's Weekly*, by such men as Mr. Jerome, D. D. Withers, the Dwyer brothers, J. B. Haggin, the Honorable William L. Scott, A. J. Cassatt, and Mr. Belmont.

As a fleet little two-year-old filly, Mr. Haggin's Firenze made her debut at Saratoga in August of 1886, winning five of her eight starts and charming the female contingent by her brilliant performances. Firenze went on to delight her followers by running second to the formidable Laggard in the Omnibus Stakes, at the same time beating the great Hanover who had nosed her out in a previous race, and finally climaxing her career by scoring a win over The Bard in the Freehold Stakes at New Jersey's Monmouth track. Firenze easily earned her title, "Queen of the Turf." As her admirers said about the stouthearted bay mare, "on a good day she could always beat the boys."

To Saratoga in the late 1800's came Lucky Baldwin, bringing his own coach-and-four across the continent. His rule was that only pretty women might ride with him to the track or out to the shady lake to "pretend to fish."

The betting was as high, wide, and handsome as the patrons themselves. The story of one day in the life of John W. "Bet-A-Million" Gates has gained momentum over the years, but it is fairly certain that he did lose close to half a million dollars in a single day at the Saratoga track, then proceeded to the gambling casino run by Morrissey's successor, Richard Albert Canfield, where he dropped another hundred thousand or so, asked to have the stakes raised along about midnight, and by dawn had won back everything he had lost at roulette and half of his racetrack losses!

The filly Firenze

21 SPRINGS

"The health-giving Springs of which the fame of Saratoga has been born, however much Fashion may have since nursed it, are all in or very near the village." A Saratoga guidebook of the 1850's thus reassured the seeker after health, adding a long list of the merits of the various waters where once "the Indian resorted for relief when laboring under disease."

But it was old Gideon Putnam who first realized the commercial value of what is now Congress Spring, and in 1804 opened his Union Hall and bought up more acreage and laid out a street one hundred and forty feet wide, appropriately named Broadway.

By 1829 signs were notifying an eager public that here was "Saratoga water—all you wish for five cents." Hathorn Spring, pictured above a half century later, was one of the most popular at the spa. In the cool and early morning hours attendants at Hathorn were busy ladling out the water from the fenced-in spring and handing it to customers at the railing, many of whom downed twenty glasses before breakfast. Judging by the breakfast menus of the time, the principal effect was to perk up appetites. The Grand Union started its guests on hot cereal and progressed through fried lake fish, steaks, cutlets or chops, omelet, cold roast beef or ham, French fried potatoes, six kinds of breads, griddle cakes with syrup, coffee, chocolate, or tea, and a choice of breakfast wines! The ritual morning promenade would seem to have been less by choice than by digestive necessity.

Some of the springs were on hotel grounds and reserved for guests. Congress Spring Park, however, was civic-owned,and in the amusing little pavilion pictured in the first of the sketches a band played morning concerts for the promenaders. The next scene is the noted Columbian Spring, excavated and tubed in the early 1800's with Jotham Holmes' Columbian Hotel conveniently near. A few yards from Congress Spring Pavillion, pictured in all its stained glass splendor with a carved "water bar" stood the sprawling Congress Hall Hotel surrounded by a shaded park.

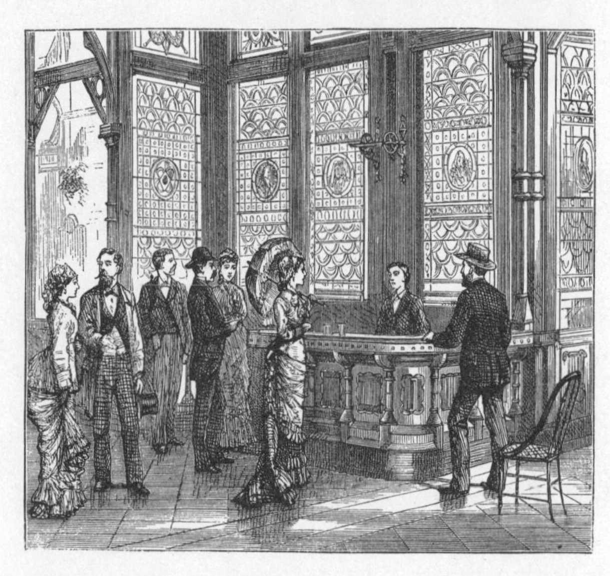

For a few stiff-laced years in the early 1800's a temperance society tried to make sure that Saratoga visitors drank nothing stronger than the waters, that orchestras played only hymns, and that dancing, that "unseemly pastime," was not tolerated in the hotels. This moral climate could not survive the take-over of the spa by pleasure-loving Southerners to whom good food and wine, light flirtation, and a lively polka were a way of life. Nor did later hell-fire preachers have any lasting effect on the high-living set which came to Saratoga in August for racing, gambling and fun.

21

CONGRESS SPRING

COLUMBIAN

WASHINGTON SPRING

CRYSTAL SPRING

GEYSER

GLACIER

ELLIS SPRING

HATHORN SPRING

PUTNAM SPRING

PAVILION SPRING

UNITED STATES SPRING

FLAT ROCK

HIGH ROCK

STAR

SELTZER

RED SPRING

"A" SPRING

EXCELSIOR

EUREKA

WHITE SULPHUR

TEN SPRINGS

"The Baden-Baden of America" was the title conferred upon Saratoga by *Harper's Weekly* (1890) featuring this end-of-season scene in one of the pavilions at the spa. "Saratoga reflects our national traits to a degree not quite true of Newport. The latter has an air of aristocratic seclusion less lively than that engendered by the commingling of classes at Saratoga . . . Amidst the whirl of gayety and frivolity and the dizzy rattle of fashion, there is an element which furnishes a substantial feature . . . noble-looking old men and sweet-faced gray-haired women give tone and quality to the wealthy rabble."

This then was old Saratoga, "a social microcosm in which our national traits were so happily portrayed in miniature."

TO THE MOUNTAINS...

Choosing a precarious perch for primping while her escort halloos from a clearing, she waits as her friends scramble up the rocky trail to have their turn at angling for a brook trout. Enormous summer hotels at this period, the late 1870's, were rivaling the spas and seaside resorts, and many sent their own stages to the nearest railroad depot to transport their guests over the steep and rocky roads.

...AND THE LAKES

The lake steamer is evidently bringing a very special visitor to the shores where a young belle of the season of 1875 waits in a leafy lookout, her curls carefully arranged, straw walking hat in hand. Lakeside hotels were springing up as rapidly as mountain resorts for a suddenly vacation-minded America, made aware by news stories, books, and advertisements of the natural beauties of their fair land.

...A PLETHORA OF PALMS

"NO INTOXICANTS ARE SOLD," states a booklet describing the Sterlingworth Hotel on the shores of Lake Chautauqua in upper New York state. And surely none were needed if the place looked anything like the palmy dreams of the artist who created these interiors. The booklet, happened upon in the famous Bella C. Landauer collection at the New York Historical Society, proved irresistible to the authors of this book. They felt that its slightly insane charm deserved a place in the annals of the nineteenth-century summer resort.

This drawing, complete with grand piano and full orchestra, is apparently meant to make quite sure that everyone knew the Sterlingworth was equipped with "incandescent electric lights for illumination." Daily chamber music was played by a "recherche orchestra in harmony with the refined tastes of its patronage." Even on a quiet day the sheer mass of indoor foliage must have given the Sterlingworth a frenetic air ... palms in elaborate vases, palms swaying over fountains, palms waving from balconies.

The ubiquitous fronds and fountain also adorned the Conservatory Cafe, pictured here on a summer afternoon when ice creams, lemonades, and soda water were quaffed by the temperate visitors.

The Sterlingworth made news in the resort world by inaugurating a winter season, and here is the artist's version of guests enjoying a sun bath in November. As the proprietors put it, "the charms of the late autumn, with the fine fishing, excellent driving, perfect scenes and restfulness . . . make the winter season, once pronounced a folly, a demonstrated success." Our uninhibited artist really let himself go on the giant palm in the foreground which must have effectively screened the sunshine pouring into the solarium.

The Sterlingworth management assured its guests that the kitchen was "detached, only one story and practically fireproof." Judging by the smoke and steam spouting forth in this scene it is as well that the place *was* both detached and fireproof. Proceeding with the reckless abandon which characterizes his approach to palms, our artist here provides ten assistant cooks for the moustachioed chef. "Famous Sterlingworth Spring Water" was used for all the cooking and for mixing the non-alcoholic fruit drinks and punches. Detached kitchens required waiters fleet enough of foot to get the food to table still reasonably hot and to whisk back the dishes from each course, on the ready to deliver the next one.

Once a party of "well-known capitalists, about seventy in number" is said to have arrived late in the evening after a day in which they "had been feasted, receptioned and banqueted to the limit of endurance." Wishing only a simple meal, the group found itself being served "a really elaborate and expensive banquet in ten courses. The guests intended to be honored sat down and managed to contain their impatience while course after course was rushed in." After two hours of this, they "incontinently rose, locked the doors that led from the kitchen, marched out and went to bed."

...AND COOKS GALORE!

...AND SO TO BED!

The writer of the Sterlingworth's promotion copy gave up any hope of finding adjectives to describe this room. He simply labeled it "Tower Bedroom" and let it go at that. If it looked anything like this, it deserved to be transported, down to the last lace pillow, to a museum of Victoriana. Potted plants, cherubim atop the carved bedstead, statuary, frescoed circular ceiling . . . a guest certainly needed all her own frills and ruffles to complete with the décor. And in keeping with the customs of the late nineteenth century, she probably brought at least a trunkful of costume changes. If she read her *Demorest's Monthly Magazine* faithfully, she learned that "early rising, a clear conscience, regular food . . . and light, comfortable clothing are the conditions of appreciative and intelligent enjoyment of the sweetness, the light, the warmth and the transcendent loveliness of an American summer . . . Lying around doing nothing but eat and drink and sleep is not intelligent enjoyment."

"A free heroic coach" was offered to take guests from the Erie Pullman vestibule coaches to the Sterlingworth, which is pictured here with all the turret towers where the lacy boudoirs were located. Perhaps someone still remembers the old Sterlingworth in its heyday. Perhaps it even looked something like this. But if only part real and the rest fancy, its rococo decor is symptomatic of the late nineteenth-century determination to provide summer guests with more and more of everything.

"Where shall we go this summer?" asked the endless pages of advertisements setting forth the pleasures of the Thousand Islands, Lake Champlain, the Adirondacks and Catskills, Lake George, the Berkshire Hills, Richfield Springs, and a hundred others. Travel articles filled the columns of *Harper's, Demorest's,* and other publications. Berkshire Springs in the hills of Oswego County, New York, offered "six lovely lakes . . . in a striking and picturesque framework of hill and wood and dale." Lebanon Springs, with mountain and valley landscape of "indescribable beauty," would also cure "Liver Complaint, Dyspepsia, Rheumatism and nervous diseases." Scenic wonders such as the flume in the White Mountains, were called the "lions" of the resorts; a major "lion" was Mount Washington and there were daily excursions there as well as to Echo Lake and Diana's Bath.

But as the Eastern resorts became more familiar and easily accessible, the mountains and lakes of the far West took on an allure for the adventurous. It became very chic during the nineties to forego a summer trip to Europe and take a transcontinental train west to "see America first."

PIKES PEAK

The DREAM BEGINS...

Colorado had been a state for less than a decade when Count James de Pourtales caught his first awed glimpse of Pikes Peak rising from the great Central Plains. The young German nobleman spent several enchanted days along the trails of South Cheyenne Cañon. The unspoiled land and aromatic air were, for him, the start of a dream. More people were coming to Colorado every year to climb the "greatest mountain in the world" and Count Pourtales decided to skim the cream from this new tourism, offering them luxury amusements as well as a "battalion of burros" . . . docile little creatures like those pictured on the preceding page during a Pikes Peak climb of the 1880's.

Looking much as he does here, with wide-brimmed hat, trim beard and pointed mustache, the count was a familiar figure as he strode over his acres and planned, in this jewel-like setting at the foot of the Cheyenne Mountain, to establish a sort of American Monte Carlo. He built an artificial lake, platted wide streets and avenues, and christened the place Broadmoor.

FIRST FLOWERING

The handsome Georgian-style casino which rose on the shore of the lake had two special assets . . . the count's young wife, a celebrated continental beauty, and the count's cellar of vintage wines and imported liquors. The countess was famous for her pearls and her Paris gowns and hats, elegant ensembles such as the one she wears in this portrait painted during the casino days.

Colorado Springs at the turn of the century was the scene of spirited polo and cricket matches and of afternoon tea on the clipped lawns of the casino, where the name Broadmoor was spelled out in bright flower beds. The titled Englishmen who made the place their favorite resort in America brought their customs with them as well as their spirited horses and Savile Row clothes. They cycled on the mile-long bicycle path, rowed on the lake, enjoyed the casino's spacious parlors and reading rooms and, not least, the well-appointed bar.

When the casino burned in 1897, a more modest structure took its place. But Count Pourtales was off in pursuit of another dream, and this time it came richly true in Arizona mining properties. He and the countess went back to the ancestral estate in Silesia, and the lake and lawns of the Broadmoor lay quiet in the sun, waiting for another dreamer to come along.

FROM CRIPPLE CREEK..

"The mountains are solid gold," was the creed of a quiet cowhand named Bob Womack who had first discovered rich gold floating in the area of Cripple Creek in 1878. Most people thought Bob was crazy, but he lived to see four hundred and seventy-five mines staked out and more than fifty thousand people setting up overnight towns of tents, paper shacks, false-front saloons and dancing halls as the drifts, stopes, and glory holes yielded their treasure.

A young Philadelphian, Spencer Penrose, was given a third interest in a mine called Cash-On-Delivery, the balance being held by his boyhood friend, Charles L. Tutt, Sr., whom he was visiting in Colorado

Italian marble, hand-painted ceilings, Della Robbia tile, carved and painted beams, and a treasure in paintings and Oriental art made the Broadmoor a conversation piece for the whole country. Below is the dining room and at right a scene on the lantern-lit terrace by the lake on opening night.

...TO CAVIAR!

Springs. Eventually the operating group included the gentlemen in the photograph above, taken in the boom year of 1892. Fifth from left is Spencer Penrose.

In the years just before World War I Messrs. Tutt and Penrose decided the time had come to make the Pourtales dream come true. They kept the name bestowed by the count on his lovely acres, but they spelled it with a small "a" . . . BROaDMOOR . . . as their special trademark. It was a name to become synonymous with luxury, with superlative foods and wines, and with a clientele which included the rich and the famous from nearly every corner of the world.

The JEWEL of the ROCKIES

Even the loftiest visions of Count Pourtales could not have measured up to this idealized painting of the BROaDMOOR executed by Maxfield Parrish. The artist is said to have protested the "moving" of the Cheyenne Mountain for theatrical effect, but his painting nevertheless does capture the beauty and drama of the resort and its sky-high park on the rim of the Rockies.

By the turn of the century,when the old casino was still a fashionable place to go, the winter season was just gaining popularity. A *Harper's Weekly* journalist, arriving in Colorado Springs for the first time, sent a rapturous report back home:

"Imagine the world flooded with warm sunshine, the mountains standing clear against a cloudless sky, a trap and a horse, a fur cape for coming home, a companion you like and a drive over the mesa. On one side the plains stretch out as far as you can see—like the ocean —on the other you can stretch out your hand to the mountains. The pale yellow wheat blows up and down on the plains, and the shadows and sunlight play up and down on the mountains. The road is hard and firm. There is the wood fire to drive home to, a cup of tea or something warmer, the blood tingling so that your face smarts, and the best feeling all through you that you have ever known. There are no troubles, and nothing really matters—only the afternoon that has passed, and *that* was pleasant. It may not be lived through again, but it need not be forgotten."

Of the terrain of the Springs itself, he noted that "it is easy to build a road . . . A space fifty or sixty yards wide is fenced off. Then you drive upon it. That is all."

He went on to the delights of piñon wood fires "which smell of the pine from whence it gets its name." He warns, however, that in that year, 1899, all the servants were investing in mining stock and watching the newspapers, so that "a poorly cooked dinner may sometimes be thus accounted for." Generally the food was excellent; wild turkey so good "it is worth a three days' journey to eat it" and a bounty of other game. There were oysters on the half shell,

too, at such effete spots as Colorado Springs, where champagne suppers were a commonplace among the gentlemen-miners from Cripple Creek. Tallyhos and later the railroad brought gay parties from Denver to the BROaDMOOR for feasts of mountain trout, smoked elk, and antelope steaks, hot biscuits made from a Colorado recipe which required the use of bear's lard, and a shortcake blanketed in sun-ripe wild strawberries, or a slice of famous Denver red chocolate cake made according to a special high-altitude recipe.

The complex of the BROaDMOOR is far vaster than Pourtales or even Penrose and the elder Tutt had dared to dream, with its golf club, theater, year-round skating arena, sports stadium, and carriage house museum. But the count's lake still shines in the sunlight, there is still Pikes Peak to climb and still some visitors who agree with *Harper's* essayist of more than fifty years ago:

> The horizon holds no mountain heights for him
> Who hath no mountain heights within his soul.

"These lines," the writer concludes, "were written in Colorado Springs and tell, perhaps, of one of the missions of Pikes Peak."

NIAGARA FALLS

"THE THUNDERER OF WATERS"

Niagara Falls' fame as a haven for honeymooners flowered in the late 1800's when the Erie Railroad provided palace cars to the Falls with compartments as frescoed, mirrored, and gilded as any bridal suite.

But the "Thunderer of Waters" as the Indians called the great cataract, had been attracting visitors for nearly a century, even when it meant a journey by steamboat, stage, canal

boat, and sundry "gigs and waggons." A visiting Englishman, Lieutenant George Kirwan Carr, arrived at the Falls in 1832 to find a General Whitney operating both the Eagle Hotel and the Cataract House. Guides took the lieutenant on the hazardous excursion behind the Falls, providing him with oilskins, and afterward with an official document to certify that he had "passed with me beneath the Table Rock, and behind the Great Falling Sheet, under the Falls of NIAGARA, to Termination Rock." Seventy-two won the certificate that season, and Lieutenant Carr concluded that "for all the disgusting impudence of the Yankees . . . the whole sight is most wonderful and truly magnificent . . . and fully repays one for a six weeks passage across the Atlantic."

By the 1870's Niagara was offering "magnificent rooms and suites" in hotels such as the International,pictured above in 1873 when it announced the opening of a wing containing three "elegant parlors" extending a hundred feet over the rapids.

A small omnibus waits outside the International Hotel. The bridge to Goat Island in this photograph is a much improved version of the precarious span built by General Whitney in 1818, a small affair which, according to a visitor of the time, "quite overhangs the Fall, and the sensation when you get to the end is something horrid . . . you feel as tho' nothing could save you, but that you *must* go over, bridge and all."

ON THE BRINK

The bride is properly timid as this honeymoon couple of 1875 approaches the brink of the Falls. Her high-piled curls were the fashion of that year, as were the plumed bonnet and billowing bustle. Her trousseau would have been incomplete without a Camellia polonaise and several pairs of thread gloves. Their bill of fare was an unexciting four-course affair of such items as boiled fish, corned beef hash, and apple pie, but they did have a choice of three champagnes in which to toast, in more ways than one, the journey they had made "to the brink."

THE GREAT CURE-ALL

"In all my travels I have never seen a place better suited for a summer residence than Long Branch."

No resort could have asked a better endorsement, since the gentleman who said it was U. S. Grant, President of the United States. Many people were in agreement with the President and suites were at a premium in the rambling hotels which crowned the choice beach acreage and offered free access to sea bathing . . . "which has become so popular that the medical profession are recommending it as the great 'cure-all.' "

In the sketch above, the New York steamer is arriving at Long Branch, and on the beach more people seem to be taking the sun than the "cure-all." The two young females surveying the sands are done up in approved costumes for the summer of 1873, gay little hats shading their complexions, long sleeves and high necks preserving the proper pallor for evening wear.

THE OCEAN HOUSE

The racy resort on the New Jersey shore was giving Saratoga serious competition in the 1870's and 1880's, in spite of an acidulous reaction from lobbyist Sam Ward, who came there during the 1882 season and decided that in general the Long Branch set was "rude, boisterous and uncivil."

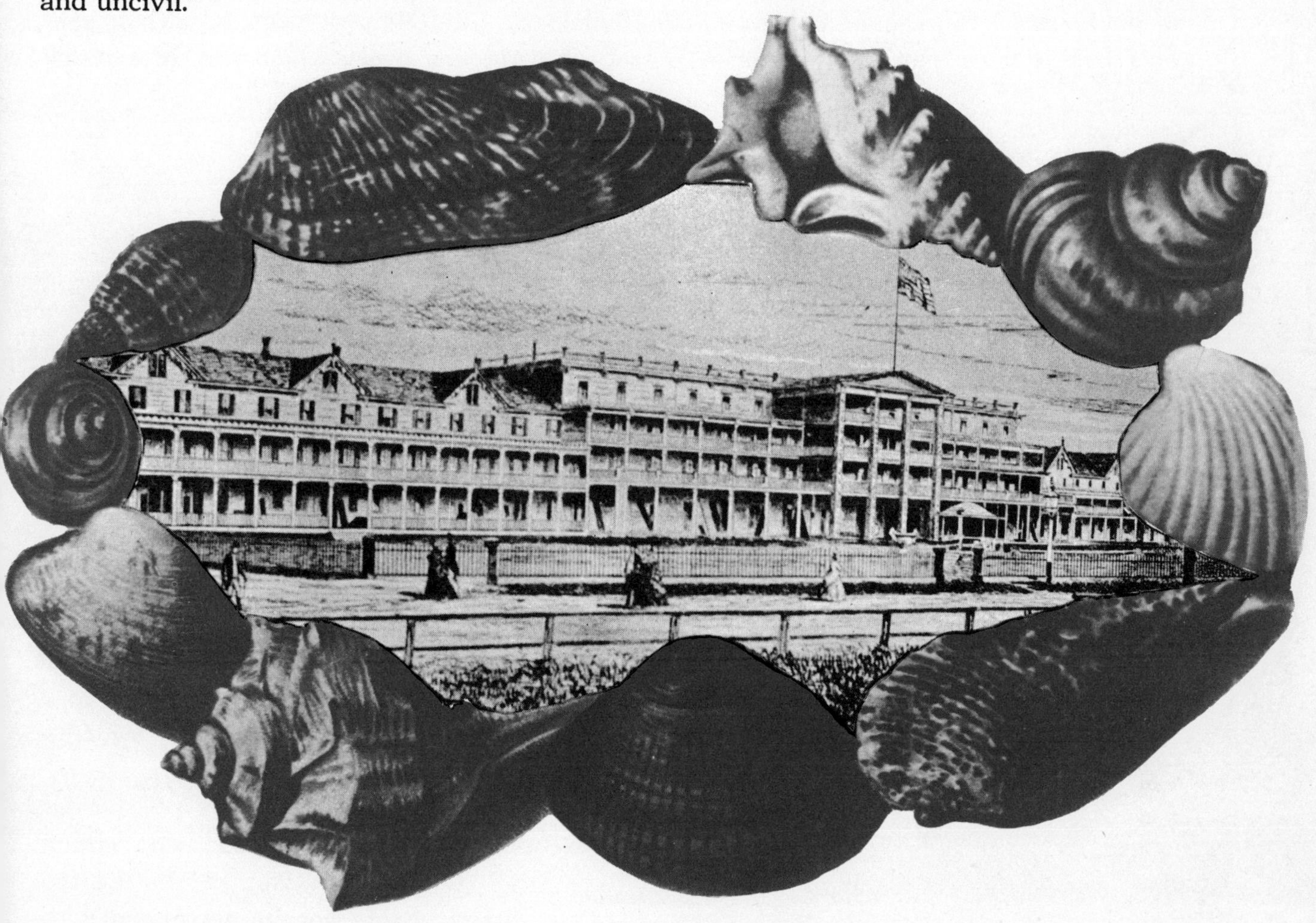

There was, however, nothing uncivil about the block-long façade of the Ocean House, and much less about its proprietors, two members of the most celebrated family of hotel keepers in America . . . the Lelands. A journalist of the 1870's, visiting the Ocean House, was delighted to find the Leland brand of hospitality awaiting him. It was just like "traveling with our own hotel keepers," he wrote. "As we go to Saratoga, the Lelands are on hand. As we exit from the cars at Long Branch, one of the first hotels that obstruct our view is the Ocean House, kept by the Lelands."

The Leland saga takes in Simeon Leland and his five sons, Vermonters whose special brand of management seemed to cast an aura of success and well-being around the thirty-odd establishments linked with the Leland name . . . among them the Palace in San Francisco, Saratoga's Grand Union, the Astor and the Metropolitan in New York. Their Ocean House in Long Branch, seen here in an appropriate frame of seashells, was renowned for its fish dinners, its wine cellar, and the fearful and wonderful shapes of its topiary garden.

The giddiest years of Long Branch were the 1870's and 80's, when the gilded domes and weather vanes of the Chamberlain Club vied in popularity with the racetrack opened at nearby Monmouth Park in 1876 by the greats of the thoroughbred world—August Belmont, David Withers, George Peabody Wetmore, the Lorillards.

Ocean Avenue was a madhouse, with bicycles whizzing in and out among clattering buckboards, traps, landaus, omnibuses, and every other known vehicle, with a generous scattering of men and women on horseback careening every which way in a flurry

Bicycles, Belles and High-Stepping Horses

of trailing riding habits, polished boots, and beribboned crops. The carriage of Colonel "Jubilee Jim" Fisk couldn't be missed, with its pair of sleek horses, one shiny black, one gleaming white, two liveried coachmen on the box in front, two uniformed boys in the back, and everything gold- or silver-plated, including the gold Fisk monogram on the horses' blinkers.

"Boss" Tweed favored Long Branch with his presence, a dubious accolade which failed to discourage such society arbiters as the Whitneys and the Goulds. Even Oscar Wilde showed up and was showered with pink roses by a bevy of pretty girls.

The caption *Harper's Weekly* chose for the rather pathetic group of females in the sketch below was, unfortunately, an undercurrent of weekday life at Long Branch as well as at countless other vacation spots where the female, young, old and in-between, outnumbered the hapless male to an alarming degree. Until the boats, carriages and cars brought weekending husbands, fiances and unattached males, such bevies as this descended upon any gentleman rash enough to attempt a rendezvous with the lady of his choice.

The accolade of President Grant was responsible for other Presidents choosing Long Branch for summer holidays. Grant had learned of the resort from Mrs. Lincoln, who made one of her rare appearances there in 1861, to be greeted by a band of small girls wearing white and carrying bouquets, and later to be feted at a reception at the Mansion House, where it was reported she behaved in regal fashion.

There was a hint, just a hint, that occasionally all was not quite well at Long Branch. An advertisement of 1880 advised that "Mosquito Fans are exquisite little affairs of the shape of a lily leaf, with a long tapering handle and beautiful decoration . . . the colors ivory white, *rose palé,* cloud blue, sea-foam green or the most delicate lilac." Should it become necessary to use this little weapon, the notice assured that "well managed, the mosquito fan will serve very well to display a fair well-rounded arm, and with motions light as air . . . keep insect marauders at a distance."

TOO MUCH OF A GOOD THING

BY EDWARD F. UNDERHILL.

TUMBLING in the waters,
  Rolling in the swell,
Splashing 'midst the breakers,
  Dashing in pell-mell;
Diving 'neath the billows,
  Sprawling in the spray,
What can be more jolly than
  The bathing at Cape May?

Here a hale old buffer,
  Laughing at the fun,
When a fat companion,
  Frightened, tries to run
From a towering breaker,
  Which, to his dismay,
Strikes him like a catapult,
  And lays him at Cape May.

There a plump-built matron,
  Short in petticoat,
Simpering like a maiden,
  Vainly tries to float;
With a cry appalling—
  'Gulfed in boiling spray—
Quick she turns a somersault
  In bathing at Cape May.

THE DINNER HOUR.

THE HALE OLD BUFFER.

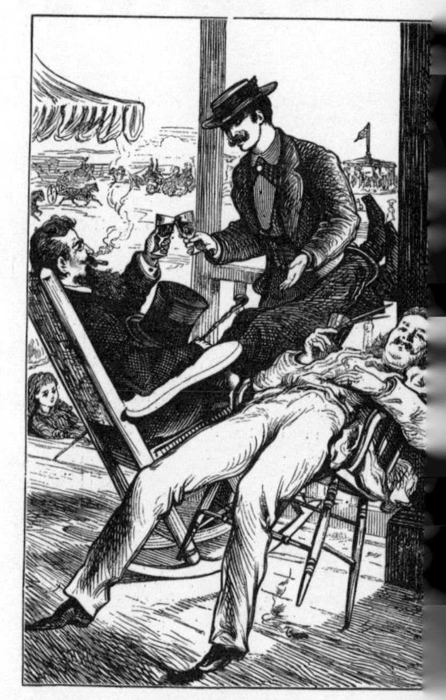

GOSSIP, COBBLERS, ROMANCE.

Tumbling in the waters,
  Rolling in the swell,
Splashing 'midst the breakers,
  Dashing in pell-mell;
Doffing briny garments,
  Donning raiment gay,
Aching voids then filling from
  The ta'le at Cape May.

Clattering of the dishes,
  Rattling knives and forks,
Jingling of the glasses,
  Popping of the corks,
Draining of the bottles,
  Stowing food away,
Don't we have a jolly time
  In dining at Cape May?

See that young dyspeptic—
  Mother's tender pet—
For each course voracious,
  Eye-teeth sharply set;
Then those fragile creatures
  Winds 'most waft away,
What an ostrich appetite
  O'ertakes them at Cape May!

ILLUSTRATED BY LUMLEY.

Now a foppish spooney,
With mustaches dyed,
Quick to show his mettle,
Plunges in the tide;
Breakers tumble o'er him,
Spoiling his display,
Sneezing, he emerges from
The waters at Cape May.

Here a rosy sea-nymph
In the water laves,
Boldly mounts the billows,
Dashing surges braves:
See the boisterous sea-king
Kiss the watery fay;
Hear her laughter ringing from
The billows of Cape May.

Hand in hand together
Then a noisy band
Move forth in the waters,
Bravely try to stand
'Gainst the shocks of breakers,
Eager for the fray—
See them quickly scamper for
The sand beach of Cape May.

FLIRTING AND CROQUET.

THE ROSY SEA-NYMPH.

THE LANCERS.

Time assassinating,
To verandas drawn,
Lounging in pavilion,
Smoking on the lawn;
Gossip, cobblers, romance,
Flirting and croquet,
Till darkness drops its mantle
O'er nature at Cape May.

Gathering in the parlors,
Rustling of the dresses,
Fascinating features,
Agitating tresses,
Gliding through the lancers—
Gayest of the gay
Are the evening pleasures that
We whirl in at Cape May.

Thus the fun continues,
Morning, noon, and night,
Till our aching eyelids
Ask for a respite;
Then we soundly slumber
Till the break of day,
Only to again resume
The frolics at Cape May.

ATLANTIC CITY

playground of the World

"Nearly every day somebody falls off the Boardwalk. In nearly every instance the parties have been flirting." Judging by the modest little "plank-walk" in this beach scene at Atlantic City, it is not surprising that people fell off it. Only a mile long and eight feet wide when it opened in June of 1870, the wooden promenade that was to make Atlantic City world famous did not even have a name. It was just there, built at the instigation of Alexander Boardman, a railroad conductor whose life had been made miserable by the quantities of sand brought aboard his returning train by excursionists.

Atlantic City was only sixteen years old when the Boardwalk made its debut. But never in its gay and tinseled career was it intended to be anything but a seaside resort. Its first season began on the Fourth of July, 1854, and there were five hotels in readiness for the occasion. Philadelphians arrived via lumbering stages over two rival routes, the Black Horse and the White Horse Turnpikes.

By the 1870's the wide sandy avenues were crowded with carriages and lined with verandaed Victorian hotels like the venerable twin hostelries, the Chalfonte and Haddon House on North Carolina Avenue (view on preceding page). People were not averse to getting around on foot in those days. A journalist of the time gave full marks to the "Philadelphia girl, fairest of the continent . . . she knows how to walk with simplicity and without consciousness of notice," while the "Philadelphia male . . . paces as if he could afford to do it."

The "bathing beauties" here are typical of the 1870's at Atlantic City, where as *Demorest's* fashion authorities noted, ". . . For bathing-dresses there is nothing better than twilled flannel, decently long and well cut . . . with a Garibaldi waist, not too full or baggy, gored skirt and full drawers gathered into an elastic. About ten yards of flannel are required." Bathing shoes and a straw hat were needed as well, for early Atlantic City rules required that the entire body be covered; until 1907 women were not allowed on the beach without stockings! The bathing dresses of the 1870's were padded at breasts, arms, shoulders, and calves for the benefit of those not naturally endowed with enough curves.

FIRSTS...

1892—The first paid lifeguards, known as the Atlantic City Beach Patrol, went to work, taking over the old volunteer Rescue Life Guard services. These two, the Jeffries brothers, were gallant members of that first squad. Volunteers still served in beach areas not protected by the Patrol, and among them was an ex-cowboy named Captain Charles E. Clark who, because of his unusual costume and his unusual record of seven hundred rescues, was known as the "Velvet-Gloved Hero."

1889—First mention of salt water taffy in the city directory. As many stories cluster around the origin of this confection as about the beginnings of pink lemonade. One such tale has to do with a David Bradley who was mixing his daily batch of taffy when a wind splashed seawater into the stuff, and presto—salt water taffy. Actually seawater is not used, although salt and water are ingredients. A typical booth is this one photographed about 1900 with the somewhat perplexing legend on the awning: "James Up To Now Salt Water Taffy." Joseph Fralinger who started his business in 1889 won the title of "Salt Water Taffy King" and his twenty-odd flavors of taffy were shipped around the world.

BESIDE THE SEA

1885—Another notable first was the rolling chair, an ingenious notion of William Hayday who had been renting wheelchairs for invalids. It occurred to him that foot-weary Boardwalk visitors might take to the idea of being whisked along the promenade at a profitable rate per hour.

1897—The marvelous configurations of the "sand sculptor" began with Philip McCord and soon this was a popular and profitable feature of the Boardwalk scene. Other notable Atlantic City firsts: First picture postcard, 1893; first amusement pier built over water, 1882; the golf term "birdie" coined at an 1899 match at Atlantic City Country Club.

1890

WATCHING THE TIDE COME IN...

"Like unto the Dead Cities of Holland, can there be decayed watering-places?" asked *Harper's Weekly* in the article featuring this Boardwalk view of Atlantic City in 1890.

"Comes there that ebb-tide of fashion which, after a time receding, leaves a resort once thronged, high, dry and deserted?"

No, the writer concluded, "We are too young yet to have any of our sea-side resorts taking on signs of decadence. The growth of Atlantic City has been marvelous. It has broken away from its Philadelphia tutelage . . . and has all the busy appearances of a well-thronged city."

...THE BATHING HOUR

About the picture, *Harper's* went on: "To see a tide come in is to spend many an hour. Tides have special physiognomies beyond scientific considerations. And so Mr. Snyder [the artist] drew a group of three, who see the ocean on its return, when it would wrestle for supremacy with the land. Far off are two figures on horseback who canter along on the smooth sea-bed. The piers are thronged. The breeze flutters the women's, the children's dresses . . . There is a pretty girl, an elegant invalid and a prosaic man . . . Is there expectancy on the part of the young lady . . . Who might it be that comes . . . Demure as she seems, she would have him burst in with the tide, the wind swelling the canvas of his yacht; and there, just there on the horizon, that white gleam of sail makes her heart beat. The pug-dog in the invalid's lap gives but one snappy bark, and there is only one more *illusion perdue*."

In the same year the glorious drawing above presented *Harper's* version of the beach on a midsummer afternoon. The crowd is due "to the proximity and summer temperature of Philadelphia" from which tens of thousands, "grip-sacks" in hand, form a daily exodus to Atlantic City.

It was in the summer of 1890 that something akin to the Loch Ness monster appeared off the Jersey coast and was quickly captured for posterity in the sketch below. The accompanying description said:

" 'The Sea Spider' is the popular name given a new machine now to be seen off shore in the vicinity of Atlantic City, but the inventor, the Rev. Ezra B. Lake, calls it 'The Ocean Tricyclemor Sea-Wagon.' The Spiders' car, holding as many as forty adventurous souls, rose

THE SEA SPIDER

on four standing metal beams, twenty-five feet above the sea surface. It was steam-propelled with three wheels, each able to move in a different direction. However, it was not for pleasure excursions that the Rev. Lake planned his extraordinary vehicle, but for an adjunct to the life-saving service! . . . There would be something imposing in the slow march of this machine through a heavy sea, the surges tearing below her, until she reached a stranded vessel." Regrettably there is no record of such a noble effort, nor even of the eventual fate of the lugubrious Spider.

By the early 1900's Atlantic City had matured into a winter and spring resort "favored by people of wealth and fashion from fourteen states." The hotels were vast and elegant, as

1880's

The Clam Was King

"All is festooned, floating, honeycombed, with the free air blowing through," reported *Scribner's* magazine of the Iron Pier in 1880. "An interminable dainty palace, pinnacled, gabled, arcaded, many-storied, raised on slender columns above the water, like a habitation of some charming race of lake-dwellers."

Bands played on the pier; steamboats unloaded crowds from New York. But Coney Island was far from a proletarian paradise in those days. It had its full quota of Lorillards and Vanderbilts, Belmonts and Lawrences, who formed the Coney Island Jockey Club in the late 1880's and raced their horses at Brighton Beach, Sheepshead Bay, and Morris Park. Their favorite gathering place was the fashionable Manhattan Beach Hotel and the clam, not the hot dog, was king. The Iron Pier served littlenecks on the half shell, clam chowder, and grilled clams, and the going price, music included, was about twenty-five cents a portion.

Political bigwigs favored the elegant Oriental Hotel, but they too liked to lunch on the "New" Iron Pier with its elaborate flowers and shrubs and cool ocean breezes. The "Old" Iron Pier was simpler and more utilitarian, with its boardwalk approach and sturdy twin towers, and just behind it that wonderful Coney monstrosity, the Elephant.

AN ELEPHANT HOTEL & AN INEXHAUSTIBLE COW!

He . . . the elephant, was a brother to Lucy, the original Margate elephant built at Atlantic City in 1882 by James V. Lafferty, who planned a chain of the metal pachyderms around the country. The one shown here was the third of the Lafferty efforts and it had several rooms inside the thigh, hip, trunk, and shoulder, a cigar store in one front leg, a diorama in the other, and a pair of telescopes atop the howdah. The various elephants burned or washed away in storms. No one has recorded the fate of the dairy company's "Inexhaustible Cow" pictured below.

"Like the Democratic Convention where no man needed a record longer than twenty-four hours, Coney Island needs no past . . . it is intensely present and actual." The *Harper's* writer who made that comment might have been setting the theme for the panorama presented in these pages, for never was Coney more "intensely present and actual" than in the 1880's. It was getting to be fashionable, a fact deplored by the same reporter:

"A year or two ago Coney Island was *sui generis,* racy with a flavor of its own . . . the people's watering place in the fullest sense. But it was *too* good."

And so to breezy dining spots like the Iron Pier, pictured here at the early lunch hour, came the "upper classes" to enjoy the food and the view.

"Did you ever see such high light and motion before?" asked *Harper's.* "The shining white pine buildings, glittering windows, sea foam, dazzling sand and spray . . . the fluttering of countless flags . . . the restless crowd."

The pier itself was twelve hundred feet long and its main floor was twenty-four feet above the sea, providing a favorite place underneath for shady dips. Theatrical people still came to Coney Island as they had back in the days of *The Black Crook* and even earlier, when P. T. Barnum escorted Jenny Lind to the Coney Island House for dinner. But the 1880's were the years of big spending, wild real estate speculation, political skulduggery, and heavy gambling . . . all topped with a frosting of millionaire sportsmen and socialites.

"...EVERY ATTRACTION THAT IS POSSIBLE TO A WATERING PLACE..."

Nobody exaggerated when they wrote about the beach at Coney Island during the 1880's. The picture above would indicate that, involving as it does practically everything that could possibly happen on a beach. Our *Harper's* correspondent, as he wandered along the sands, found "a plaintive individual" who invited him to step into a weighing chair, another who "blandly urges us to test the strength of our lungs on his blowing machine. . . . An acrobat has cleared a space and is tying himself in double bow-knots . . . a cluster of singers with bones and banjo fling themselves into the melodic frenzy of 'Camp-Town Races.' " The children are galumphing around on burros, a vender is peddling "sun glasses," a tallyho whisks a gay crowd along the sands, a Punch and Judy show is in progress, and some people even wade into the surf. All in all, it is a frivolous, frolicking day in the sun . . . a Coney Island day circa 1880.

...EVEN AN ELECTRIC LIGHT!

Nighttime at Coney Island was a special enchantment, and bathing by the extraordinary calcium light hoisted on a fifty-foot pole was an excitement that began in the Centennial year of 1876, the date of the drawing below which shows a fairly raucous group of surf devotees at play. The turreted and bannered structure is the Manhattan Beach Hotel. By the 1880's the whole resort was blazing with gas or arc light, presenting, according to a newspaper account, "an almost fairy-like aspect . . . the Concourse glittering with its countless lamps, the attractive music, the enthusiastic crowd of visitors, combined with the sound of the breaking surf and the exhilarating sea air." At the Manhattan Beach Hotel there were "some beautiful effects of light, purple glasses being used, which gave a weird appearance to the surf and to those enjoying it."

SEASIDE CARAVANSERAIS

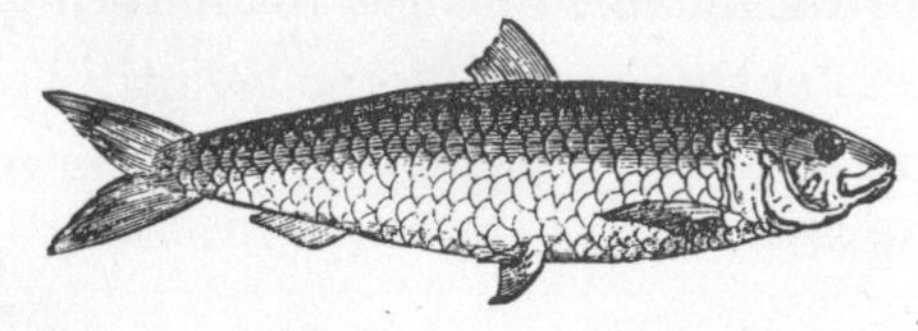

"... to secure the regular patrons from the crush..."

The luxury hotels where high-spending and high-living guests sought respite from the rush and crush of Coney Island excursionists were mostly located at Brighton and Manhattan Beaches. If the patrons were haughty, the waiters were haughtier; according to *The Steward's Handbook:*

"There's the waiter at the seaside
With his life of gilded ease;
He's the one who's always waiting
For those customary fees.

He will starve you in submission
If his tips you should refuse,
But treats you like a monarch
If you give to him his dues."

The waiters at the Manhattan Beach Hotel, which claimed in the 1880's to be "the most fashionable in the United States," knew the whims of their regular guests, and which ones preferred the crab bisque for which the chef was famous, the delicate white-bait, bluefish baked in wine, and the meringue glacé. The Manhattan Beach (on the opposite page, top) had its own amphitheater and was summer headquarters for such exclusive New York clubs as the Union League, Union University, and the Jockey Club. The Oriental (opposite page, bottom) had a reputation for a more sedate clientele. It made a point of not inviting transients, since it catered principally to wealthy families who took suites for the season. The Brighton Beach Hotel (above), a vast Gothic structure, creamy white with red trim, not only fancied transients, it even provided a picnic room for them, with airy piazzas surrounding it. The dining room opened on three sides to the sea and in fine weather meals were served on the verandas. "Eastlake sets in dark green raw silk with lambrequins to match" were used throughout the carpeted parlors. Band concerts and fireworks were on the entertainment program all summer long, picnics and clambakes were the order of the day as within a single decade hotels sprang up "like Aladdin's palace" for miles along the ocean.

A HOTEL ON WHEELS...

The year was 1888. Luna Park, Dreamland and the Shoot-the-Chutes, and all the rest of the Coney Island razzle-dazzle were still more than a decade away. But there was gambling aplenty, tough saloons down West Brighton way, with ten-cent champagne, and the three tracks as Gravesend reported a $15 million handle for the season.

The Brighton Beach Hotel found itself in this year threatened by the encroaching surf, its curving walks eroded, and its foundations dangerously shaky. So the management decided to put it on wheels and move all seven million tons of it to a safer spot. During the winter, gangs of workmen laid twenty-four parallel railroad tracks, raised the hotel and fitted it on a fleet of flatcars. Blocks, hawsers, chains, and stays held the huge building steady. On a Monday morning in April crowds of visitors arrived to watch the spectacle. Promptly at eight-forty-five a half dozen puffing engines went into action and the Brighton Beach, as pictured above, began to move. Amid tremendous excitement the first stage of the journey was launched. The "hotel on wheels" traveled one hundred and twenty-four feet that day, and another two hundred and fifty in subsequent "hops." Finally it was set down safely, "laughing defiance to the merciless sea."

Everyone remembered the boats to Coney Island with fond nostalgia. John Erskine in his memoirs told of a boyhood journey "on a gallant vessel of the fleet maintained by the Iron Steamboat Company . . . the first cool shock of ocean air as the sidewheeler paddled down the bay." A harp and a violin played "music haunting and wistful." Just as memorable was the boat trip back home, although, as a *Harper's* writer recalled it, there were squalling children and scolding mothers, "careless young folk in the corner" laughing, flirting, and singing, while "from dampened garments rises a vapor of soaked humanity, mingled with a flavor of lager, whiskey, oranges, peppermint and tobacco. . . . When we come out on the damp deck at Twenty-third Street the clouds have broken and rolled off . . . the city lights are glimmering about us, the air is sweet and cool" . . . and thus ends a summer's day of long ago at Coney Island.

THE RUSH FOR THE LAST BOAT

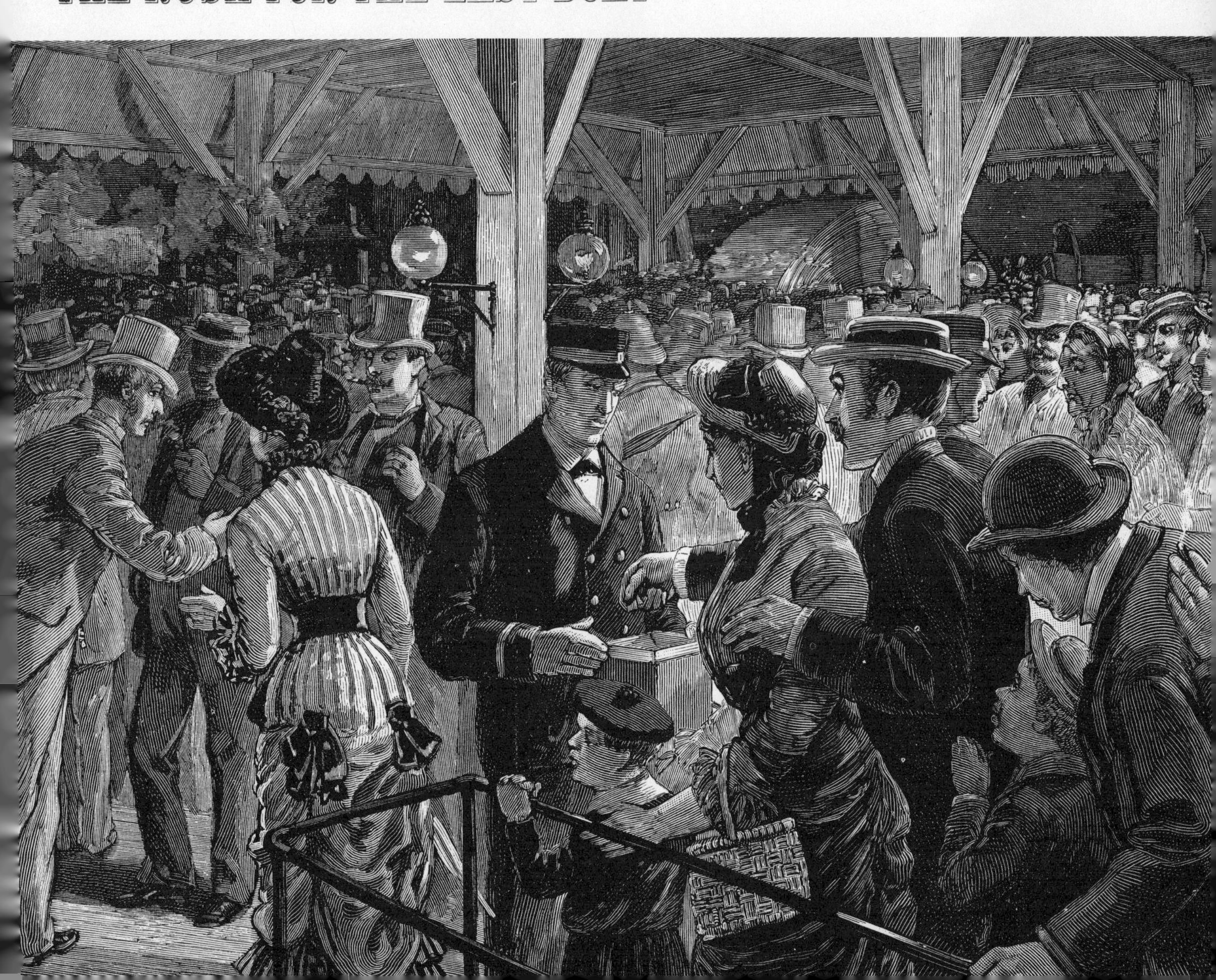

When the great nineteenth-century resorts were in full Victorian flower, Florida was just a place down South, Palm Beach was just that . . . a beach with palms . . . and Miami wasn't even on the map.

BLIZZARD TO BALMY BLISS

Perhaps it was the frigid northern winters and blizzards like the one buffeting New York (left), but more likely it was Henry M. Flagler's new railroad that turned all eyes toward the balmy sands of Palm Beach. The railroad opened in a blaze of publicity in the late winter of 1894 and Florida rapidly gained momentum as *the* new winter playground. By the turn of the century steamship lines were vying with luxury trains in luring people to the "shining sands and sunlight . . . where palms and dancing waves beckon to the fatigued and the leisurely alike."

It was smart to be exotic; in St. Augustine "a lady created a sensation by appearing in public with a chameleon resting on her head-dress, and held there by a delicate silver chain. When touched by other than its owner, its throat puffed up and curious waves of color passed over the whole body." Diamonds were all right, of course, but since nearly everybody at the luxury Florida hotels had them, it was chic to appear in something different such as the chameleon or the new "red-clawed soldier crabs" from Mexico, coated with mother-of-pearl or plated with gold and fastened to the dress by a pin and chain.

Atlantic Coast Line
Via Washington and Richmond
Florida, Cuba, Nassau, Jamaica, Porto-Rico, Augusta, Charleston, Savannah
ROUTE OF THE CELEBRATED
"New York and Florida Special" and
"Florida and West Indian Limited"
ABSOLUTELY THE QUICKEST ROUTE
Winter Excursion Tickets, good until May 31, 1900, now on sale.

Hotel Ponce de Leon, St. Augustine

"Palms, vines, roses, all the trailing plants of **Florida**" grew in profusion along the sunny walks of this lovely roof garden atop the Hotel Alcazar in St. Augustine in the winter of 1888.

"IS ST. AUGUSTINE NEVER TO BE SATISFIED?"

The answer put to this question by *Harper's Weekly* in 1887 seemed to be a decisive No. Certainly Mr. Flagler was not to be satisfied when he decided to give his Ponce de Leon a luxurious sister hotel, the Alcatraz, complete with roof garden, domed rotunda, towers, minarets, and arcades. Above the dining room on a balcony an orchestra played while bejeweled women in evening gowns and their escorts in summer formal attire dined on broiled red snapper and turtle steak and that Florida delicacy *Pompano en Papillote.* They were sampling guava and toying with the tangy taste of grapefruit, which as late as 1897 was still such a curiosity in the north that a lot of twenty-five boxes was bid up to $156.25 by a New York dealer.

Mr. Flagler's first grand gesture in Florida was the Ponce de Leon. Built in Spanish Renaissance style at a cost of $1,230,000, the Ponce de Leon opened in January, 1888, its towers, arched windows and colonnades agleam with electric lights, then a sufficient novelty to make front-page headlines. It had another unusual feature: it was built of poured concrete made from ground coquina hauled over from a nearby island. This material gave the exterior "a pearly lustre . . . and

HOTEL PONCE DE LEON

in the shade, superb effects." On opening day it looked as much as it does in the photograph at upper right, with flashy equipages drawing up before the entrance, and on that occasion a special omnibus drawn by white horses to bring guests of honor from the depot. There were cannon salutes, band concerts, and waving flags. Exotic as the Ponce de Leon appeared from the outside, inside the guests felt right at home, for here were the fringed velvet and brocade, the lace antimacassars, the flowered carpets so dear to the Victorian heart. The view of the lobby on the right tells the story.

1903

"The wealth of one man, Henry M. Flagler, has converted Palm Beach into the most beautiful mile or two of water-front on any sea . . . it has been called the American Riviera, but the Riviera has nothing to compare with it in gorgeous tropical setting" (*Harper's Weekly*, 1897.)

1879

The idyllic palm garden above, "arched with the fronds of palms and dreamlike in its beauty" . . . was the sort of inducement offered at the Royal Poinciana (at right) which rose in six stories of luxurious suites with a dining room that seated two thousand persons. It opened in the late winter of 1894. Two years later the Flagler Bridge connected the island of Palm Beach to the mainland and over it rolled private cars fairly brimming with Social Register names.

The Royal Poinciana, painted a pale yellow, offers a decorative backdrop for the ladies pictured at left as they stop to chat on the broad stairway after one of the six- or eight-course luncheons which everyone sat down to at one o'clock. Mornings were spent on the beach, and the rules were strict: modest bathing dresses and black stockings for the women, who, however, were perfectly free in the evening to display all the flesh they were forbidden to bare to the morning sun.

No horses were allowed on Mr. Flagler's enchanted island. But guests averse to trudging everywhere on foot were offered the curious conveyance shown in this photograph of 1903 . . . a chair mounted on three wheels, somewhat like a tricycle and piloted from the rear by a uniformed attendant.

With the star of Palm Beach in its ascendancy during the early 1900's, the season began to stretch well beyond a few weeks in December. There was gambling at Bradleys' Beach Club, golf, tennis, fishing, and sailing. Luxury yachts began to make Palm Beach a regular stop and millionaires' estates monopolized the precious beach properties.

As a visiting journalist noted, Florida offered "orange groves outside of Spain . . . pleasant skies forgetful of southern France, Italy or Egypt, and with only a journey of hours Americans can now, within their own country, buy the exact climate they want."

1891
HOTEL del CORONADO

"People go into the surf on Christmas Day as well as on the Fourth of July, and in January as well as in June." With that accolade to the climate, *Harper's Weekly,* sometimes inclined to be a bit snide about people, things, and places of the West, admitted southern California and especially the Hotel del Coronado, to its list of resorts for the elite. The 1880's had seen a real estate explosion in southern California when the newly completed Santa Fe Railroad began a war with rival lines to attract passengers. Trains roared into Los Angeles and San Diego, disgorging passengers who had paid as little as eight dollars, and at the height of the competition, one dollar each to ride all the way from the Missouri Valley.

By 1891, the time of the photograph above, the Del Coronado was located in a boom area. Sleepy little San Diego, a few miles away, was bursting at the seams with more than fifty thousand new residents, many of them saddened victims of investment in towns that never were.

The city of San Diego, circled by distant mountains, nestled on the harbor just across from the broad white sands of the Del Coronado beach. "Never hot in summer nor cold in winter at Coronado," said an advertisement. Well, perhaps not exactly cold, but the beach promenaders in this picture seem to be fairly well supplied with long-sleeved jackets and only one lone figure can be discerned sampling the surf. There was central steam heat and many rooms had open fireplaces as well . . . just in case. Still, it was the climate that southern California had to sell, and it did a magnificent job of it. Meteorologists declared it was "Mediterranean plus" and the Coronado stated with finality that its beach in summer was "ten degrees cooler than any of the five world-renowned famous Mediterranean resorts." And all this for three dollars a day and upward, plus such gourmet delights as abalone steaks and avocado salads. Visitors from the East were especially charmed with this land of the "sun-down sea" where the sudden and dramatic sunsets brought tropical nights for dancing and even a daring Del Coronado innovation of the 1890's, the midnight swim.

"THE SITUATION IS UNIQUE"

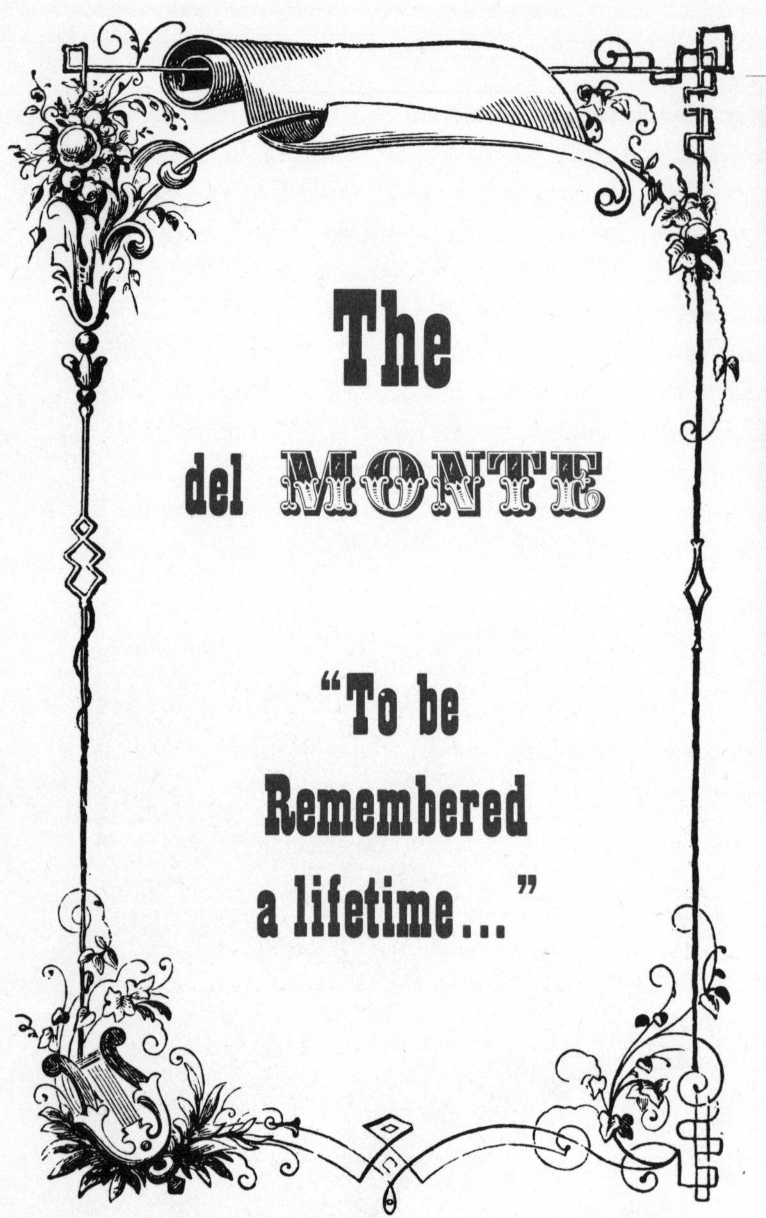

The del MONTE

"To be Remembered a lifetime..."

A bride of the 1880's, arriving at sunlit Monterey Peninsula and discovering the delights of the honeymoon suite at the Hotel del Monte, sent the postcard reproduced above to her family back in the Middle West . . . and all she wrote was, "it is to be remembered a lifetime."

That surely was the aim of the proprietors who persistently ignored the existence of resort hotels in "that other part" of the state to the south. It was their view that only at Del Monte could "the incomparable beauties of California and the health-giving qualities of the climate be fully enjoyed." The hotel's gardens comprised one hundred and twenty-six acres of live oaks growing in fantastic shapes, pines, lawns of grass and creeping ivy, calla blossoms, heliotropes "as tall as trees," and miles of shady walks and bridle paths. The hotel itself was turreted and pinnacled in pseudo-Gothic style. The winter season, November through February, was fashionable in the 1890's and rates at the Del Monte ranged from sixty-five dollars per month for a single room to one hundred and seventy-five for the small parlor suites. There was a ladies billiard room, a music parlor, ballroom, and mirrored dining room where the menu offered meat, vegetables, melon, milk and cream from its own "plantations," as well as venison, quail, mountain trout, and salt-water fish.

The Del Monte operated its own lodge up on the Carmel River "in the wildest mountain region where deer hunting and trout fishing are the best in the State." It maintained its private track "for gentlemen's races" and nearby a polo grounds where "when contests are announced the driveways are crowded with drags, tallyhos and traps of every description."

Guests were whisked from the railway station to the Del Monte in a hotel stage which deposited them at the vine-draped main entrance shown at right, where two young visitors are setting forth for a pony-cart drive while their elders look on from the veranda.

By the early 1900's the transcontinental trains were advertising "California only three days away" from Chicago, were boasting of "electric lights everywhere . . . bath rooms, with hot and cold water, soap and REAL bath towels."

After a meal in the plain but spacious and airy Del Monte dining room (above), the more sedentary ladies would gather in groups like the one above to gossip away the afternoon in the mild California sun. An occasional young lady in frilly white carriage costume might perch on the railing for a moment to assure Mama or Grandma that she was behaving with propriety.

A Palmy Plunge at the Delmonte

The Del Monte was probably the first hotel to boast a glass-roofed indoor bathing pool, complete with palms, but not—judging by the above picture—with female bathing beauties.

In the summer of 1888, a young lady staying at the Del Monte reported to the *San Francisco News Letter* that everyone there was wearing white, which is "awful trying in the daylight to women going down the grade to the 30-milestone." Men were in white, too—snowy flannels and linen and, for tennis, brightly colored lengths of surah. The weekly mail was a big event, according to the *News Letter's* correspondent, with "letters from Europe telling of more princes being captured by American heiresses."

A Burlingame socialite, E. D. Beyard, who loved running down from the city to meet his friends at the Del Monte, initiated a tallyho service in 1901 between that hotel and the Palace in San Francisco. It was enormously popular, the four matched horses hauling the brightly painted coach down to Monterey in the morning and back late that night.

The Del Monte organized trips for its guests along the exotic shoreline of the Peninsula where the Monterey cypresses, twisted by the winds of centuries into bizarre shapes, were fine conversation pieces, as was the old Mission San Carlos Borromeo with its Moorish dome, dating back to 1770 when it was founded by the pioneering missionary, Fray Junipero Serra.

The fact is that Americans were becoming conscious of their own history and many families at the turn of the century were taking a summer off from the conventional trip abroad to go "abroad" in their own country instead. Actually, although the great resort hotels were still flourishing, their day in the sun was nearly over. The automobile, the airplane, the desire to see more places in less time . . . all these spelled the end of long lazy summers and of places like Del Monte and Del Coronado which were once "to be remembered a lifetime."

Seal Rocks, the Golden Gate, and endless miles of the sparkling Pacific Ocean stretched away from this lovely esplanade when Adolphe Sutro and his guests took the air after lunch or tea at the Sutro mansion. They leaned on the white marble parapet, adorned with Italian statuary brought around the Horn in the 1880's, and looked down on the famous Cliff House. There the dancing was always a little livelier, the stakes at poker a little higher, the flirtations a little naughtier than in more staid establishments in the city. Sutro, a millionaire mining engineer and Mayor of San Francisco from 1895 to 1897, enjoyed the gay goings-on at the hotel down the cliff. At times he must have been uneasy about his own property, for Cliff Houses burned and exploded with alarming frequency in the late nineteenth and early twentieth centuries. Like its turreted, multi-storied predecessor, this Cliff House too has vanished. The tallyhos filled with gay excursionists, the parasoled ladies, the young dandies in linens and white flannel, the lilt of a dance band . . . they are only nostalgic souvenirs, as are so many of the scenes and places in this book. The statutary on Sutro Heights is broken or scattered. Tourists munch hot dogs where the Cliff House stood, a skating rink has replaced the pool where galleries of young women spectators watched their beaus disporting in the water.

Yet such change is inevitable for a nation on the move, impelled by its own restless energy to destroy almost as recklessly as it creates. As the buildings rise higher, as concrete and steel and neon lights take over, Americans tend to look back to try to recapture the audacious dreams, the follies and triumphs of their country's past, part of which we hope have come alive in the pages of this book.

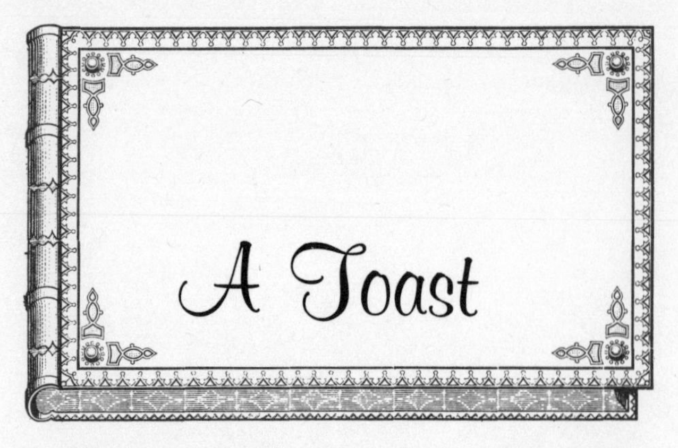

This book began in the winter of 1954 (although no one, including the authors, was aware of it), when the New York Historical Society acquired the fine Arnold B. Shircliffe collection of menus and other related memorabilia. This formed the basis for an exciting exhibition, and one of the authors of this book went day after day to see it, taking notes and having photostats made of especially intriguing documents, which he assembled into a scrapbook for reference use in his interior designing work. It then occurred to him that here was the nucleus of a book picturing the whole colorful past of America's hostelries and resorts.

Now that the book is a reality, both the authors want to say a heartfelt "thank you" for the help they have had along the way.

First comes Arthur M. Carlson, knowledgeable curator of the New York Historical Society's great picture collection; his assistants, Betty J. Ezequelle and Paul Bride, and the society's able librarian, E. Marie Becker. The Bella C. Landauer Collection and the unfinished collection of W. Johnson Quinn were invaluable.

In this same area of source material, we are indebted to the Museum of the City of New York, especially to A. K. Baragwanath, picture curator, and Grace M. Mayer, former curator; to the New York Public Library; and to the Long Island Historical Society in Brooklyn.

The Hotel de Paris story could not have been told so well pictorially without the generosity of Fred and Jo Mazzoola, of Denver, owners of one of the best historical archives in the State of Colorado.

Hotel people who helped enthusiastically, included Eve Brown, public relations director of the Plaza; Ed Seay, formerly of the Waldorf-Astoria; Fred Townsend, manager, Palmer House, Chicago; Carl A. Mahlman, manager, Brown Palace, Denver; Philip D. Shea, publicity director, Sheraton Corporation of America; Veneta Weber, public relations, Broadmoor, Colorado Springs; Tom Menaugh, advertising director, Fred Harvey chain; staff, Atlantic City Chamber of Commerce.

Special thanks, too, to Henry Brown (for a lucky lunch), Ruth Le Clair *(encourageur par excellence)*, Mrs. George F. Newstadt (for enduring faith), Gilbert Weist, proprietor of Michael's Pub, New York (for spiritual and temporal nurture) . . . and finally, all those unknown people who saved postcards, made scrapbooks, took photographs, drew maps, assembled directories, collected bound volumes of old magazines—in short, those who made possible the authors' own collection of Americana.

Hail... and Fare Thee Well!

THE AUTHORS

List of Illustrations

Page

2. Washington Hotel Adv., 1819, Portland, Me.
2. Green Dragon Announcement, 1803, Boston
2. Indian Queen Opening Announcement, *circa* 1700
4. Regulations of the House, *circa* 1802
7. Wright's Hotel Adv., 1832, Syracuse, N.Y.
10. Wright Tavern, Concord, Mass., 1733
11. Maj. Pitcairn Sipping Blood, Wright's Tavern, 1776
12. Tavern bill, Genl. Quarter-Sessions, N.J., rates for food and lodging, 1790
14. "Fit Persons" to Keep Publick Houses, Penn., 1797
14. 1786 license form for ordinary-keeper, Frederick City, Md.
16. Union Tavern, bill, Georgetown, Columbia, 1812
16. Bill from Heiskell's Hotel, Philadelphia, undated
16. Tilton's Tavern, bill, Portsmouth, N.H., 1777
17. Buckhorn Tavern, N.Y.C., 1812
18. View along Bouwerie, N.Y.C., showing Gotham Inn, 1860's
18. Shakespeare's Tavern, 1820's
18. Halfway House, N.Y.C., 1860's
19. Fraunces Tavern, Pearl & Water Sts., N.Y.C., before restoration, 1880's
19. Fraunces Tavern, as it looks now, after restoration
20. View of Long Room, Fraunces Tavern, N.Y.C., Colonial period (top)
20. Long Room, Fraunces Tavern, N.Y.C., before restoration, 1893 (bottom)
21. Hurlgate Ferry Hotel, 86th St. & East River, N.Y.C., early 1800's
21. Adv. for 25¢ meals, American Hotel, Rochester, N.Y., 1870's
22. Coffee House Slip, foot of Wall St., N.Y.C., 1805
23. Invitation from Mr. Colles for meeting to discuss Mohawk navigation, Apr. 5, 1786 (top)
23. Invitation for dinner honoring R. R. Livingston, Tontine Coffee-House, N.Y.C., Dec. 2, 1805 (bottom)
24. Indian Queen Tavern, Philadelphia, *Harper's Weekly* (many years later, 1890's)
25. Brown's Coffee House, 71 Pearl St., N.Y.C., 1840's
26. Bill of Fare, Bank Coffee House, 11 Pine St., N.Y.C.
27. Markoe House, kept by Mrs. S. Howell, N.Y.C., Colonial period
28. Boardinghouse cartoons, *Harper's Weekly,* 1873 & 1898
30. Mrs. Mann's Boardinghouse, 61 Broadway, N.Y.C., 1832
36. City Hotel, Broadway below Trinity Church, N.Y.C., 1790's
37. City Hotel, N.Y.C., table-d'hôte menu 1846
38. Adv., 1880's, Washington Hall, 282 Broadway, N.Y.C., near City Hall, from early directory
39. Holt's Hotel, Water & Pearl Sts., N.Y.C., here called United States (after Holt's bankruptcy, 1830's)
40. Pacific Hotel, 162 Greenwich St., N.Y.C., early adv., 1836
41. Astor House, Broadway at City Hall Park, N.Y.C., 1836
42. From early N.Y.C. directory, showing both sides of Broadway at City Hall Park
43. Typical Caution sign from hotel bedroom when gas lighting was introduced
44. Decorated Astor House parlor in its later years
45. Astor House, Ladies Ordinary Menu, 1839
46. View of Astor dining room, Barclay St. side, 1844
47. Astor House Bill of Fare, 1849
48. Astor House Rotunda, 1901
49. Astor House dining rooms, Vesey St. side, 1913
50. Metropolitan Hotel, Broadway, Spring & Prince Sts., N.Y.C., old lithograph, 1850's
51. New Russian Baths, 18 Lafayette Pl., N.Y.C., lithograph, 1883
52. Banquet of N.Y. Dramatic Fund Assoc., Metropolitan Hotel, 1856
53. Metropolitan Hotel, Custom-Designed Silverware
54. Stereopticon view, Niblo's Gardens, court, Metropolitan Hotel, 1880's (top)
54. Niblo's Gardens, Temple of Music in background, Metropolitan Hotel, 1880's (bottom)
55. Main entrance, Niblo's Garden Theater (in later years)
56. Main entrance, St. Nicholas Hotel, Broadway at Broome and Spring Sts., *Ballou's Pictorial,* 1855
57. Tiffany's, Lower Broadway, N.Y.C.
58–63. Double-fold picture of St. Nicholas Hotel dining room
59–62. Menu for 5 o'clock dinner, Wed., Jan. 19, 1876
64–65. St. Nicholas, a letter "from Jennie to her sister," on facsimile of hotel stationery, 1856
66. Fifth Avenue Hotel, N. W. Corner, 23rd and Fifth Ave., opp. Madison Sq. Park, N.Y.C., 1859
67. Fifth Avenue Hotel Corridor, 1880's
68. Centennial Fourth, celebration in front of Fifth Avenue Hotel
69. Fifth Avenue Hotel Reading Room, 1870's
70. Fifth Avenue Hotel, Grand Dining Room
72. Hoffman House, S. W. Corner, Broadway and 25th St., N.Y.C., 1880's
73. Cigar box top for Hoffman House five-cent Bouquet cigars, 1880's
74. Hoffman House, remodeling in 1882
75. Hoffman House, Famous Bar, 1880's
75. Bouguereau's "The Nymphs and Satyr" (in frame)
76. Hoffman House Banquet Hall, 1882
77. Broadway scene in February thaw, outside Hoffman House, *Harper's Weekly,* 1872
78. Early electric light, Madison Square, N.Y.C., 1882
79. Gilsey House, N. E. Corner, Broadway and 29th St., N.Y.C., 1871
80. Cartoon of Tenderloin "Cop"
81. A Hot Summer's Day on Broadway, *Harper's Weekly,* 1901
82. Midnight in the Tenderloin, early 1900's
83. Fifth Ward Museum Hotel, W. Broadway & Franklin St., N.Y.C., 1820's (top)
83. Fifth Ward Museum Hotel, Public Room and Bar (bottom)
84. Windsor Hotel, N.Y.C., Fifth Avenue entrance, 1870's
85. Windsor Hotel, cor. Fifth Avenue & 46th St., 1873
86. Windsor Hotel Lobby (top)
86. Windsor Hotel Billiard Room (bottom)
87. Ruins of Windsor Hotel, morning, March 18, 1899
88. Adv. Trade Card, 1890's (top left)
88. Advertisements, *Harper's Weekly,* 1890's (middle & bottom right)
89. Grand Union Hotel, N.Y.C., with Grand Central Station in background, 1899
90. Fashion plate, traveling clothes, *Demorest's Magazine,* 1876
91. Stereopticon Viewer of Grand Union Hotel, for Guests
92. Grand Union Oyster Bar, closing day, May 3, 1914 (top)
92. Grand Union Horseshoe Corner, closing day, May 3, 1914 (bottom)
93. Grand Union Hotel, showing auction sign, May 12, 1914
94. Buckingham Hotel, cor. 50th St. & Fifth Ave., N.Y.C., St. Patrick's Cathedral to left, 1876
95. Buckingham Hotel Ladies Parlor, 1876
96. Buckingham Hotel (insert), bridge leading to breakfast room, 1876
96. Buckingham Hotel Grand Dining Room, 1876
97. Hotel Buckingham Breakfast Room, 1876
98. Adv. for Woman's Hotel, N.Y.C., *Harper's Weekly,* Apr. 13, 1878
99—101. Portfolio, Woman's Hotel, N.Y.C., *Harper's Weekly,* Apr. 13, 1878
102. Woman's Hotel, New York, news item, explains change to hotel for general public, 1878
102. Woman's Hotel, New York, two cartoons lampooning "no pets" rule which defeated hotel, *Harper's Bazaar,* 1878
103. Park Avenue Hotel, N.Y.C., main entrance (from adv. brochure, 1870's)
104. Park Avenue Hotel, N.Y.C., dining verandah, 1890's (top)
104. Park Avenue Hotel, courtyard with bandstand, 1870's (bottom)
105. Hotel Vendome, Broadway & 41st St., N.Y.C., bar on opening day, October, 1889
105. Adv. for Vinous Rubber Grapes, 1887
106. Hotel Vendome, New York, two illustrations of New Year's Day collation, Jan. 1, 1889
107. Waldorf-Astoria Hotel, New York, two statues which are now in Park Avenue lobby, flanking steps leading to Sert Room
108. Waldorf Hotel, N.Y.C., 33rd St. main entrance, 1890's
109. Col. John Jacob Astor in automobile, *Harper's Bazaar,* 1899
110. Waldorf-Astoria Hotel, N.Y.C., Fifth Avenue & 34th St., early 1900's
111. Waldorf-Astoria Hotel, New York, carriages at main entrance colonnade, 1890's
111. Waldorf-Astoria Hotel, Ladies Lounge, 1890's
112. Portrait of Mrs. John Jacob Astor, 1899 (insert)
113. Telephone booth, believed to be first long distance, *circa* 1890
114. Waldorf-Astoria, gentlemen's Cafe showing famous "Bulls and Bears," *Harper's Weekly,* 1890's
115. Fashion plate, afternoon dress, 1890's
116. Autographed order by Oscar of the Waldorf
117. Oscar of the Waldorf, photographed in later years
117. Menu for breakfast, hand-written by Oscar, June 23, 1924

118. Waldorf-Astoria, view of one of the kitchens
119. Waldorf-Astoria, table setting in manner of old Waldorf, with original china, gold flatware, crystal glasses
120. Waldorf-Astoria, view of corner of roof garden
121. Waldorf-Astoria, King Henry IV of France drawing room in one of suites (top)
121. Waldorf-Astoria, Francis I bedroom of a suite (bottom)
122–23. Waldorf-Astoria, painting of Peacock Alley, *Harpers Weekly,* early 1900's
124–25. After the theater, stopping at the Waldorf-Astoria for supper, *Harper's Weekly,* 1901
126. Waldorf-Astoria, Horse Show Ball, 1890's
127. Table especially set at the Waldorf for *Harper's Bazaar,* 1899
128. Fashion plate, evening wear, *circa* 1890's
128. Waldorf-Astoria, first Assembly Ball, *Harper's Weekly,* 1902
129. Waldorf-Astoria, Grand Ballroom set up for banquet honoring Prince Henry of Prussia, 1902
130. Waldorf-Astoria, historic clock by Goldsmiths of London, now to be seen in the main lobby
131. Waldorf-Astoria, late revelers hailing hansom cabs
132. Departure of a steamer for Liverpool, "The Last Good-Bye," *Harper's Weekly,* 1870's
133. The *S.S. Oceanic,* White Star Line, 1870's
134. The new ocean steamer *Germanic* of the White Star Line (top)
134. The *Newport* of the N.Y. and Havana Line, *Frank Leslie's Mag.,* 1880 (bottom)
135. "Homeward Bound," by Winslow Homer, *Harpers Weekly,* 1870's
136. "Plaza Hotel," New York, painting by Everett Shinn, 1908
137. Plaza (first), "A May Day on Central Park Plaza," 1890
138. Drawing of Plaza, Vernon Howe Bailey, *Harper's Weekly,* 1906 (top)
138. Plaza Hotel, opening day register, Tues., Oct. 1, 1907 (bottom)
139. Newspaper story of apartments for millionaire residents of Plaza
140–41. Pastel drawing of the Plaza's famous Palm Court
142. Plaza Hotel, motor cabs, new French "taximeters" on opening day (top)
142. Section of Plaza's main lobby exquisitely wrought mosaic floor (bottom)
143. Pastel drawing of Plaza's Rose Room, site of present Persian Room
144. Plaza Hotel, the pastry kitchen
145. Plaza Hotel, the bottling room
146. Section of paneling in Plaza's Oak Room showing plaque marking George M. Cohan's favorite corner
147. Plaza Hotel, the wine vaults
148. Newspaper story, "50,000,000 Worth of Hotels"
150–61. Fulton Market, N.Y.C., holiday season of 1877, *Harper's Weekly*
152. Washington Market, New York, mid-1800's, *Harper's Weekly*
153. Washington Market, New York, mid-1880's, *Harper's Weekly*
154–55. South Street, New York, 1878, *Harper's Weekly*
155. Provision list of William G. Thring Hot House Products, 1911
156. Gov. De Witt Clinton appoints Ichabod Postwick to inspect meat, Columbia Cty., N.Y., 1817
157. Manhattan Abattoir, *Harper's Weekly,* 1877
158–59. Chicago stockyards and shipments to N.Y., *Harper's Weekly,* 1882
161. Fulton Market, New York, fish-landing slip, 1870's, *Harper's Weekly* (top)
161. Fulton Market, New York, view, early morning, *Harper's Weekly* (insert)
162. Opening of the Oyster Season, *Harper's Weekly,* 1872
163. Oyster barges along East River, New York, 1870's
164. Canning oysters, *Harper's Weekly,* 1872
165. Clamming along Great South Bay, *Harper's Weekly,* 1877
166. Candling eggs before shipping to New York market, *Harper's Weekly,* 1870
167. Landing tropical fruits, East River wharfs, 1870's, *Harper's Weekly*
168. Unloading melons from Southern sloops, 1870's, *Harper's Weekly*
169. Broadside issued by M. L. Faulkner, prop., Rochester, Vt., 1885
170. City Hotel, Reading, Penn., view of dining room, 1890's
171. Huff's Hotel, Winona, Minn. Terr., prior 1858
172. Morris House, Indianapolis, Ind., Bill of Fare, 1861
172. Waitress with dinner bell, wood engraving, *Demorest's Mag.,* 1870's
173. Lahr House, Lafayette, Ind., 1880's
174–75. Belmont Hotel, Springfield, Mass., register, 1878
177. Hotel de Paris, Georgetown, Colo., exterior view (top)
177. Hotel de Paris, Georgetown, Colo., carved room key rack (bottom)
178. Hotel de Paris, Georgetown, Colo., section of lobby
179. Hotel de Paris, Georgetown, Colo., view of dining room
179. Hotel de Paris, Georgetown, Colo., oyster menu (insert)
180–81. On the Way to New Diggings, *Harper's Weekly,* 1874
181. Georgetown, Colo., view of town and environs, 1874
182. Hotel de Paris, Georgetown, Colo., portrait of prop., Louis du Puy
182–83. Hotel de Paris, Georgetown, Colo., view of bed chamber
183. Hotel de Paris, Georgetown, Colo., portrait of Sophie Gally
184. Tombstone marking graves of Louis du Puy and Sophie Gally
185. California Terminus, Central Pacific R.R., Oakland, Calif., *Harper's Weekly,* 1871 (bottom)
185. Railroad Building on the Great Plains, *Harper's Weekly,* 1875 (center)
185. Boston Harbor, view, masthead, *Ballou's Pictorial,* 1856 (top)
186. Isaiah Rogers, portrait, later years, date unknown
187. Architectural rendering of Tremont House exterior from book by Gray & Bowen, Boston, 1830
188. Description of Tremont House with Architectural Illustrations (Gray & Bowen, Boston, 1830)
188. First floor plan of Tremont House from book by Gray & Bowen, Boston, 1830 (upper left)
188–89. Dining-room plan of Tremont House from book by Gray & Bowen, Boston, 1830 (center)
189. Tremont House, Boston, opening night dinner menu, Oct. 16, 1829
190. Tremont House, Boston, banquet for Col. N. A. Thompson, *Gleason's Pictorial,* 1852
191. Tremont House, Boston, Bill of Fare, Aug. 25, 1844
192. Burning of Tremont Temple seen from the cupola of *Ballou's Pictorial,* office, 1856
193. Metropolitan Horse R.R., Tremont St., Boston, *Ballou's Pictorial,* 1856
194. Continental Hotel, Philadelphia, 1876
194. Girard House, Philadelphia, 1876
194. The Rush for Rooms at the Philadelphia Hotels, *Harper's Weekly,* 1876
195. Crush on Opening Day at Elm and Belmont Aves., Philadelphia, *Harper's Weekly,* 1876
196. National Hotel, Washington, D.C., *Gleason's Pictorial,* 1852 (top)
196. Washington, D.C., Board of Health Notice, May, 1857 (bottom)
197. Willard's Hotel clam bar, said to be largest in world, Washington, D.C., from trade card, 1870's (center left)
197. Willard's Hotel, Washington, D.C., 1900's (bottom right)
197. Willard's Hotel, Washington, D.C., 1870's (center right)
197. Ebbitt House, Washington, D.C., 1860's (top right)
198. Dining salon, Mississippi River Steamboat "Red Wing," 1850's (top left)
198. Bill of Fare, Gentleman's Ordinary, St. Charles Hotel, New Orleans, La., Sun., March 16, 1845 (insert)
199. New St. Charles Hotel, New Orleans, La., *Gleason's Pictorial,* 1853
200. Menu, Lindell Hotel, St. Louis, Mo., July 4, 1865 (insert)
200. The levee at St. Louis, Mo., *Harper's Weekly,* 1871
201. Burning of Lindell Hotel, St. Louis, Mo., *Harper's Weekly,* 1867
202. Original Palmer House, Chicago, 1871
202–3. Chicago in Flames, the Rush for Life Over Randolph St. Bridge, *Harper's Weekly,* 1871
203. Building new Palmer House, Chicago, 1873
204. Exterior of new Palmer House, Chicago, main entrance, 1880
205. Promenade costume, 1870's (insert)
205. Grand stairway, Palmer House, Chicago
206. Drawing of grand dining room, Palmer House, Chicago, 1870's
207. A silk-fringed, printed menu, Palmer House, Chicago, 1880's
208. Ornamental frame taken from 1880's menu card, Palmer House, Chicago
209. Mrs. Potter Palmer, a portrait (left)
209. Discount card of 1891, issued by Palmer House, Chicago (right)
210. One of many elaborate bedrooms, Palmer House, Chicago
211. Roof garden of the Palmer House, Chicago
212. Interior of parlor car, *circa* 1870 (top left)
212–13. Atchison, Topeka & Santa Fe Depot, Topeka, Kan., 1880 (center)
213. Staff of Fred Harvey Hotel, Wallace, Kan., 1880's
214. Fred Harvey, a portrait
214–15. Three Harvey Girls at Rosenberg, Tex., 1908 (bottom)
215. Group of Harvey Girls at lunchroom, Syracuse, Kan., 1880's (top)
215. Group of Harvey Girls, Chanute, Kan., 1910 (in oval)
216. Fred Harvey lunchroom in R.R. depot, Houston, Tex., early 1900's
217. Fred Harvey eating house, Guthrie, Okla., 1890's (top)
217. 1889 Fred Harvey dining-car menu cover and back (bottom)
218. Brown Palace Hotel, Denver, Colo., from brochure, 1892
219. Brown Palace, Denver, main lobby from which ten-story court rises, brochure, 1892 (bottom)
219. Brown Palace, Denver, construction detail, portion of court, brochure, 1892 (center)
219. Brown Palace, Denver, banquet hall, top floor, brochure, 1892 (top)
220. Fashion plate, *circa* 1890's, *Harper's Bazaar*

220. Brown Palace, Denver, sitting room of bridal suite, and section of bedroom
221. Brown Palace, Denver, one of the "modern" bathrooms, brochure, 1892
221. Fashion plate, *circa* 1890's, from a tailor's style chart
222. Brown Palace, Denver, looking toward Rockies from top-floor dining room, brochure, 1892
223. Brown Palace, Denver, dining room, ready for dinner, brochure, 1892
224. A typical forty-niner, from contemporary engraving
224. Palace Hotel, San Francisco, time of opening, 1875, engraving
225. Newsboys on galloping ponies, *Harper's Weekly,* 1870's
226. Palace Hotel, San Francisco, Grand Court, 1875
227. Palace, San Francisco, top floor, Grand Court, showing statuary, hanging baskets and skylight, 1875
228. Palace Hotel, San Francisco, mahogany and red marble bar, 1870's
229. Palace Hotel, San Francisco, looking into Grand Court through colonnades, 1870's
230. Palace Hotel, San Francisco, dining room at rear of Grand Court, 1880's
232. Palace Hotel, San Francisco, "cosey corner," Grand Court, 1880's
232. Fashion plate, carriage costume, *Frank Leslie's Ladies Journal,* 1870's
233. Palace Hotel, San Francisco, three views of elaborate suites, 1880's
234. Palace Hotel, San Francisco, as flames engulf the hotel during the San Francisco fire, from photograph, 1906
235. Proclamation by Mayor E. E. Schmitz, Apr. 18, 1906, after disaster
236. Palace Hotel, San Francisco, in ruins after fire. Note tent restaurant in left foreground; photograph, 1906
237. Mohawk Lake House, N.Y., 1870's, adv. lithograph
238. Deagle's Hotel, Macomb's Dam, Westchester, N.Y., adv. brochure, 1850's
239. Sybil's Cave, Hoboken, N.J., early 1800's, engraving
240–41. "Out of Town," drawn by Thomas Nast, *Harper's Weekly,* 1870's
242. Fashion plate, lake resort costumes, 1870's, *Demorest's Magazine*
243. Aerial view, White Sulphur Springs prior to Civil War, lithograph
244. White Sulphur Springs, taking the waters, *Harper's Monthly,* 1878
245. Promenade at "Old White," main building in rear, *Harper's Monthly,* 1878
246. Paradise Row, White Sulphur Springs, *Harper's Monthly,* 1878
247. "A Reminiscence of the White Sulphur Springs," *Harper's Weekly,* 1870's
248. A delightful summer picnic of the 1870's, *Harper's Weekly*
250. United States Hotel, Saratoga, N.Y., lobby, *Frank Leslie's Ill. News,* 1876
250. Saratoga, N.Y., crush along Broadway prior to boat races, *Frank Leslie's Ill. News,* 1876
251. Grand Union Hotel, Saratoga, N.Y., afternoon promenade on Broadway, *Frank Leslie's Ill. Weekly,* 1875
252–53. United States Hotel, Saratoga, N.Y., elm-shaded garden, *Frank Leslie's Ill. News,* 1874
255. United States Hotel, Saratoga, a concert on verandah, *Frank Leslie's Ill. News,* 1876
256–57. Fashion plate, *Frank Leslie's Ladies Journal,* 1873
258–59. Union Hotel, Saratoga, N.Y., dining hall, *Frank Leslie's Ill. News,* 1864
260. Grand Union Hotel, Saratoga, N.Y., stereoscopic view of parlor, 1870's (top)
260. Grand Union Hotel, Saratoga, N.Y., ballroom, *Frank Leslie's Ill. News,* 1876 (bottom)
261. Morrissey's Gambling House, Saratoga, N.Y., *Every Saturday,* 1871
262. Jockeys exercising horses prior to races, Saratoga, N.Y., *Frank Leslie Ill. News,* 1875 (top)
262. A start for the mile and three-quarters dash, Saratoga, N.Y., *Frank Leslie's Ill. News,* 1875 (bottom)
263. French fashion plate, *Revue de la Mode,* 1890
264. The filly *Firenze* (bottom)
264. Leonard W. Jerome, portrait (top)
265. Hathorn Spring, Saratoga, N.Y., *Frank Leslie's Ill. News,* 1876
266. Music pavilion, Congress Park, Saratoga, N.Y., *Harper's Bazaar,* 1878 (upper left)
266. Congress Spring pavilion, Saratoga, N.Y., interior view, *Harper's Bazaar,* 1878 (lower left)
266. Columbian Spring, Saratoga, N.Y., *Harper's Bazaar,* 1878 (upper right)
266. Congress Park, Saratoga, N.Y., *Harper's Bazaar,* 1878 (lower right)
267. Taking the Waters at Saratoga, *Harper's Weekly,* 1890
268. Holiday Excursion in Mountains, *Harper's Weekly,* 1878
269. "Up in the Crow's Nest," *Harper's Weekly,* 1875
270. Sterlingworth, Lake Chautauqua, N.Y., concert hour in ballroom, 1890's
271. Sterlingworth, Lake Chautauqua, N.Y., conservatory cafe (top)
271. Sterlingworth, Lake Chautauqua, N.Y., winter sun bath (bottom)
272. Sterlingworth, Lake Chautauqua, N.Y., kitchen
273. Sterlingworth, Lake Chautauqua, N.Y., tower bedroom
274. Sterlingworth, Lake Chautauqua, N.Y., cover ill., brochure
275. "Climbing Pike's Peak by Burro," *Harper's Weekly,* 1888
276. Broadmoor Dairy Livestock Co., Colorado Springs, Colo., adv., *Colorado Springs Gazette,* Jan. 1, 1888; first business enterprise in area
276. Count James de Pourtales, a portrait (insert)
277. Countess Berthe Pourtales, a portrait (insert)
277. Original casino on lake, Colorado Springs, 1891
278. Prominent mining men in Cripple Creek, Colo. Spencer Penrose fifth from left, 1892 (top)
278–79. Broadmoor, Colorado Springs, dining room at opening, June 29, 1918, drawing by Vernon Howe Bailey
279. Broadmoor, Colorado Springs, dining on terrace, 1918, drawing by Vernon Howe Bailey
280–81. Famous Maxfield Parrish painting of Broadmoor, Rocky Mountains in background
282. International Hotel, Niagara Falls, N.Y., 1873
283. International Hotel, Niagara Falls, N.Y., with omnibus, 1880's (top)
283. "On the Brink," *Harper's Weekly,* 1875 (bottom)
284. Ad. trade card, Ocean Pier, Long Branch, N.J., 1881 (top)
284. Fashion plate, *Demorest's Magazine,* 1873 (insert)
285. Ocean House, Long Branch, N.J., 1870's
286. Ocean Avenue, Long Branch, N.J., *circa* 1870
287. "Too Much of a Good Thing," *Harper's Weekly,* 1870
288–89. "The Humors of Cape May," N.J., *Harper's Weekly,* 1871
290. "The Bathing Hour," Atlantic City, N.J., from *A Century After; Picturesque Glimpses of Philadelphia and Pennsylvania,* 1876 (top)
290. N. Carolina Ave., Atlantic City, Chalfont (left), Haddon House (right), 1870's (bottom)
291. Fashion plate, *Demorest's Magazine,* 1870's
292. Jeffries Brothers, first Life Guards, 1892 (upper left)
292–93. "James Up To Now Salt Water Taffy Stand," Boardwalk, Atlantic City, 1889
293. Roller chair parade on Boardwalk, Atlantic City, 1880's
294. "Watching the Tide Come in at Atlantic City," *Harper's Weekly,* 1890
294–95. "The Bathing Hour on the Beach at Atlantic City," *Harper's Weekly,* 1890
296. The "Sea Spider," *Harper's Weekly,* 1890
297. Crowds at Steel Pier, Atlantic City, *Harper's Bazaar,* 1900 (top)
297. Aerial view: Marlborough-Blenheim and Brighton, Atlantic City, 1900
298. Musicians entertain passengers en route to Coney Island
298. Boat preparing to leave N.Y.C. for Coney Island, 1870's, *Harper's Weekly* (top)
299. Iron Pier restaurant, Coney Island, 1880's
300. Elephant Hotel, Coney Island (top)
300. "The Inexhaustible Cow," Coney Island (bottom)
301. View from the Iron Pier, Coney Island
302–3. "On the Beach at Coney Island," *Harper's Weekly,* 1878
303. Bathing by electric light at Coney Island, Manhattan Beach Hotel in background
304. Manhattan Beach Hotel, Coney Island, 1880's (top)
304. The Oriental Hotel, Coney Island, 1880's (bottom)
305. Brighton Beach Hotel, Coney Island, 1880's
306. Steam engines moving Brighton Hotel, *Harper's Weekly,* 1888
307. "The Rush for the Last Boat," *Harper's Weekly,* 1880's
308. "The Blizzard of 1899," *Harper's Weekly* (top)
308. Clyde S.S. Company adv., 1908 (center)
308. Worth resort costume, 1894 (insert)
309. Atlantic Coast Line adv., 1900's (insert)
309. Hotel Ponce de Leon, St. Augustine, Fla., *Harper's Weekly,* 1887
310. Roof garden, Hotel Alcazar, St. Augustine, Fla., *Harper's Weekly,* 1888 (circle)
310. Hotel Alcazar, St. Augustine, Fla., *Harper's Weekly,* 1888 (bottom)
311. Ponce de Leon Hotel, St. Augustine, Fla. (Spanish without), 1887 (top)
311. Lobby, Ponce de Leon Hotel, St. Augustine, Fla. (Victorian within), 1910 (bottom)
312. Wood engraving of palm garden (top)
312. Royal Poinciana, Palm Beach, Fla. (bottom)
313. On steps of Royal Poinciana, Palm Beach, Fla., 1903 (top)
313. Getting about at Royal Poinciana, Palm Beach, Fla., 1903 (bottom)
314. Aerial photograph, del Coronado Hotel, San Diego, Cal., 1901
315. "On the Beach at del Coronado, San Diego, Cal.," *Harper's Weekly,* 1890
316–17. Main entrance, del Monte Hotel, Monterey, Cal., from brochure, 1890's (top)
317. Guests and pony cart, del Monte, Monterey, Cal., brochure, 1890's (bottom)
318. Lady guests on a verandah, del Monte, Monterey, Cal., brochure, 1890's (bottom)
318. Del Monte dining room ready for guests, brochure, 1890's (top)
319. Indoor swimming pool, del Monte Hotel, Monterey, Cal., *Harper's Weekly,* 1890's
320. Morning Drive, del Monte Hotel, Monterey, Cal., brochure, 1890's
321. View of Sutro Heights, overlooking Cliff House, Seal Rocks, and Pacific Ocean, San Francisco, Cal., *Harper's Weekly,* 1890's

Index

A

Adams, John, 6, 16
Adams, Maude, 113
Alcazar Hotel, St. Augustine, Fla., 310
Astor family, 42, 43, 49, 108, 109, 112, 116, 127, 128, 193
Astor House, New York, 41-49, 187, 193, 285
Astoria, Oregon, 109
Astoria Hotel, New York, 109
Atlantic City, N.J., 290-97

B

Bailey, Vernon Howe, artist, 138, 278, 279
Bangor House, Maine, 187
Barnum, P. T., 25, 301
Barrymore, Ethel, 143
Battle House, Mobile, Ala., 187
Bear Market, New York, 152
Belmont, August, 261, 264, 286, 299
Belmont, Mrs. Oliver H. P., 127
Belmont Hotel, Springfield, Mass., 174
Berkshire Springs, Oswego, N.Y., 274
Bernhardt, Sarah, 208, 232
Beyard, E. D., 320
Billings, C. J. K., 139
Blaine, James G., 69
Blashfield, Edwin H., 113
Boardinghouses, 27-30
Boardman, Alexander, 290
Boldt, George C., 108, 110, 112, 113, 115, 116, 117, 119, 130
Boston, Mass., 86-93
"Bouwerie Boys," 18
Boyden, Dwight, 189
Boyden, Simeon, 189
Bradley, David, 292
Bradley, Martin Ball, 128
Brady, "Diamond Jim," 147, 257
Brady, James T., 52
Bread and Cheese Club, 36
Breslin, Col. James S., 80, 81
Brighton Beach, Coney Island, 299, 305, 306
Broadmoor, Colorado Springs, Colo., 275-81
Brown's Coffee House, New York, 25
Brown Palace, Denver, Colo., 218-23
Brown, "Unsinkable Molly," 223
Bryce, Mrs. Lloyd, 128
Buckingham Hotel, New York, 94-97
Buffalo Bill, 223
Burnett Hotel, Cincinnati, Ohio, 187
Burnley, Mrs. Hardin, 112
Burns Coffee House, New York, 36
Butler, Benjamin F., 73
Butler, Nicholas Murray, 143

C

Calhoun, Henry C., 245
Canfield, Richard Albert, 264
Captain Flagg's Inn, Weston, Conn., 6
Carnegie, Andrew, 56
Carol of Rumania, 119
Caruso, Enrico, 233, 234
Cassatt, A. J., 264
Cataract House, Niagara Falls, N.Y., 282
Centennial Exposition, Philadelphia, Penn., 194-95
Central City, Colo., 180
Chalfont and Haddon House, Atlantic City, N.J., 291
Chamberlain Club, Long Branch, N.J., 286
Chapman, Mrs. William Rogers, 130
Cheyenne Mountain, Colo., 276
Chicago, Ill., 202-11
City Hotel, first, New York, 1794, 32
Claflin, Tennessee, 78
Clarendon Hotel, Saratoga, N.Y., 250
Clay, Henry, 245, 251
Cleveland, Grover, 69, 205
Cliff House, San Francisco, Cal., 321
Clinton, DeWitt, 18, 156
Coenties Slip, New York, 6, 25
Coffee Houses, 22-26
Cohan, George M., 146
Coleman House, New York, 81
Coleman, Robert, 81
Coles, Robert, 5
Colorado Springs, Colo., 277, 280, 281
Columbian Hotel, Saratoga, N.Y., 266
Commercial Club, Chicago, 206
Coney Island, N.Y., 298-307
Congress Hall, Saratoga, N.Y., 250, 251, 266
Congress Spring Park, Saratoga, N.Y., 266
Conklin, Roscoe, 205
Continental Hotel, Philadelphia, Penn., 194
Cooper, James Fenimore, 18, 36
Cripple Creek, Colo., 278
Crum, George, 259
Cushman, Charlotte, 70

D

Damrosch, Walter, 108
Deagle's Hotel, Macomb's Dam, Westchester, N.Y., 238
del Coronado Hotel, San Diego, Cal., 314-15
Delmonico's, 82, 117, 232
del Monte Hotel, Monterey, Cal., 316-20
Denver, Colo., 179, 180
de Paris, Hotel; *see* Hotel de Paris
Depew, Chauncey M., 112, 143
de Reszke, Jean, 208
De Tocqueville, 42
Dillon, Sidney, 181
Dodge, Grenville, 181
Dom Pedro, "The Magnificent," ex-emperor of Brazil, 95, 227
Drake, John, 139
Drew, John, 113, 143
du Puy, Louis, "French Louis," 177-84
Dwyer brothers, 264
Dyer, Elisha, Jr., 128

E

Eagle Hotel, New York, 25
Eagle Hotel, Niagara Falls, N.Y., 282
Eisenhower, Dwight D., 223
Electricity, first in hotels, 78, 270, 303
Elephant Hotel, Coney Island, 299, 300
Elevators, first in hotels, 66, 90, 102
Emerson, Ralph Waldo, 190
Erskine, John, 307
European trip circa 1870's, 132-35
Everett, Edward, 189
Everett House, New York, 78
Exchange Hotel, Richmond, Va., 187

F

Fashions
- men's, 23, 115, 116, 173, 253, 255-57
- women's, 90, 112, 205, 232, 246, 248, 283, 284, 287, 291, 308, 309, 313, 319

Field, Jacob, 114

Fields, James T., 190
Fifth Avenue Hotel, New York, 66-71
Fifth Ward Museum Hotel, New York, 83
Fillmore, Millard, 245
Fish and seafood, for hotels, 161-65, 179, 299
Fish, Mrs. Stuyvesant, 127, 143
Fisk, Jim, "Jubilee Jim," 77, 261, 286
Fitch, Diantha, 141
Fitch, John, 23
Flagler, Henry M., 250, 309, 310, 311, 312, 313
Ford, Henry, 93
Ford, John, 253
Ford, Simeon, 43, 51, 89, 91
Fraunces Tavern, 19-20
Freehold Stakes, Monmouth, N.J., 264
Fuller and Gage, 95
Fulton Market, New York, 151, 161
Fulton, Robert, 25

G

Galli-Curci, 129
Gally (Gallet), Sophie, "Aunt Sophie," 183, 184
Galt House, Louisville, Ky., 187
Garden, Mary, 223
Gardner, Peter, 81
Garfield, James A., 205
Garrison, Gen. William L., 228
Gas illumination, dangers of, 43
Gates, J. W., "Bet-A-Million," 114, 139, 142, 264
Gates, Mrs. John W., 139
Georgetown, Colo., 177-84
Gilsey, Henry, 81
Gilsey House, New York, 79-82
Girard House, Philadelphia, Penn., 195
Georgetown, Colo., "The Silver Queen," 177-84
Globe Hotel, Philadelphia, Penn., 195
Goelet, Mrs. Ogden, 127
Gould, Jay, 181, 250, 253
Gould, Mrs. George J., 139
Grand Central Station, New York, 89
Grand Hotel, Saratoga, N.Y., 250, 285
Grand Union Hotel, New York, 88-93
Grand Union Hotel, Saratoga, N.Y., 232, 250, 251, 255, 259, 260, 265
Grant, U. S., 194, 195, 205, 206, 207, 228, 284, 287
Gray, Asa, 190
Gray's Ferry, Philadelphia, Penn., 238
Greenaway, Edward M., 230

H

Haggin, J. B., 264
Halfway House, early curb service at, 18
Halleck, Fitz-Greene, 18
Hanna, Mark, 117
Hardenbergh, Henry J., architect, 109, 142
Harder, Jules, chef, 232
Harriman, Mrs. Oliver, 139
Harvey, Fred, 212-17
Harvey Houses, 212-17
Hawthorne, Nathaniel, 196
Hay, John, Secretary of State, 129
Heiskell, Thomas, 16
Held, Anna, 112, 232
Heyworth, Mrs. Young, 139
Hoffman House, New York, 72-78, 117
Holmes, Jotham, 266
Holmes, Oliver Wendell, 190
Holt, Mary, 39
Holt, Stephen, 39
Holt's Hotel, New York, 39
"Hotel," first use of term, 31, 32
Hotel de Paris, Georgetown, Colo., 177-84
Hotels; *see* individual listings
Houseman, A. A., 114
Howard, Capt. Dan., 72
Huff's Hotel, Winona, Minn. Terr., 171
Hung-chang, Li, 116
Hurlgate Ferry House, 21

I

Inns, Colonial, names of, 6
International Hotel, Niagara Falls, N.Y., 282-83

J

Jefferson, Thomas, 16
Jerome, Leonard W., 261, 263
Jessups, Benjamin, 40
Josselyn, John, 8

K

Kalakaua, David, King of Hawaii, 227
Keene, James R., 114
Kemble, Madame Fanny, 189
Kipling, Rudyard, 205
Kitchener, Field Marshal Viscount, 129
Knickerbocker, side-wheeler, 21

L

Lafferty, James V., 300
Lahr House, Lafayette, Ind., 173
Lake Chautauqua, N.Y., Sterlingworth Hotel, 270-74
Lake, Rev. Ezra B., 296
Langtry, Lily, 232
Laperreque, Eugene, chef, 76, 144
Latrobe, John H. B., 246
Lauder, Sir Harry, 223
Leland brothers, 53, 230, 232, 285
Letard, Chef, 143
Lincoln, Abraham, 7, 44, 73
Lincoln, Mrs. Abraham, 287
Lind, Jenny, 25, 301
Lindell House, St. Louis, Mo., 200-1
Lipton, Sir Thomas, 117
Long Branch, N.J., 261, 284-87
Longfellow, William Wordsworth, 190
Lorillard, Pierre, 250, 261, 286, 299
Low, Will H., 113
Lowell, James Russell, 15

Mc

McAdoo, William, Police Commissioner, 80
McClellan, Gen. George B., 228
Macomb's Dam, Deagle's Hotel, Westchester, N.Y., 238
McCormack, John, 129
McIntyre, P., 38
McLean, Evalyn Walsh, 223

M

Manhattan Abattoir, 157
Manhattan Beach Hotel, Coney Island, 299, 303, 305
Mansion House, Long Branch, N.J., 287
Marvin, James, 253
Maxwell House, Nashville, Tenn., 187
Meat markets, wholesale, 156-60
Merchant's Coffee House, first directory, 22
Merchant's Exchange, New York, 187
Metropolitan Horse Railroad, Boston, 193
Metropolitan Hotel, New York, 50-55, 285; *see also* Niblo's Gardens
Mills, Mrs. Ogden, 127
Modjeska, Helena, 205, 208
Monmouth Park, N.J., 286
Monroe Tavern, Lexington, Mass., 15
Monterey, Calif.; *see* del Monte Hotel
Moon's Lake House, Saratoga, N.Y., 259
Morgan, Anne, 128
Morgan, J. Pierpont, 112, 117
Morris House, Indianapolis, Ind., 172
Morrissey's Clubhouse, 261
Moulton, Mrs. Mace, 112
Murphy's Stages, 21

N

Nahant Hotel, Nahant, Mass., 239
Nast, Thomas, 73, 239, 240, 241
National Hotel, Washington, D.C., 196
New Orleans, La., 198-99
New York, N.Y., 36-147
Niagara Falls, N.Y., 282-83
Niblo's Gardens, New York, 50, 52, 54, 55; *see also* Metropolitan Hotel
Nicholas, R. C., 40
Norton, Charles Eliot, 190

O

Ocean House, Long Branch, N.J., 285
Oelrichs, Mrs. Herman, 143
Oliver, William, 114
Omnibus, 77, 264

Ordinaries, 4-5
Oriental Hotel, Coney Island, 299, 305
Oscar of the Waldorf, 116-19, 124, 127, 130
Oysters and clams, for hotels, 162-65, 179, 299

P

Pacific Hotel, New York, 40
Palace Hotel, San Francisco, Cal., 224-36, 285, 320
Palm Beach, Fla., 308, 309, 312, 313
Palmer, Mrs. Edwin, 112
Palmer, Potter, 202, 203, 204, 208
Palmer, Mrs. Potter (nee Bertha Honore), 204, 208, 209, 211
Palmer House, Chicago, Ill., 202-11
Park Avenue Hotel, New York, 103-4
Parrish, Maxfield, artist, 280-81
Patti, Adelina, 232
Peirce, Benjamin, 190
Penn, William, Jr., 24
Penrose, Spencer, 278, 279, 281
Philadelphia, Penn., 194-95
Phillips' Ordinary, Virginia, 4
Pierce, President, 52
Pike's Peak, Colo., 275, 276, 281
Piretti, Domenico, chef, 96
Pitcairn, Maj., 10
Plaza Hotel, New York, 136-47
Ponce de Leon Hotel, St. Augustine, Fla., 309, 310, 311
Ponselle, Rosa, 129
Pourtales, Count James de, 276, 277, 279, 280, 281
Pourtales, Countess Berthe de, 277
Prince of Wales, at Fifth Avenue Hotel, 67
Provisions, for hotels, 149-68
Prussia, Prince Henry of, 129
Pullmans, first, 171
Putnam, Gideon, 265

Q

Quinn, W. Johnson, 105

R

Ralston, William Chapman, 225
Read, Wall & Co., 72
Recipes, drinks, 10, 11, 12, 13, 22, 75, 197, 245, 259
Recipes, food, 71, 116, 144
Reunion Hotel, 89
Riley, Thomas, 83
Robinson's Hotel, 89
Rockefeller, John D., 253
Rogers, Isaiah, architect, 42, 186-89, 193, 199
Roosevelt, Gov. Theodore, 129, 223, 234
Royal Poinciana Hotel, Palm Beach, Fla., 312, 313
Royall, Mrs. Anne, 27, 44
Russell, Edmund, 112, 113
Russell, Lillian, 147, 263
Russia, Prince Henry of, 119
Russian Baths (new), New York, 51

S

Sachem's Head Hotel, Guilford, Conn., 239
Sage, Russell, 181
St. Augustine, Fla., 309
St. Charles Hotel, New Orleans, La., 187, 199
St. James Hotel, New York, 81
St. Louis, Mo., 200-1
St. Nicholas Hotel, New York, 56-65
Saltus, Col. Nick, 36
San Diego, Cal.; *see* del Coronado Hotel
San Francisco, Cal., 224-36
Sante Fe Railroad, 213
Saratoga, New York, 249-67, 285
Saratoga Springs; *see* Saratoga, New York
Schelcher, Edward, chef, 103
Schlippenbach, Baron, 112
Schmitz, E. E., Mayor of San Francisco, 234, 235
Schumann-Heink, 129
Scott, Gen. Winfield, 73
Scott, Hon. William L., 264
Shakespeare Tavern, New York, 18
Shanley's Lobster Palace, New York, 82
Sharon, Sen. William, 225, 231, 232
Sheridan, Gen. "Little Phil," 205, 225
Sherman, Gen. William T., 205, 206, 228
Siam, Crown Prince of, 119
Simmons, Edward, 113
Sloane, Tod, 257
Smith, Mrs. James Henry, 139
S.S. Germanic, White Star Line, 134
S.S. Oceanic, White Star Line, 133
S.S. Red Wing, Mississippi steamboat, 198
S.S. Rising Sun, first steam-crossing of Atlantic (1818), 133
S.S. Savannah, first New York to Liverpool steam sailing (1819), 132
Sterlingworth Hotel, Lake Chautauqua, N.Y., 270-74
Sterry, Fred, 142
Stetson, Col. Charles A., 46
Stevens, Paran, 66
Stewart, A. T., 98, 103, 260
Stewart, Mrs. Alexander T., 98, 103
Stokes, Edward S., 75
Storm, Col., 114
Stowe, William, 114
Subway, first in New York (1873), 84
Sutro, Adolph, 321
Sybil's Cave, Hoboken, N.J., 239
Szechenyi, Count Laslo, 141

T

Table Rock, Niagara Falls, N.Y., 282
Taverns, 7, 10-16
Taylor, T. S., 114
Termination Rock, Niagara Falls, N.Y., 282
Terry, Ellen, 232
Toney's, 82
Tontine Coffee House, New York, 23
Tontine Hotel, New Haven, Conn., 239
Train trip (*circa* 1880's), 212-17
Transcontinental Hotel, Philadelphia, Penn., 195
Travers, William R., 261, 263, 264
Tremont, first designed hotel, Boston, 32
Tremont House, Boston, Mass., 186-93
Trollope, Frances, 33
Tschirky, Oscar (Oscar of the Waldorf), 116-19
Turner, Charles Y., 113
Tutt, Charles L., Sr., 278, 281
Twain, Mark, 205, 206
Tweed, Boss, 73, 286
Tyler, John, 245

U

Union Hall, Saratoga, N.Y., 259, 265
United States Hotel, Saratoga, N.Y., 250, 251, 253, 255, 259

V

Van Buren, Martin, 245, 251
Van Cortlandt, Col., 19
Vanderbilt family, 108, 137, 139, 141
Vegetables and fruits, for hotels, 167-68
Vendome, Hotel, New York, 105

W

Waldorf-Astoria Hotel, New York, 107-131
Waldorf Hotel, New York, 108-9
Wall, Berry, 257
Walsh, Clara Bell, 141, 147
Wanamaker, John, 250
Ward, Sam, 197, 285
Washington, D.C., 196, 197
Washington, George, 7, 20
Washington Hall, New York, 38
Washington Market, New York, 152, 153
Wasserman, Jesse, 114
Webster, Daniel, 189, 245
Welling, R. W. G., 128
West India Co., 6
Wetmore, George Peabody, 286
White Star Line, 133, 134, 135
White Sulphur Springs, 243-48
Wilde, Oscar, 286, 205
Willard family, 197
Williston, James R., 114
Windsor Hotel, New York, 84-87
Winthrop, Gov., 4
Withers, D. D., 264, 286
Womack, Bob, 278
Woman's Hotel, New York, 98-103
Woodhull, Victoria, 78
Woodward, William E., quoted, 163